MW01199078

Resistance from the Right

Justice, Power, and Politics

COEDITORS
Heather Ann Thompson
Rhonda Y. Williams

EDITORIAL ADVISORY BOARD
Peniel E. Joseph
Daryl Maeda
Barbara Ransby
Vicki L. Ruiz
Marc Stein

The Justice, Power, and Politics series publishes new works in history that explore the myriad struggles for justice, battles for power, and shifts in politics that have shaped the United States over time. Through the lenses of justice, power, and politics, the series seeks to broaden scholarly debates about America's past as well as to inform public discussions about its future.

A complete list of books published in Justice, Power, and Politics is available at https://uncpress.org/series/justice-power-politics.

Resistance from the Right

Conservatives and the Campus Wars
in Modern America

· ·

LAUREN LASSABE SHEPHERD

The University of North Carolina Press Chapel Hill

© 2023 Lauren Lassabe Shepherd
All rights reserved
Set in Charis by Westchester Publishing Services
Manufactured in the United States of America

Library of Congress Cataloging-in-Publication Data
Names: Shepherd, Lauren Lassabe, author.
Title: Resistance from the right : conservatives and the campus wars
    in modern America / Lauren Lassabe Shepherd.
Other titles: Justice, power, and politics.
Description: Chapel Hill : The University of North Carolina Press, [2023] |
    Series: Justice, power, and politics | Includes bibliographical references
    and index.
Identifiers: LCCN 2023004232 | ISBN 9781469674483 (cloth) |
    ISBN 9781469674490 (paperback) | ISBN 9781469674506 (ebook)
Subjects: LCSH: Education, Higher—Political aspects—United States—
    History—20th century. | Conservatism—United States—
    History—20th century.
Classification: LCC LC173 .S48 2023 | DDC 379.73—dc23/eng/20230201
LC record available at https://lccn.loc.gov/2023004232

Cover illustration: Protest against Students for a Democratic Society,
Harvard Yard, Cambridge, Mass., April 22, 1969 (AP Photo).

For my parents. Dad, I owe my earliest political ideas to you.

Thank you for encouraging us to ask for more concepts.

In memory of my grandparents, Mary and Ramie, who didn't care much

for history or politics but indulged my need to know their stories.

I believe that if and when the menace of Communism is gone, other vital battles, at present subordinated, will emerge to the foreground. And the winner must have help from the classroom.

—William F. Buckley Jr., *God and Man at Yale*, 1951

Contents

Illustrations

Acknowledgments

Doing the research for this book was a very personal endeavor, but it was certainly not one taken alone. Mentors, colleagues, Twitterstorians, family, and friends have contributed in countless ways that have made the research and writing processes more fulfilling. I hope not to have forgotten anyone here.

This project was first conceived as a paper in a graduate history of higher education course. Thomas O'Brien, Lilian Hill, Kyna Shelley, and Holly Foster encouraged me to transform it into a full-time research project. The Graduate School at the University of Southern Mississippi, the Committee on Services and Resources for Women, and the Dale Center for the Study of War and Society offered travel expenses to numerous archives as the project became my dissertation. I thank Dean Karen Coats, Alison Abra, and members of both grant committees for their faith in my scholarship.

I am deeply grateful to dozens of archivists and facilitators who helped locate source materials. Extra special thanks to Chris Marino and staff at the Hoover Institution who accommodated an unforeseen eleventh-hour flight change, then evacuated a roomful of historians during a San Mateo County wildfire. Thank you for keeping us all safe! I do not know who scanned my remaining boxes and folders, but they are owed a tremendous debt of gratitude for saving the day.

For their invaluable archival expertise and kindnesses, I also thank Sara Lipka and Tim Bloomquist at the *Chronicle of Higher Education*, Nick Herold and Meghan Lee-Parker at the Richard Nixon Presidential Library, Amy McDonald and Megan O'Connell at the Rubenstein Rare Book and Manuscript Library of Duke University, Sarah Cooper at the University of Wisconsin–Madison archives, Alexandra Bainbridge and Meredith Anne Weber at Pennsylvania State University's Special Collections Library, Holly Roper at the University of North Carolina at Chapel Hill's Wilson Special Collections Library, Clara Wilson at the North Carolina State University Special Collections Research Center, Laura Kristina Bronstad at the University of Tennessee Libraries Special Collections, Ken Barr at the Alabama Department of Archives and History, Dalton Alves and Rachel Burley at the Gelman

Library Special Collections Research Center of George Washington University, Rebecca Petersen May at Wake Forest University Special Collections and Archives, Alex Boucher at the University of Alabama Libraries Special Collections, Ann Case at Tulane University Special Collections, Ryan Semmes at the Congressional and Political Research Center of Mississippi State University, and Frank Smith, Jessica Perkins Smith, and Nekita Gandy at the Mississippi State University archives.

Greg Schneider kindly provided me with transcripts of his interviews with Young Americans for Freedom (YAF) executives and the unpublished papers of YAF's first historian, the late John Andrew, who passed just as this project began. Thanks also to Isaac Kamola and Ralph Wilson for sharing sources related to libertarian projects and ideas, and for providing feedback on chapters 2 and 7. I would also like to thank Mark Rudd and Robert Friedman, who are not conservatives, for their perspectives and source material.

Alumni of the College Republicans, Intercollegiate Studies Institute (ISI), YAF, and other late 1960s student clubs, as well as their partners and children, provided oral interviews and shared their memorabilia to bring this story to life. I am humbled by their enthusiasm and willingness to contribute their memories and artifacts. Several invited me to their homes to meet their families during interviews. Others chatted and dined with me at meetings of the Liberty Fund, the Philadelphia Society, and the Conservative Political Action Conference (CPAC). For their formal and informal conversations, I am forever indebted. While this project cannot possibly please all readers, I hope those oral history narrators will find my representations of their views truthful and accurate, even if they disagree with the conclusions I draw from them. I especially hope participants will find my treatment of white supremacists within their groups (and broadly under the banner of conservatism) fair, even if they personally do not share those views. To these narrators: I acknowledge that, for some, your political views have changed since your young adult years. The story I provide here is about those whose views have led them toward authoritarianism. Please know that I have done my best to distinguish you from those whose present-day vision is still to dismantle our nation's pluralist democracy and public higher education along with it.

Several historians helped develop my arguments within. Chats with colleagues during conferences of the American Historical Association, the Organization of American Historians, the History of Education Society, the Organization of Educational Historians, the Southern History of Education

Society, and the American Political History Conference at Purdue University were invaluable. I am particularly grateful to Michelle Nickerson, Seth Blumenthal, Ellen Schrecker, and Larry Glickman, who each offered feedback during our panels at Society for U.S. Intellectual History (S-USIH) conferences. Glickman and Geoffrey Kabaservice provided vastly different perspectives on the conclusion chapter, helping me frame my most critical arguments therein. Nancy MacLean offered so much encouragement and astutely pointed out where my passive voice was hiding critical parts of the account. Adam Laats assured me that my argument here about a right-wing Astroturf backlash in higher education did not contradict his excellent work on grassroots backlashes of the K–12 realm. My sincere thanks to all for your kind words and thoughtful suggestions.

The S-USIH Hannah Arendt Group for Shitty First Drafts offered a regular sounding board for my ideas as the manuscript developed; thank you to Tim Lacy, Rebecca Brenner Graham, Ethan Miller, and Andrew Seal. Matt Lassiter and Douglas Bristol provided helpful feedback during the proposal-writing process. John R. Thelin, Jonathan Schoenwald, Rick Perlstein, Kenneth Heineman, Rebecca Klatch, Kate Jewell, and Tyler Bridges each offered clarifying answers to tedious questions. Feedback from anonymous reviewers at the *History of Education Quarterly* helped me further clarify my arguments in chapters 6 and 9. Neil J. Young, Chad Walters, and many others previously mentioned read chapters and offered excellent comments in areas that intersected with their expertise. Brian Rosenwald was instrumental in condensing excerpts for the *Washington Post*'s Made by History column.

Emily Grecki and Leo Costigan at Wolf Street Editorial provided careful copyediting and polish to the manuscript at different stages. Emily, you were so patient with my multiple emails. Thanks to Michelle Witkowski and team at Westchester Publishing Services for the final copyedits. Kelly Clancy gave astute comments and gentle responses to a few half-baked and panicked ideas. Nick Osborne offered fantastic remarks on the entire project and, at its final stages, provided invaluable insights, allowing me to "tinker around the edges." Thanks also to Bridgette Werner for her exceptional indexing skills.

To every historian and other academic who read chapters or excerpts of the book: your collective additions, cuts, questions, musings, comments, criticisms, and praise constitute the final draft of this book in ways that I could not have constructed on my own. Thank you.

This project would likely still exist as a dissertation and several essays saved to my computer without the examples of others who inspired me to transform it into a book. Laura Portwood-Stacer and Melody Herr were invaluable mentors through this process. Beth English assured me acquisitions editors are eager for research that helps contextualize the present political moment. Thank you for urging me to "just hit send."

Many thanks are owed to my wonderful acquisitions editor, Andrew Winters; his team; and the anonymous reviewers for their support and enthusiasm. I could not have imagined a better advocate than Andrew, more keen readers than those who responded to my drafts, or a better home for this book than UNC Press. I am so appreciative to Heather Ann Thompson and Rhonda Y. Williams for warmly welcoming the book into the *Justice, Power, and Politics* series.

Most importantly, I am grateful for the unwavering support of my family and friends (as well as sweet distractions from our pets, Jack, Tchoup, Oscar, Willis, and Margot). To my Pilates, yoga, and other fitness instructors, thank you for absorbing my anxieties and offering me hours of peace through exercise, laughter, and friendship. To my biggest cheerleaders—James, Mom, Ronnie, Dad, and Wendy—thank you for everything. Grayden, Tate, Colin, Caroline, Adrienne, Trey, and Barbara: This is the book! I hope y'all like it. You don't have to read the whole thing.

Resistance from the Right

Introduction

· ·

On an unseasonably cool May 3, 1967, thousands of young people gathered in Hanover, New Hampshire, to hear George Wallace, the pro-segregation ex-governor of Alabama and candidate for president, deliver an address to the students and faculty of Dartmouth College. All 1,400 seats of Webster Hall were filled, with an additional 1,000 bystanders gathered outside the hall, tuned in to the campus radio broadcast. But the segregationist's speech was inaudible over boos and shouts of "Wallace—Racist" by members of Students for a Democratic Society (SDS) and the Afro-American Society (AAS). White audience members barked back "Shut up!" and goaded the SDS and the AAS to "Get out!" As SDS and AAS members began a walkout, some of the most raucous members of the crowd outside broke past police barricades and entered the auditorium. Hecklers shouted "Here comes the lynch mob!" as students burst into the hall and stormed the center aisle. Alabama state troopers brought in as reinforcement whisked Wallace offstage to his getaway vehicle, which was immediately surrounded and assailed by rocks and pounding fists.[1]

The commotion was contrived on the speaker's part as much as the audience's. The students wanted a spectacle of dissent. Wallace wanted their spectacle of dissent as a talking point: "They were trying to turn the car over and blow in the top," said the victimized segregationist to a reporter at the *Chronicle of Higher Education.* "That's academic freedom. That academic freedom will get you killed."[2] Wallace, a man who could "strut sitting down," often welcomed hostile activists to his populist rallies. Allowing them to demonstrate first, he would follow with a clever announcement from the stage: "You young people seem to know a lot of four-letter words. But I have two four-letter words you don't know: S-O-A-P and W-O-R-K."[3] To a Harvard professor, he once quipped, "If you can't distinguish at Harvard between honest dissent and overt acts of treason, then you ought to come down to Alabama, we'll teach you some law down there."[4] While Wallace's Dartmouth visit was indisputably antagonistic, a minority of voices in the crowd shouted his defense in defiance of AAS and SDS protesters. These students arrived in earnest, eager to hear the presidential candidate notorious for promising "segregation now, segregation tomorrow, segregation forever!" Shortly after the debacle, a Dartmouth faculty committee voted to suspend the anti-Wallace demonstrators for the remainder of the spring term.[5]

That a segregationist was invited to speak at an Ivy League college during the height of the civil rights movement was a curiosity, but it was not exceptional. Wallace's appearance at Dartmouth represents part of a longer story about conservative and right-wing backlash directed at higher education.[6] The right's grumblings that the academy functioned as a breeding ground for anti-Americanism were articulated throughout the 1930s and 1940s by anti–New Deal businessmen lamenting Keynesian economic solutions emanating from the ivory tower. These complaints were perhaps most popularly articulated in the 1950s by students who would become leaders of the postwar conservative movement: William F. Buckley Jr. and M. Stanton Evans. As Yale students, Bill Buckley and Stan Evans were themselves no strangers to the Ivy League. They were founding members of the Intercollegiate Studies Institute (ISI, then called the Intercollegiate Society of Individualists). The organization was created in 1953 by writers at the *Freeman* and *Human Events* magazines and bankrolled by the William Volker Fund as a foil to the Intercollegiate Socialist Society. With Buckley, the "enfant terrible of the right," as its first president, ISI functioned as an intellectual bulwark against a perceived liberal indoctrination on American campuses two decades before Wallace's invitation to Dartmouth.[7]

After leaving Yale, Buckley and Evans each produced book-length polemics condemning the humanist, liberal establishment dominated by progressives in America's oldest institutions, whom they dubbed elitists. In *God and Man at Yale: The Superstitions of "Academic Freedom"* (1951), Buckley eloquently chided the university's hypocrisy in soliciting financial contributions from Christian "individualists" while "persuading the sons of these supporters to be atheistic socialists."[8] In *Revolt on the Campus* (1961), Evans echoed these charges against socialism, further complaining that the campus was "a world in which a student of conservative inclination found himself badly in need of help, counsel, and information."[9] To provide these services, Buckley and Evans designed a second student organization—one with more temerity and punch than the highbrow ISI.

Buckley and Evans identified a small group of apprentices ideal for their project. Some were students who were volunteering alongside movement conservatives to draft Barry Goldwater, the cowboy senator from Arizona, as the Republican presidential nominee. Others were fighting to preserve the unpopular anticommunist loyalty oath requirement for recipients of National Defense Education Act funds. Still more were scouted by right-wing faculty, such as law and economics professor Gordon Tullock at the University of South Carolina, who sensed students' distaste for liberalism in their coursework.[10] Buckley shepherded these protégés with their various grievances to his family estate in Sharon, Connecticut, in September 1960. Out of this inaugural gathering came the activist youth organization Young Americans for Freedom (YAF). United by strident anticommunism, Christian moralism, and disdain for bureaucracy and planned economies, these student foot soldiers began a movement, under the direction of Buckley and others, to advance a provocative and antagonistic brand of conservatism before their professors and peers. In this context, George Wallace's invitation to Dartmouth—along with more recent lamentations of "wokeism" and critical race theory—can be understood as a major battle in conservatives' decades-long war against the academy and the cultural changes that liberal education champions.

The account that follows tells how right-wing students of the late 1960s, following the guidance of anti–New Deal elders who sponsored them financially and professionally, participated in an astroturf mobilization against a so-called liberal establishment in higher education during their time on campus—an era typically associated with the New Left antiwar and Black Power student movements. It describes how young conservatives, who became known as the New Right in the 1970s, used the skills they learned in college to consciously drive American politics and culture further to the authoritarian right, with the Republican Party as their vehicle. These former students include familiar Republican Party officials and strategists (Newt Gingrich, Bill Barr, Jeff Sessions, and Karl Rove), conservative and right-wing activists better recognized by historians (Pat Buchanan, David Duke, Tom Charles Huston, and Paul Weyrich), and less well-known architects of the nation's antidemocratic political shift (Morton Blackwell, R. Emmett Tyrrell Jr., David Keene, and others). This cohort of movement leaders cut their political teeth as college students engaged in a campus-based struggle against the peace and Black Power movements. When they left college in the 1970s, they represented the "Madison Avenue types" who, according to AFL-CIO president George Meany, were "trained in mass psychology and propaganda techniques, who have a computerized mailing list, a printing press and a government-subsidized mailing permit."[11]

But the history that follows is not of a vast right-wing conspiracy, as Meany implied. Rather, it is about the overt development of a broad network of men and institutions committed to restoring the United States to a preexisting—even imagined—time when plutocratic white Christians dominated the educational, political, and cultural spheres. Though the movement was chartered and set forth by only a few dozen powerful conservatives, it was not done in secret—quite the opposite. These movement makers have loudly proclaimed their service to the counter-left revolution.[12] They have been prolific writers on the topic of their own success. The reason for this book is that liberals and progressives have generally failed to take the Right's self-aggrandizing seriously, at least when it comes to revealing their own inner workings in the academy. This has been to the detriment of not just our public colleges and universities but our cultural and political spheres more broadly, as the New Right has committed to slashing liberal institutional powers to satisfy their preferences and seal their own advantages.

Conservatism seeks to maintain social and political conditions that bolster the already powerful.[13] *Resistance from the Right* tells the story of stakeholders in American higher education reacting to challenges to their power from the New Left and Black Power student resistance movements of the late 1960s. This narrative centers the political and cultural Right in their pursuit to maintain status quo conditions that, in their perception, benefited them. As we have come to understand conservative backlash against 1960s student activists, familiar stakeholders of the Right include college administrators and trustees; politicians; courts; business, church, and community leaders; the National Guard; and the police. This account provides a deeper investigation into another group of campus stakeholders: reactionary college students themselves. During these years, the student Right mobilized through traditionalist, libertarian, evangelical, and political campaign groups to join forces with sources of authority to thwart revolution in the academy and punish those who used direct action to bring it about. The organizations of the college Right included YAF, ISI, College Republicans, and Campus Crusade for Christ International. By the end of the decade, each of these groups had become, to some degree, beholden to ideas promoted by YAF. What bound them together through the Vietnam War and civil rights era, they claimed, was anticommunism. What they were actually united by was something much less sinister: liberalism.

The 1960s student Right is usually mentioned in the footnotes of historical studies of the New Left and Black Power movements as part of the collective backlash forces that progressive activists faced. Historical monographs that do attend to the student Right have established an important baseline for gauging the identities and activities of conservative youth, but their scope is limited to YAF and ISI alone, with broad coverage of the organizations' histories throughout the entire decade of the 1960s and beyond, rather than a focus on their reactionary roles during the late years of the campus wars.[14] These monographs are now over two decades old.[15] Providing an updated evaluation, *Resistance from the Right* considers previously unanalyzed sources to offer a more thorough investigation, while tightening the chronology to spotlight the college Right's most combative years. This study also widens the discussion of college conservatism beyond YAF and ISI, incorporating other political, evangelical, libertarian, and white supremacist student groups into a more comprehensive analysis.[16]

If general readers recall the student Right during the late 1960s protest era at all, they are usually remembered as a weak, disaffected cadre of reactionaries throwing counterweights at the radicalism inherent in the New Left. YAF is perhaps the only notorious group historians name when mentioning the student Right. This is understandably so. As a small and generally ineffective force on their own, conservative students experienced real power only when they enhanced and elevated the voices of existing authorities. But the student Right's relative weakness in comparison to the student Left ironically became an efficiency once these young people understood that they did not need to be popular to wield power. So long as they tapped into existing channels of authority, winning over their peers was not necessary to achieve their desired ends.

This understanding was formative in developing the New Right's organizing techniques, not just during their time on campus but for the rest of their careers as the next generation of movement leaders. They understood that democracy presented a challenge to their unpopular positions (in favor of the Vietnam War and against social justice causes). But they also realized that in a democratic system, the *illusion* of popularity remained essential. Conservative baby boomers thus discovered that they needed only to appear popular—to claim to represent a youth silent majority or to cast doubt on the legitimacy of actual majorities—while relying on external powers to uphold structures that privileged them. In the context of national backlash to the New Left and Black Power movements, the collegiate Right internalized how existing power structures functioned, then used this understanding to shape the conservative movement they would carry forth from within the Republican Party.

This book complicates our understanding of right-wing backlash as populist, since the narrators within were college students at a time when higher education was inaccessible to most. The inclusion of Ivy League and other elite institutions throws this dynamic into even further relief. It challenges assumptions of conservative backlash as grassroots by exploring the students' impressive financial support. The Right's campus mobilization was less an organic youth endeavor than a top-down directive from funding giants in the larger movement, primarily leaders associated with the Foundation for Economic Education, the Mont Pelerin Society, and writers at *National Review, Modern Age, Human Events, Commentary,* and *Public Interest* magazines. Major benefactors included Harold Luhnow of the William Volker Fund, businessman Charles Koch, former New Jersey governor Charles Edison, banking and oil magnate Richard Mellon Scaife, philanthropist Henry Salvatori, and others connected through direct mail operations by fundraisers Marvin Liebman and Richard Viguerie. In addition to funding, young conservatives received regular mentorship and direction from elders such as Buckley, Goldwater, Ronald Reagan, William Rusher, Strom Thurmond, and a host of other prominent white male writers, politicians, evangelical leaders, segregationists, and anticommunist conspiracists.

Since graduating college in the early 1970s, many former members of the student Right (including all fifty-six participants interviewed in this study) have populated the academy, the legal system, politics, the media, think tanks, state and federal agencies, and private industry, serving as economic, political, and cultural influencers. They willingly share that throughout their professional careers, they have purposefully expanded their ideological influence to guarantee an enduring resistance to liberalism in whatever arena they hold power. The New Right's coalition of former YAFers, College Republicans, and ISI students have gone on to found think tanks, operate and fundraise through political action committees, and exercise their organizational talents to bring new constituents, including the religious Right, into the Republican Party. For decades, these alumni have trained new generations to elevate traditionalist and libertarian grievances in United States politics and have relentlessly waged culture wars to return to what they consider more desirable social and economic conditions of the past.

Understanding how the New Right was educated and how they continue to work as activists is not just important to anyone studying the history of the Republican Party, American conservatism, or social movements more broadly; it is fundamental to studying higher education. The people discussed here are not just former college students—they are powerful present-day leaders who have dedicated their careers to fundamentally reshaping liberal higher education, including college founders, college presidents, faculty of various disciplines, and leaders of educational think tanks and youth activist training organizations. Other alumni included in this study work outside higher education but have nonetheless held influence over education policy, including two former attorneys general, members of Congress, White House staffers spanning the Nixon to Trump administrations, federal judges, conservative lobbyists and advisers, members of conservative media and advising enterprises, lawyers, activists, and others who view liberalism in the academy as a problem deserving intense scrutiny and sanction.

To construct a narrative of the campus wars from the conservative perspective, *Resistance from the Right* looks to oral histories from former college students (representing YAF, ISI, College Republicans, ROTC programs, and other groups) and their mentors. Most of the interviews were conducted in participants' homes and workplaces; at the 2018 annual meeting of the Philadelphia Society in Fort Worth, Texas; at meetings of the Liberty Fund in Indianapolis, Indiana, in 2018 and Chicago, Illinois, in 2019; at an alumni reunion during the 2019 Conservative Political Action Conference in Oxon Hill, Maryland; and virtually in 2020. My own interviews are supplemented with transcripts of interviews with YAF mentors—including William F. Buckley Jr., William Rusher, and Richard Viguerie—conducted by historian Gregory L. Schneider between 1994 and 1997. The nearly five dozen interviews are enhanced by archival collections from the Hoover Institution at Stanford University and the Lyndon Johnson and Richard Nixon presidential libraries; news coverage from the *Chronicle of Higher Education*, the *New York Times*, and regional and community print journalism; chapter artifacts from public and private university special collections nationwide; and the personal collections of memorabilia and literature offered by interview participants.

The story unfolds chronologically from 1967 to 1970—the peak of the campus wars—to show how the collegiate Right adapted and enhanced its strategies for countering the Left over the course of a few years. Though this is not an exhaustive list of their endeavors, it illustrates the general perspectives, motives, interests, and behaviors of conservative students of the baby boomer generation. Their activities as college students not only informed their future politics (and the future character of the Republican Party), but also gave shape to subsequent policies, precedents, and laws that limit perceived progressivism in the academy today.

This book is organized thematically into two parts. Part 1, "Coalition Building," broadly tells of the student Right's efforts to mobilize, with guidance and funding from older mentors who supported their fight to shield the campus from changes demanded by peace and civil rights activists. It offers a comprehensive examination of the student Right's decision to transition from the promotion of conservative ideas to reactionary resistance against their political foils as college conservatives defined what it meant to "act like" an American, placing antiwar and racial justice activists outside the definition.

Chapter 1 situates the academy in the context of national politics, discusses contemporary student demographics, and introduces the ideological contours of the student Right. An examination of federal funding for institutional military research explains faculty and administrative imperatives to repress antiwar dissent. This chapter is most helpful to those with an interest in the 1960s landscape of higher education.

Chapter 2 explores the conservative rationale for "balancing" the academy through right-wing educational nonprofits. These nonprofits, especially ISI, offered seminars and free literature to equip students with traditionalist counterarguments in their classes. ISI and other organizations provided generous fellowships to ensure a continuous conservative pipeline into the professorate. Detailed instruction manuals from movement elders, and specially crafted press releases directly from the Nixon administration, guided the students in creating content for alternative campus newspapers and radio programs.

Chapter 3 chronicles YAF executives' efforts to make student conservatism appear more widespread to support their claim that the Right represented a campus majority. An exploration of the backlash to peace demonstrations in the fall of 1967 and support for war industry recruitment demonstrates how the Right's independent attempts to organize were initially disjointed and inefficient. Organizing broadly around the principle of "anticommunism" (which meant anti-liberalism) helped groups like YAF reach new constituencies. This chapter further covers students' appropriation of New Left slogans and symbols and discusses how the guise of humor helped conceal white supremacy. Finally, it details how the Right strategically captured moderate College Republican clubs and student government associations.

Chapter 4 details conservative mobilization against antiwar and civil rights demonstrators at Columbia University in the spring of 1968 and the anti-leftist majority coalition organizational model that emerged in its aftermath. Under this model, the leading conservative group abandoned its multiple objectives (as outlined in the Sharon Statement) to reorganize around the singular idea of stopping the New Left. This model was revolutionary, and became a fundamental part of the Right's mobilization thereafter.

Part 2, "Law, Order, and Punishment," elaborates the transition in student focus from recruitment to demands for punishment and, in some instances, violence against their opponents. It also demonstrates how the vanguard conservative club, YAF, fully committed to the singular aim of resisting an ill-defined Left to attract new recruits under the banner of a unified student silent majority.

Chapter 5 analyzes student participation in campaigns for law-and-order and segregationist Republican Party presidential nominees throughout the fall of 1968. Chapter 6 explores the backlash against civil rights demands and calls for Black studies programs and departments in 1969. These two chapters most fully explore how resistance to racial justice was inherent to college conservatism during these years, though it is a theme that recurs throughout the book.

Chapter 7 recounts the censure and expulsion of libertarians from YAF for pointing out common ground with the New Left on certain issues related to conscription, civil rights, and police brutality. It demonstrates how, ideologically, students on the Right chose whatever rhetorical defenses they needed to protect traditionalist values and were willing to exile long-standing members who challenged these inconsistencies. In response, traditionalists expanded their outreach among other students by enthusiastically supporting campus athletics against the New Left charge that contact sports were a proxy for war.

Chapter 8 explores conservative defenses of the Vietnam War and campus ROTC programs. YAF's nationwide Freedom Offensive campaign encouraged students to become legally and physically assertive in anticipation of leftist demonstrations by threatening lawsuits against their colleges' trustees and students while goading radicals into physical altercations.

Chapter 9 analyzes the Right's support for the invasion of Cambodia and the massacre of Kent State University students in the spring of 1970. It also examines the Right's lawsuits designed to force institutions to remain open during campus strikes, demonstrating the movement's willingness to use the courts to bend administrators to their political will.

In these years, radical demands for peace and racial justice emboldened the student Right to challenge progressives' claim of majority representation, reframe their arguments, and focus on the Left's less respectable tactics to create suspicion around campus antiwar and civil rights initiatives. Through alliances with powerful figures of the larger conservative movement and corporate sponsors who delivered, among other things, financial support and the assurance of legal, physical, or carceral punishment against their adversaries, campus conservatives harnessed multiple forces to ensure a battery of checks against progressivism in the academy.

Over the past several decades, alumni of these groups and others who have been inspired by authoritarian rhetoric and techniques have served as college and university trustees, have been members of governing boards, or have shaped university policy and precedent through financial gifts or legislative appropriations. Traditionalist trustees, legislators, and alumni continue to use their influence to remove tenure protections in state colleges and universities, deny tenure for and pressure the resignation of outspoken faculty, revoke scholarships from student protesters, and force campuses to remain open during the COVID-19 pandemic. Red state legislators encourage students to record and report their professors for perceived political bias in the classroom. As this research demonstrates, the current panic from the Right over student culture; curricula; and faculty hiring, tenure, and promotion is part of a longer historical pattern. Conservatives' ability to gain power over the academy, implement the Right's favored restraints, and punish those who threaten their minoritarian capacity is not a recent phenomenon but part of a longer iterative process. The Right has developed, refined, and expanded these strategies through sixty years of practice.

Part I   Coalition Building

··

Throughout the late 1960s, conservative college students worked to cultivate an anti-leftist mood on campus and in local and national politics by
calling attention to the perceived victimization of white Christian traditionalist students by atheist, Black, and Jewish left-wing revolutionaries. While
exposing a prevailing progressivism among faculty, graduate assistants, and
student body representatives, conservatives began to assemble anti-liberal
campus clubs and create their own sources for counter-messaging via print
and radio. Intellectual direction and financial support for this new campus
"conservative countersphere" came from mentors and donors in the larger
conservative movement.[1] Campus leaders and their media and industry
sponsors organized extracurricular workshops to train students to become
more intellectually and legally combative against their adversaries. Movement conservatives' mentorship fused intellectual conservatism with the
populist sentiments of students and gave academic justification for reactionary pro-war and anti–civil rights impulses. Graduate fellowships sponsored by the Intercollegiate Studies Institute (ISI), the Institute for Humane
Studies, and other organizations began the now longstanding tradition of
placing conservatives in doctoral programs to ensure that the Right maintains a presence in academia for generations. This section examines how
students on the right defined what it meant to be a conservative—and how
to "act like," in their estimation, an American. It also describes several key
strategies students on the right used for organizing, recruiting, counter-
messaging, and building coalitions with other student clubs and sources of
authority on and off campus from 1967 to 1968.

1 Soap and Work

On a Sunday night in March 1967, an excited crowd packed Harvard University's Sanders Theatre to witness a performance of the Sing-Out Kids, a youth auxiliary of the Moral Re-Armament evangelical group. The Up with People! production opened dramatically as 130 beaming teenagers burst onto the stage in a Broadway-like chorus of the "Star Spangled Banner." At the invitation of the Harvard-Radcliffe Young Republicans, the Sing-Out Kids choir was entertaining a mostly white audience made up of students and housewives and their children. The performance featured songs such as "You Can't Live Crooked (and Think Straight)," "Freedom Isn't Free," and "What Color Is God's Skin?"—a soliloquy by one of its few Black troubadours. The gleaming show troupe of straight, "freshly scrubbed" youth in blazers and jumpers smiled as cast members delivered scripted statements about abstinence from drinking, smoking, and dating to the Harvard audience. When the production concluded, the crowd of satisfied mothers and young audience members rewarded the ensemble with a polite standing ovation.[1]

Other Harvard-Radcliffe students left the theater snickering. An opinion editorial in the campus *Crimson* dubbed the performance "overtly anti-intellectual" and "very simple for 18-year-old Midwestern minds." The standing ovation was "strictly emotional. A successful Sing-Out creates an hysterical atmosphere where rationality is lost to powerful feelings of patriotism and goodness in the catchy rock beat of the songs."[2] The *Crimson* writer's condescending review was a typical response to obtuse displays of patriotism and morality on college campuses in the countercultural 1960s. But outside the ivory tower, the Sing-Out Kids enjoyed popularity with mainstream audiences.[3] That they were asked to perform by Harvard-Radcliffe Young Republicans indicates their appeal to a certain demographic of elite students as well.

At the time of the performance, the liberal mood that appeared to prevail in higher education was deteriorating across the country. The year 1962 marked the beginning of a critical decline in liberalism from which the United States only momentarily rebounded in 2018. Liberal mood has

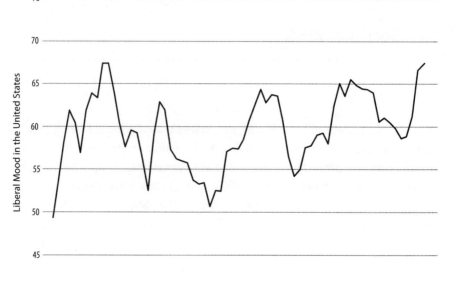

Public policy mood (liberalism). The liberal mood has only just begun to rebound from its postwar peak preceding American intervention in the Vietnam War. Still, preliminary data for 2020 and 2021 are anticipated to show "a moderate conservative movement from the 2018 high point of liberal sentiment." See James A. Stimson, Public Policy Mood (Liberalism), 1952 to 2020, http://stimson .web.unc.edu/data/.

continued to deteriorate since that recent high point. Between 1967 and 1970, the national desire for liberalism plunged. Although there was a brief uptick from 1970 to 1973—the era corresponding with American withdrawal from the Vietnam War—liberalism in the American mood continued to depreciate through the 1970s. Even when it began to swing back toward liberalism in the 1980s, scores remained close to those of the early Vietnam War years. As the American mood became less liberal, conservative politicians capitalized on the opportunity to gain more power, sparking a "conservative ascendancy" in American politics that has lasted into the twenty-first century.[4]

Ironically, in the historical memory of American higher education, these years are synonymous with widespread liberalism on campus. Common recollections of college life in the late 1960s and early 1970s include antiwar demonstrations, the creation of ethnic and women's studies programs, and the deconstruction of social norms in appearance, dress, and recreation. Progressive changes in higher education from 1967 to 1970 are better understood as feats accomplished *despite* an apathetic campus majority and a boisterous antiliberal assault from the political, cultural, and religious Right.

A Turning Point in American Higher Education

In the early postwar period, white college students were largely disengaged from national and international politics.[5] For those interested in these issues, debates between peers on opposite ends of the political spectrum were generally peaceful. The University of California at Berkeley's Free Speech Movement of 1964 is exemplary of left-right student cooperation against the common enemy of oppressive administrators and in loco parentis restrictions. As the decade waned, however, common ground was lost over American intervention in Vietnam's civil war, the extent to which universities should aid military research, and demands for representative curricula. By 1967, students on the Left and the Right arrived at an impasse over these and other issues.[6] News outlets referred to extremism on either political end as the "New McCarthyism," with each side attempting to stifle and discredit its opposition. A 1967 assessment by the *Chronicle of Higher Education* determined that students would rather burn books by authors they disliked than read them.[7]

Even at historically Black colleges and universities (HBCUs), where nonviolent direct action had been the tradition for dissent, 1967 marked a turning point as some activists introduced militant tactics to their demonstrations. Leadership changes in civil rights organizations like the Student Nonviolent Coordinating Committee (SNCC) resulted in explicit calls for Black nationalism and militant resistance. SNCC chair Stokely Carmichael advised Black students to disassociate from white liberals, as whites in the movement, he argued, conceded white supremacy.[8] Alongside Carmichael, SNCC's H. Rap Brown and Black Panther Huey Newton echoed calls for Black Power. At Berkeley, Carmichael insisted students burn their draft cards, openly carry firearms, shout communist slogans, and refer to police as "pigs." Conservatives pointed to Black militarism, a response to white supremacy, as a reason to harden existing oppressive systems and escalate violence against demonstrators who resisted these structures.

For the student New Left, the Vietnam War and anti-Black racism were causes for unraveling order and abandoning the legacy of scholarly debate.

As American aggression in Southeast Asia escalated under the Johnson and Nixon administrations, the federal government appeared indifferent to student demands to end the war and—especially—the draft. Political and social inaction were the catalysts for violent, radical activism from some leaders among the mostly white New Left. Crusading against a military-industrial complex, students burned their draft cards, occupied campus buildings where military research was being sponsored by the Department of Defense, and bombed Bank of America branches to protest the company's financial involvement in the war. Black Power student strikers shut down campuses to demand increased minority student enrollment, scholarships, faculty diversity, and the creation of Black studies programs and other representative curricula. For some Black and white activist leaders, militancy and violence were purposeful in publicizing their needs.[9]

As students on the left became radicalized, students on the right became intensely reactionary. And while some of the most extreme right-wing students did respond to perceived threats from the Left with violence, conservatives generally did not need to match radicals' hostilities, as they were confident that they had the violence of the government on their side via the police and the National Guard. Instead, conservative students committed to countering resistance from the Left by celebrating administrators and other authorities who firmly refused demands for peace and social justice.

Managing Student Affairs

Throughout the 1960s and 1970s, matters of student conduct that disrupted the classroom and campus, including demonstrations and other acts of dissent, were generally handled by staff within academic affairs departments. The modern use of student affairs professionals trained in theories of college student development, counseling, conflict resolution, social justice, and crisis management was not yet commonplace, and this would not change until after the academy's upheaval in the era described here.[10] Exponential growth in enrollments throughout the 1960s meant a slightly more diversified student body in terms of race, gender, socioeconomic status, and age. Many students accessing new need-based grants and work-study programs, including a number of Vietnam veterans, became the first in their families to seek a college education. As the public university student corps became older, less white, less affluent, and less male, administrative staff found themselves gravely unprepared to manage complex matters of student conduct using traditional methods designed with wealthy young white men in mind.

By 1967, administrators and community leaders expressed concern that students' unruly conduct could spill into surrounding cities and create a burden that local police would be unprepared to meet. Violent protests sparked negotiations between administrators and city mayors regarding town and gown boundaries for student and non-student arrests, establishing precedents for campus security personnel to arm themselves with guns.[11] Toward the end of the decade, campus security officers were entrusted with authority equal to that of city police, and they expanded their territories of patrol outside of the campus perimeter. Nationwide, campus and municipal police escalated demonstrations into riots that often ended in National Guard occupations of universities and surrounding neighborhoods. By mid-1970, reactionary police and state military forces had killed students at South Carolina State College (now University), the University of California at Santa Barbara, Kent State University, and Jackson State College (now University), and arrested and injured thousands. Police and military escalations, such as the infamous Kent State massacre in May 1970, led to additional policies and laws that stymied student ability to assemble for dissent.

College Student Demographics

Though the national student body was beginning to diversify, American college campuses were still mostly composed of full-time students between seventeen and twenty-two years old who were middle class, Christian, unmarried, and overwhelmingly white (95 percent of undergraduates were white in 1969).[12] This demographic was even more pronounced at southern campuses, where integration was violently challenged through massive resistance.[13] Most public institutions were diversifying by socioeconomic class more quickly than by gender or race, as many white women and Black students were still educated in women's colleges and HBCUs.

By 1970, a quarter of all students were accessing benefits provided by the Johnson administration's Great Society educational programs. The Higher Education Act of 1965 (HEA) provided federal financial aid to students who had been historically underrepresented in college, including the poor. In addition to offering guaranteed federal student loans, HEA offered work-study opportunities and, for the first time, need-based Educational Opportunity Grants that deemphasized achievement to qualify. With so much funding provided to higher education in the postwar years, enrollment soared from 2.5 million to 8.8 million between 1955 and 1974, an increase of over 350 percent in less than twenty years.[14]

Citing a study by the American Council on Education, a *Chronicle of Higher Education* profile of the class of 1970 offers a glimpse into the academic and social life of students in the late 1960s. Nearly half (46.3 percent) reported a parental income of greater than $10,000 (about $95,000 in 2023). Almost half of all students—43.9 percent at public and 49.6 percent at private universities—reported that the qualifier "liberal" was "very descriptive of [my] college's atmosphere," though students identified their own politics as liberal (19.1 percent) or conservative (15.3 percent) at similarly low rates. Politically interested but not activist, 70.7 percent reported voting in student elections, but only 15.3 percent had attended a campus demonstration in the past year. This cohort was ambitious, politically astute, and driven by recognition. Student objectives ranked as "very important" included the following: "to be an authority in my field" (66 percent), "to keep up with political affairs" (57.8 percent), "to succeed in my own business" (53 percent), and "to obtain recognition from my peers" (42.6 percent). Half (51.8 percent) asked questions in class. Most (60.1 percent) claimed to have an above-average understanding of others, while ranking their own social self-confidence as low (29.8 percent). A majority (63.5 percent) attended church regularly. Half drank beer (53.5 percent) or wine (44.4 percent). Less than half (42.5 percent) had experienced a blind date.[15]

Given these statistics, popular depictions of students in the 1960s as unruly and countercultural at best, or radical and violent at worst, mischaracterize the broadly square, affluent, and Christian student body. This is not only a historical misunderstanding but also a contemporary one, as evidenced by political and media depictions of particularly bold and unrepresentative youth actors such as Abbie Hoffman and Bernardine Dohrn and their associated organizations, the Youth International Party and Weather Underground. Such mischaracterizations afforded the leaders of the growing conservative movement, and the students they mentored, strawman adversaries to unite against.

Conservative students and their elder sponsors extended the typecast depiction of the violent radical to the broader antiwar and civil rights student movements and called for their demonstrations to be criminalized. During the Cold War years, influential white men at the head of the movement hyperbolized liberalism as a less conspicuous but nonetheless dangerous iteration of Marxist ideology. Fearful of students' assertive calls for justice, a combination of conservative forces—including other students, administrators, trustees, legislators, federal investigators, businesses, churches, and those who simply identified themselves as taxpayers—worked to cultivate a pro-war, anti–civil rights attitude on campus and more broadly across the American public.

An effect of this increasingly revanchist mood was that college administrators expressed general suspicion of liberal–left goals, which manifested in punishment and resistance to educational reform measures. Progressive aims toward educational justice—such as diversifying the faculty and student body and creating Black, Chicano, gender, and other area studies programs—were effectively delayed as administrators', trustees', and other stakeholders' positions were conditioned by the Right's insistence that these changes would be anti-American and destabilizing to the social order. But Cold Warriors did understand the value of area studies programs, such as Russian and East Asian studies, which they encouraged as useful pedagogical tools for combating communism. Area studies were almost universally acknowledged as essential for advancing social (and in the Right's case, geopolitical) interests—it was a matter of whose interests they served.

Student Culture and Politics

Counterculture and the New Left

Given that popular perceptions of 1960s college life and the Right's sloganeering against their classmates and adversaries involved caricatured versions of student types, it is useful to get a sense of student characteristics as contemporaries envisioned them.

The term *counterculture* refers to cultural changes of the 1960s in youth dress, physical appearance, music, drug use, sexuality, and communal living. It is associated with the emergence of psychedelic Day-Glo art, tie-dyed shirts, love bead necklaces, bell-bottoms, ripped jeans, slogan T-shirts, and the affirmative expressions "far out" and "right on." The counterculture movement rejected materialism while promoting naturalness in food, health, and appearance.[16] Those who exuded the counterculture ethos were called hippies.

Hippies and the New Left were not mutually exclusive. Sociologist Rebecca Klatch explains that as a counter*culture*, there were many more hippies than New Left activists, and there were far fewer New Left activists who identified as militant.[17] While having overlapping tastes in dress and music and similar habits of recreational drug use, New Left activists were assertive in their politics, whereas hippies preferred nonparticipation in, or "dropping out of," society. Most conservatives failed to make the distinction and regarded the broad liberal–left spectrum with disdain. The Right regularly denounced anyone to their left as a "pinko," implying a degree of association with "red" communism.

The New Left describes a cohort of young, mostly white, activists seeking revolution in favor of liberal participatory democracy to correct social, political, and economic inequalities. They further demanded an end to Cold War militarization. The New Left's cumbersome missions were expressed fully in Students for a Democratic Society's (SDS) Port Huron Statement, but essentially their aims were antiwar, anti-capitalist, and antiracist. To reach these ends, the New Left led regular demonstrations on and off campus. After 1967, demonstrations frequently morphed into total strikes, with students occupying administration buildings or pledging to skip class until an injustice was corrected.

New Left clubs included SDS, the National Mobilization Committee to End the War in Vietnam (the Mobe), the Youth International Party (Yippies), and SNCC. New Left leaders had become increasingly frustrated that their peaceful demonstrations and teach-ins of semesters past were not effecting change. The belief that universities were institutions of an oppressive system, combined with administrators' unsympathetic reactions to their demonstrations, sparked militancy among some leaders. Police and state militaries were magnetized to antiwar and Black Power events, which were growing larger in terms of participation and national interest, and violence came to characterize the events in media headlines. After 1967, each of these groups was infamous for acts of domestic terrorism by a small number of their members, and all of them were known by their respective local police forces.

Conservative elders, such as Virginia Board of Education chair and future Supreme Court justice Lewis F. Powell Jr., stoked public outrage against student demonstrators by linking single-campus demonstrations to global communist plots. Powell claimed that New Left organizations were "communist oriented and supported," though their "dominant philosophy" was nihilism. Representing the Right's thought leaders, Powell maintained that leftist students cynically offered no solutions other than destruction against existing institutions. Organizations like SDS "set the pace" for the broader New Left and were able to draw thousands of "regular" students into their schemes for revolution. Regular students, who were merely "motivated by naïve idealism and taken in by the slogans," would soon become "the shock troops of revolution" if radical leaders were allowed to carry on unpunished, and if administrators failed "to build a broad base of support among students in the main stream of campus life."[18] This logic on the part of the Right justified their calls for administrative and law enforcement retribution. At stake was not just the campus but every American institution that the self-proclaimed revolutionaries were after, starting with the universities. Powell's logic further exemplifies the Right's understanding of how communism spread and how to combat its appeal through containment, which they applied to the lowest organizational unit: the classroom.

Squares, Squishes, and Jesus Freaks

The values conservatives promoted were exemplified by the Sing-Out Kids' evangelical show troupe, including patriotism, abstinence, and a dismissive racial color blindness. For conservatives, student life in the late 1960s was a carryover from the culture of the 1950s. Libertarian activist Jerome Tuccille claimed that a hypothetical meeting of Young Americans for Freedom (YAF) at New York's Waldorf-Astoria in the mid-1960s would have felt like "entering a time capsule and being transported ten or fifteen years into the past." One would find themselves "surrounded by a brigade of Pat Boones."[19] Young men on the right dressed in slacks, ties, vests, and blazers or corduroy jackets. They sported meticulously groomed crew cuts. Spiro Agnew wristwatches and Adam Smith neckties were fashionable adornments of square men. In the era of popular mini shift dresses and relaxed hairstyles, many college women on the right still wore long skirts and tightly coiffed updos to class.[20] Southern college women, especially, embraced the 1950s and early 1960s bouffant style, as well as the flipped bob popularized by First Lady Jacqueline Kennedy.

Students of mature dress and traditionalist demeanor referred to themselves as squares. Squares always appeared neat and clean, dressed modestly, attended church, studied, and listened to Christian worship and popular music. They loathed their bearded, bell-bottomed peers, whose causes disrupted class and campus life and whose countercultural dress and attitudes bent or violated traditional gender norms. Squares often pointed to the long hair of effeminate pot smokers and draft dodgers as an affront to the masculine standard. They revered the machismo of performers Ronald

Reagan, John Wayne, and Pat Boone, and the femininity of peers such as Rosemary McGrath, chair of the Greenwich Village YAF and known as "La Pasionaria of the Right," and Nancy Jones, the "Square Cher," whom they elevated to celebrity status within their social circles.[21]

Central to square identity was "acting like" an American—presenting oneself according to affluent white Christian heteronormative standards (discussed in chapter 3) and, as necessary, exhibiting a performative style of patriotism. College squares were deeply affronted by antiwar and civil rights activists' natural hairstyles and overall countercultural ethos. Squares stereotyped their adversaries on the left as unwashed and unmotivated, often parroting politicians' condemnations of hippies as unfamiliar with soap and work.[22] Deserving of the punishments they received from administrators and police, conservative movement leaders characterized campus activists as little more than "spoiled work shirkers who lived off illegitimate extractions from taxpayers."[23]

According to former YAF chair and executive director of the Republican Party of Texas Wayne Thorburn, squares mostly represented "more a social statement against the hippies than a well thought out political movement in any way."[24] A few squares attempted to begin a Square Power movement (to counter calls for student power and Black Power), creating a logo of a square with an upward pointing arrow.[25] Those who were antiradical but not quite square enough were given the negative designation "squishes." For the most devout square, a politician's worthiness was determined by an index from Americans for Constitutional Action. "It was commonly regarded, 'What's his ACA rating? Oh, 72 percent? He's kind of squishy.' If someone wasn't solidly conservative, they were a squish," recalled Thorburn.[26] "Solid" traditionalists had little tolerance for nuance in attitude and often purged squishes from their ranks, especially libertarians (discussed in chapter 7).

Conservative in their Christianity but culturally liberal, Jesus freaks were a squishy Christian youth subculture best remembered for their collective, hippie-like lifestyle.[27] Squares found common ground with the Jesus freaks' stance on morality but were skeptical of communal living, which they believed too closely mirrored the "freeloading" counterculture. Campus Crusade for Christ International was even more religiously conservative and far less countercultural. Almost all Campus Crusaders of the era were white and from middle-class to wealthy families. Their dress was rooted in square style, with hints of countercultural embellishments. A *New*

York Times reporter described Crusaders' dress as composed of "button-down shirts, moderately long hair, sideburns—neatly trimmed. . . . Bodies are healthy, athletic and tanned." Students themselves were "friendly extroverted campus leaders" whose good looks often won them financial gifts from approving business donors.[28]

Black Conservatives

Conservatives were practically identical in terms of demographics. Almost entirely white, most were ethnically northern European, Protestant or Catholic, middle class, and male. Of the three known Black members of YAF and the Intercollegiate Studies Institute (ISI) during these years, Jay Parker was the most prominent. Parker was a traditionalist who served on YAF's national board. After college, he cofounded the Lincoln Institute and its magazine, the *Lincoln Review*, to study how policies implemented by Democrats were "harmful to the long-range interests of blacks."[29] YAF alumnus Lee Edwards has memorialized Parker as "the founding father of the Black conservative movement in America."[30] Indeed, Parker mentored today's most prominent Black conservative, Supreme Court justice Clarence Thomas. Parker helped secure Thomas's first job in politics during the Reagan administration. As a testament to Parker's influence in his political and professional life, Justice Thomas delivered the eulogy at Parker's funeral.[31] Other Black conservatives Parker is known to have had close relationships with through the Lincoln Institute include Anne Wortham, Walter Williams, and Thomas Sowell, though these three do not appear to have been members of activist college organizations.[32]

The only other Black YAF member who appears in the archival record and whom participants interviewed in this study remembered was Myrna Bain, who founded the YAF chapter at Hunter College in New York and whose opinion pieces were featured in the *National Review*. However, Bain went on to become a professor of Black studies at City College of New York and a feminist activist for LGBTQ women of color.

William Barclay Allen, now professor emeritus of political science at Michigan State University, appears to be the only Black student affiliate of ISI in these years. With approximately 20,000 members in YAF and 100,000 members in the College Republican National Committee during this period, the three Black students were quite exceptional among the Right's campus organizations.

Between 1963 and 1969, women constituted approximately 48 percent of undergraduates nationwide, though their enrollments were not evenly dispersed, as women's colleges were still popular, especially in the Northeast and the South. Because college was viewed as a pathway to the workforce, women's education was often perceived as gratuitous. Most women were married by the age of twenty-two with the expectation that they would not join the workforce at all, or at least not until their youngest child reached the age of schooling, and that any jobs they would take would not require a college degree.[33] Even within the most progressive New Left and civil rights groups, women participants were still relegated to "women's work," such as note-taking, coffee making, envelope stuffing, and errand running. Sexism was blatant, and almost all organizational leaders were men.

Some conservative women did show interest in the second-wave feminist movement of the era. University of North Carolina YAF member Elizabeth Knowlton explored progressive arguments within the pages of the *Carolina Renaissance*. Offering a conservative defense of women's liberation, she acknowledged that issues raised by white feminists regarding marriage, children, housework, wage difference, and general social discrimination could resonate with women on the right. She organized meetings on the Chapel Hill campus so that other conservative women could "discuss these problems and work out their own types of solutions."[34]

Women interviewed for this study had divergent views of the role gender played within their conservative groups. Some expressed that sexism was not an issue in YAF, citing the fact that there were women on YAF's national board and in state chair positions. Others expressed that gender issues never arose. However, regarding campus life and in loco parentis policies, one participant remembered appreciating the curfew and entrance and exit logs in her women's residence hall, stating, "I liked knowing that if something happened to me and I didn't make it home, somebody would be looking for me. If I was on a date that wasn't going well, I had a hard stop to it. I liked having that back up. As I recall, you had to come down to the lobby to meet a guy." Rather than championing solutions to end violence against women, she represents those on the right who believed dangerous conditions were inevitable and that paternalistic policies were necessary to protect her and other women students from expected nighttime assaults and dating violence.

Remembering the dress code at the University of South Carolina, another YAF alumna, Patricia Thackston-Ganner, who became a professor of social work at Limestone University—a private Christian college in Gaffney, South Carolina—laughingly recalled that "women couldn't wear pants to class in '67, that's how backwards we were!" She also remembered nightly curfews in the residence hall, as well as the requirement to get a library pass to conduct research past nine o'clock at night. Unlike other interviewees, she asserted that YAF had "huge gender differences. [Male YAF leaders] would be talking to a group of us and never caught the eye of the women. I think they thought we weren't worth paying any attention to." Most of the women in YAF were friends, Thackston-Ganner remembered, "because there were so few of us." She expressed that after being elected as the South Carolina state chair, she had "the worst experience," explaining that "someone made a smartass remark about me 'sleeping [my] way to the top' to become state chairman. There was a real issue with women being in charge. Because they saw feminism as a liberal progressive stance, not as a right earned."[35]

Regardless of how they regarded feminism, most women students seemed interested in conservatism for reasons that had little to do with advancing women's position in society. For one woman, it was the Right's "data-driven" and "sane" ideas, such as unregulated capitalism. She recalled that her political conversion occurred when she heard YAF executive Don Devine speak at a seminar hosted by The Fund for American Studies (TFAS). She expressed that Devine's TFAS remarks at the University of Tennessee made a revolutionary impression on her: "That was the first time I heard a conservative speak and was able to say, 'Yeah, this guy makes sense. This guy is sane and sensible and not extreme.'" She reflected that "the only other thing out there at the time was *National Review*, or the more popular stuff you were more likely to run into was [the] John Birch [Society], which was ideologically fine, but it had an edge that sounded extreme." Devine's talk was "very data-based, where he cited surveys and opinion polls, but it was new then and I hadn't heard anything like that before. He marshaled facts and figures that, I said, 'Oh wow, I'm not the only one who feels this way.' We aren't crank pot weirdos, we're real. He presented it in a dispassionate, academic way and had substance and was encouraging."

For those like Thackston-Ganner, joining YAF was strongly related to her feelings about the Vietnam War and her family's own military service: "I had friends fighting in Vietnam and I wanted them to come home, of course, under a flag that's honored. My dad was in the reserves and went through the Berlin Wall crisis, we lived through the Cuban Missile Crisis, and I was used to that. I had some different feelings."[36] YAF alumna Judith Thorburn, who founded and chaired the SUNY Stony Brook (now Stony Brook University) chapter, stated that her grandfather's capture and imprisonment during the Russian Revolution shaped her anticommunism.[37] Like other baby boomers, many students on the right were children of World War II and Korean War veterans and believed that men of their generation had inherited a duty to serve in Vietnam. That peace activists of their age resisted this duty was a supreme affront.

Ideologies of the Campus Right

Squares, squishes, Jesus freaks, and Campus Crusaders partially made up the larger category of student conservatives. Conservatism in the context of this study describes the student reactionary movement, both intellectual and activist, as standing against the emancipation of oppressed groups to preserve a traditionalist racial hierarchy and against social habits that too closely resembled collectivism and moral relativism. Student conservatives thus best defined themselves by the ideas, cultural changes, and peace and justice organizations they were against.

Because they were united mainly by what they reviled, conservative groups were often ideologically out of sync with one another in the ideas they promoted. While conservatives characterized their own identities as anti-leftist, that was not always true in economic matters: for example, many were perfectly fine with America first protectionism. While harboring a deep suspicion of the Central Intelligence Agency and the State Department, they appealed to these sources of power for help against radical groups and routinely received what they asked for. While being pro-war in the name of anticommunism, they opposed both conscription and the policy of Vietnamization. And while championing economic productivity, they were ardent enemies of the minimum wage, labor unions, and New Deal programs designed to strengthen the social safety net and stabilize the national economy.

Students interested in conservatism's intellectual and capitalist foundations joined clubs such as ISI, Students for Individual Liberty, and other campus-specific literary and philosophical societies (though these clubs frequently worked alongside activist and partisan groups). As part of their activities, students read and recited the ideas of Austrian economists Friedrich Hayek and Ludwig von Mises, as well as conservative social commentators such as William F. Buckley Jr., Russell Kirk, and Ayn Rand. Within this intellectual community, religion's role in society and government was a subject of intense debate. For example, conservative heroes Buckley and Kirk chastised higher education for its secularism, while Rand was a prolific atheist.

Those interested in political organizing or campus activism joined the College Republicans, YAF, or ad hoc election campaign groups (usually started by College Republicans or YAFers). College Republican members attended workshops to learn the tenets of campaign organizing through the affiliate Republican Party or the Young Republican National Federation.[38] College Republicans organized mock elections on campus (the national voting age would not be lowered from twenty-one to eighteen until 1971) and volunteered to canvas their communities to register right-leaning voters. For hardline squares more dedicated to activism than electing GOP squishes, there was YAF. Often out of stride with the Republican Party, which in the 1960s still embodied many moderates and some liberals, YAF represented the vanguard group waging a three-front war against liberalism: on campus; in Washington, D.C.; and internationally in eastern Europe and Southeast Asia.

Small groups among the campus Right included violent white supremacist organizations, such as the Nazi paramilitary Minute Men at the University of Minnesota, who were "armed to the teeth" with automatic weapons.[39] Youth for Wallace, a student and young adult campaign organization that aimed to elect segregationist George Wallace in the 1968 presidential election, described themselves as "dedicated self-sacrificing young people who are ready to fight, and die if necessary, for the sacred cause" of eliminating "wretched liberals." The organization's purpose was "to liquidate the enemies of the American people on the campus and in the community," according to its president, Dennis C. McMahon.[40] Members assured they would not concede in the "never-ending fight against 'ones' who would destroy our country."[41] At Louisiana State University, self-proclaimed fascists of the White Youth Alliance led by student David Duke spewed anti-Jewish diatribes each week from Free Speech Alley, projecting Nazism on everyone within listening distance.[42] Students of these clubs antagonistically advocated for white studies programs and made graphic violent threats against Black and Jewish New Left organizers.

Student conservatism can further be understood as an amalgam of two major factions, traditionalists and libertarians, both of which were represented in all the aforementioned clubs. The largest cohort of student squares were the traditionalist social conservatives—those with "an enduring inclination to favor stability and preservation of the status quo over social change."[43] In the South, for instance, traditionalists rejected the power of the federal government to enforce de jure civil rights guarantees that would unravel the tradition of segregation on their campuses and in private business. Among traditionalist students were white supremacists and Christian nationalists, many of whom threatened or enacted violence to maintain the contemporary social structure. Traditionalists found role models in writers such as Brent Bozell, Richard Weaver, and Kirk, whose commentaries on Christianity and a hierarchically ordered society affirmed (as well as informed) their own preferences. Traditionalists were in favor of a hawkish foreign policy, particularly regarding American offensive strategies to contain communism. The most militant anticommunist traditionalists were influenced by activist Fred Schwarz, Rep. Walter Judd (R-MN), and writers Whittaker Chambers and James Burnham.

White supremacists like Duke carried copies of Hitler's *Mein Kampf* around campus and regurgitated the racial pseudoscience of Carleton Putnam's *Race and Reason* to their unwitting teachers and classmates. These students' ideas were shaped by the *Liberator*, the newsletter of the National Socialist White People's Party, and pamphlets produced by White Citizens' Councils and the John Birch Society.

Libertarians were supporters of a weak, decentralized federal government, maximized personal liberties, limited taxes, and an isolationist foreign policy. Protection of private property and a deregulated capitalist economy were foundational libertarian beliefs. Within the libertarian camp, ideological factions existed between objectivists and anarchists. The largest faction was the objectivists, followers of Rand's ideology of rational self-interest. Libertarians viewed the federal government and its ability to exercise regulation as a threat to personal liberty and capitalism. They praised economists Milton Friedman, Frank Chodorov, and Hayek, whose research argued that well-intentioned government spending programs were harmful attempts to control individuals through economic coercion.[44] Extreme libertarians who favored a total dissolution of the United States government were anarchists or anarcho-capitalists, identified by their all-black or military fatigue attire. The most extreme anarchist libertarian students sought direction from political economist Murray Rothbard and writer-activists like Karl Hess III and his son, Karl Hess IV.

Whether traditionalist or libertarian, leaders on the right understood that their students represented an ideological minority on campus. J. Alan MacKay, a former national chair of YAF, recalled that in the 1960s, "getting up in public and saying, 'I'm a conservative' was the equivalent of today getting up in public and saying, 'I'm an alcoholic.' You might get some sympathy for it, but basically people would regard you as human refuse."[45] But it was precisely this perceived stigma that helped unite strange bedfellows. As Lee Bebout explains with respect to right-wing extremists, "Seeing oneself as a victim is a crucial thread that weaves ideologies, identities, and historical moments together."[46]

Faculty, Administrative, and Legislative Backlash

College faculty and administrators were not impartial observers as student ideologues battled for campus hegemony. Citing a Carnegie Commission faculty survey during the 1968–69 academic year, the *Chronicle of Higher Education* reported that 22.5 percent identified as moderately conservative, and 2.2 percent as strongly conservative. A majority 54.1 percent disapproved of the "emergence of radical student activism in recent years." Everett C. Ladd, an associate professor of political science at the University of Connecticut at the time, explained that while most faculty were politically liberal, "there is a striking and clear shift toward a more conservative attitude where the faculty's immediate self-interest is involved."[47] While many junior academics and graduate teaching assistants were generally tacit supporters of New Left causes, older professors often issued the charge of emotional immaturity against student protesters, whose activism was considered impudent.[48] Historian Ellen Schrecker explains that faculty may have been the most interested constituency on campus seeking an end to the disruptions, as many identified "their own professional well-being and perceived status with their school's." In this spirit, "loyalty to their institutions was the key factor that determined how they responded to the student troubles."[49] Like-minded faculty and administrators, who were also mostly white and almost entirely men, offered support to conservative student organizations like YAF, ISI, and College Republicans on several campuses. College faculty and deans accounted for dozens of YAF's nearly 200 national advisers.

Some administrators also had low tolerance for dissent. From 1967 to 1969, the president of the University of Florida fired four untenured faculty members and one staff member for speaking or publishing about faculty roles in student demonstrations and for refusing to sign an anticommunist loyalty oath.[50] In a YAF *New Guard* article titled "Academic Freedom OR Academic Anarchy?" Michael Mescon, then dean of Georgia State University's

College of Business Administration, argued for the social responsibility of faculty to remain politically neutral: "The college professor as a highly educated person must recognize that his classroom pronouncements carry far more weight than those of individuals engaged in other vocations. For this reason, he should exercise exquisite caution in what he says and does."[51]

Even for administrators not directly tied to the Right's campaign against the New Left, managing progressive student demands proved exasperating, especially at the nation's most prestigious campuses. After dozens of antiwar and civil rights strikes, presidents at prominent institutions such as Brown, Cornell, Duke, Penn State, and the City College of New York announced their resignations or retirements.[52] The president of the University of Colorado resigned shortly after a fistfight broke out on campus between members of SDS and a conservative coalition; nearly forty students had attacked newspaper and television crews.[53] After angry letters streamed into his office, the university's director of development claimed the incident had cost nearly $1 million in alumni donations (worth nearly $8.3 million in 2023).[54]

Showing similar frustration, Princeton University president Robert Goheen opened his September 1968 welcome allocution with an indictment of the New Left for assailing the university as racist and authoritarian. "Misguided and dangerous" activists, Goheen charged to the crowd of 1,800 students and faculty, "believing that the end justifies the means, have little or no hesitation about inviting political and social turmoil to the campus."[55] By April 1969, the *Chronicle of Higher Education* had posted 270 presidential vacancies at American colleges for the upcoming academic year. Most of the outgoing presidents cited an inability to manage campus demonstrations as their reason for resignation or retirement.[56]

Even the nonviolent antics of radical students wore down administrators, such as when SDS members interrupted an address by the University of Maryland's president by playing the state song on kazoos. As this was the group's second major interruption of normal procedures that semester, President Wilson H. Elkins proposed that trustees bar SDS from campus as "restless, destructive rebels without anything constructive to offer."[57] As real estate investor Maurice Gordon prepared to make a $500,000 donation to fund the construction of a nursing school building at Boston University, the student newspaper claimed he was a "slum lord" for making his personal wealth through rental properties in the city's Black communities. SDS's demonstration against the benefactor prompted him to withdraw the donation, and university president Arland Christ-Janer publicly apologized "with embarrassment."[58]

Residents in campus-adjacent cities also voiced their disapproval with the student Left by demanding that they be drafted instead of enrolled in college. Regarding an Oklahoma University SDS member who participated in an antiwar demonstration, a town newspaper op-ed implored the local board to draft the student "and cut his hair and make a man of him instead of letting him and others like him be deferred and running around looking like a bum and demonstrating against our country." Near Oklahoma State University, one local suggested a "McNamara Scholarship" for students "who wish to go where the grass looks pinker." In both cases, the discontented writers identified themselves not as alumni but as taxpayers. Besides aghast locals, civic and church groups were the largest sources of praise for administrators whose retributive styles were both heavy-handed and public.[59]

In response to their constituents' demands, state politicians took steps to address campus radicalism in their higher education systems, often becoming frustrated by governing limitations that stymied their political will. At a regents meeting, California governor Ronald Reagan became furious when the board refused to address his concerns over matters of hiring and promotion, course supervision, and faculty code of conduct—all issues procedurally resolved by the campus-level academic senate rather than state legislators. Reagan lamented the regents' lack of accountability to taxpayers, describing their inaction as disdainful, timid, and vastly out of touch with California voters.[60] However, several lawsuits against universities had been easily won by students expelled for exercising constitutionally protected rights to speech and assembly.[61] But procedures and legalities were secondary considerations; visibly demonstrating disdain for campus radicals and peaceful demonstrators made politicians like Reagan and administrators like Goheen and Elkins popular among resentful taxpayers, who promised to take their frustrations to the polls.

College and University Defense Research

The biggest source of university presidents' frustration with radical activists was the financial cost of their dissent. This cost was sometimes direct, as when students destroyed property as part of their protests. Indirectly, their habit of attracting negative press would drive off major alumni gifts.

Enormous federal grants from the Department of Defense and the National Science Foundation were critical to university researchers, and the war-related products derived from these public funds were a constant target of peace activists.

In the fall of 1968, research-intensive institutions like the Massachusetts Institute of Technology (MIT) accepted nearly $80 million in research funding, with the following institutions receiving between $30 and $40 million: Columbia, Harvard, Stanford, Michigan, Wisconsin, and the Universities of California at Berkeley and Los Angeles.[62] The values of these grants in 2023 would be more than eight times what they were in 1968. MIT's fall 1968 grant, for example, would be valued at over $850 million today. Federal military investments had important regional effects as well. Southern public campuses, such as the University of Alabama, received $55 million between 1958 and 1967.[63] The research centers these grants supported employed hundreds of people whose pay and federal benefits were unmatched compared to other employment options in the southern private sector.[64]

In the South, where 42 percent of the domestic military payroll was spent, and where most young men were drafted from, antiwar dissent was conspicuously less common on public campuses.[65] Several southern public universities even pooled federal resources with military and space research centers to maximize funding. In the Gulf South region, for example, the University of Alabama and the University of Florida shared faculty and other resources with NASA, the US Army's Redstone Arsenal, and Cape Kennedy.[66] The promise of hundreds of millions of dollars in funding shared among multiple campuses helped ensure that administrator, trustee, and faculty interest in war-related research continued and that the destruction of campus property or research centers carried harsh penalties.

Conservative Students Begin to Mobilize

This is the context in which the campus wars between the New Left and the reactionary Right took a violent turn, with repercussions affecting higher education and American politics for decades. By 1967, peaceful interactions between students on the left and the right were no longer the exception. Neither side represented a majority of students, as both radicalized further apart on the ideological spectrum the longer the Vietnam War raged and racial unrest exploded on campus and in nearby communities. For the progressive New Left, radicalization was directed at oppressive structures that supported the war as well as at civil and economic inequality. For the student Right, radicalization was spurred by opposition to the Left's anti-war and social justice causes. The Right also positioned itself against the Left's more popular demands for cultural change, which seemed to enjoy broader support on campus. Traditionalist conservatives could see that the student body was becoming older, less affluent, less white, and less male. The visibility of "unwashed" hippies and their disheveled dress, recreational drug use, and demonstrations for peace and justice meant changes to the cultural landscape that the Right found intolerable. But these changes did not inspire criticism from the average university student, despite conservatives' unrelenting and overreaching association of New Left radicalism with the typical marijuana user.

In the context of an apathetic student body, the exasperation of administrators and politicians with the extreme Left's radicalism was ripe for exploitation by the college Right. Understanding that their opposition to the peace and civil rights student movements was not shared by most of their peers, campus conservatives frequently looked elsewhere for sources of power that they could successfully leverage against the Left. This dynamic was on full display in an open letter that Rutgers–Newark YAF wrote in 1968 to students, faculty, administrators, and alumni: "We will not complain to you about misery or oppression, but rather in this era of self-inflicted guilt, we intend to extol the glories of our campus, state and society. Take, for example, the gentlemen on the Board of Governors and on the Board of Trustees. Among them are successful businessmen, respected members of their communities, even millionaires."[67] Attempting to charm authorities with flattery and drawing a contrast between the New Left's less desirable methods of demonstrating and their own supposedly agreeable character, while sidestepping the substantive questions about peace and social justice, the student Right in the late 1960s began to develop reactionary strategies for their own version of resistance.

2 Eggheads for the Right

· ·

In 1968, tens of thousands of college students directed anti–Vietnam War and antiracism demonstrations on their campuses. Nationwide, radicals bombed university buildings and seized administration halls almost daily. Stupefied administrators frantically suspended classes in concern for student safety. Citing a report by the National Student Association (NSA), the *New York Times* publicized the upheaval, highlighting how during the spring term alone, at least 221 demonstrations were held at 101 colleges involving 38,911 participants. There were 59 building takeovers and 42 sit-ins. Four hundred and seventeen students were arrested, 124 expelled, 60 suspended, and 34 placed on probation.[1] As shocking as the dispatch was, the NSA's report failed to include two major spring strikes at Columbia University, in which 800 additional students participated in building takeovers, resulting in 712 arrests and 73 suspensions (discussed in chapter 4).[2]

Conservative political leaders united on the rhetorical offensive, doling out punitive solutions for the problems exploding across college campuses. Governor Ronald Reagan admonished University of California faculty for permitting riotous demonstrations, alleging that absent professors tinkered in their labs while graduate assistants inspired "insurrection." He had already fired UC system's president, Clark Kerr, and threatened the board of regents. Now he warned the professorate: "obey the rules or get out."[3]

A few academics and intellectuals echoed Reagan's intolerance. Russell Kirk blamed "Behemoth" universities, such as his own Michigan State, for enrolling ill-prepared undergraduates.[4] In the *National Review*, Dartmouth College English professor Jeffrey Hart (the publication's future editor) blamed "the habitually antagonistic, and sometimes even treasonous," relationship between the academy and the public.[5] In the pages of the *Public Interest*, New York University's Irving Kristol assailed the "New Class" of intellectuals as "the vehicle of radicalism" and "a threat to the sturdy virtues of Middle America."[6] William F. Buckley Jr. quipped that he would rather be governed by the first 2,000 names in the Boston phone book than by the Harvard faculty, and assailed "the submissive ghettoes that are the American universities."[7] The uprisings, they claimed, were caused by junior academics hell-bent on upending the social order.

Balancing the Academy

Given that these "treasonous" "insurrections" were apparently inspired by younger faculty and their even younger teaching assistants, movement conservatives believed they needed to direct their offensive from inside the classroom itself.[8] The only viable solution to the problem of permissive liberalism among the educated was to subvert the leftist academy with ideas and agents of their own—that is, to produce so-called eggheads in service to the Right. They needed to get trusted allies behind the lectern and their own version of the great books on the syllabus.

Though this resistance took on a sudden urgency, it was not new. Since the 1940s, anti–New Deal businessmen who were united through the international free-market Mont Pelerin Society and bankrolled by the William Volker Fund had been training academics to produce anti-Keynesian scholarship, but their efforts were concentrated in economics departments.[9] Now conservative leaders believed the time was ripe for expanding the intellectual arm of their political project into other branches of the social sciences and humanities. Not only were they after faculty in new disciplines, but they placed greater emphasis on nurturing undergraduates—malleable cohorts of *future* intellectuals—for the cause.

The infrastructure needed for this long-term project already existed; it just required more attention and funding. Beginning in the 1930s, right-wing movement leaders founded multiple nonprofits to promote their ideologies: the American Enterprise Institute, the Foundation for Economic Education (FEE), the Intercollegiate Studies Institute (ISI), the Institute for Humane Studies (IHS), the Liberty Fund, and The Fund for American Studies (TFAS), among others. The nonprofit model ensured that large gifts from philanthropist ideologues and wealthy business interests remained tax deductible.

The idea of achieving intellectual balance was central to the Right's critique of the liberal university, as well as its justification for subverting it. Though a political tactic, the quest to achieve ideological symmetry was posed as a philosophical and pedagogical commitment; thus, organizers and donors marketed each of these foundations as educational, rather than political, solutions. Their mission was to fill the social and intellectual void of young scholars, who, by the Right's estimation, were not receiving objective schooling for lack of conservative representation among college faculties. To communicate their ideas to college students and faculty, FEE, ISI, IHS, and similar right-wing projects offered books, magazines, pamphlets, and other media as correctives to standard university curricula. In the context of unparalleled disruption on campus, movement conservatives turned greater attention to these associations, offering more money and more advertising to expand their outreach and enhance their effectiveness.

The Intercollegiate Studies Institute

During the period of the campus wars, ISI was the most influential of the balance-seeking nonprofits. By 1968, it had more than 30,000 club members and a presence at over 190 campuses.[10] Headquartered in Philadelphia, the group had regional offices in Indianapolis and Los Angeles, each staffed with a director and a secretary. Older regional directors supported area clubs and arranged lecture tours at campuses such as Stanford University.[11] Regional directors recruited conservative intellectuals, including Kirk and Milton Friedman, to teach at their seminars and prepared intensive weeklong summits. ISI sourced its speakers by identifying sympathies for classical liberalism or objections to progressivism in various publications, then invited these faculty to become associates. By the end of the decade, the organization had a well-developed speakers' bureau it provided with travel expenses and honoraria.[12]

ISI's fellowships, lecture tours, summer seminars, and other expenses were funded through national direct mail campaigns and corporate donors in Chicago, Indianapolis, Pittsburgh, and Washington, D.C. One of ISI's greatest financiers and a fellowship namesake, "guardian angel" Henry Salvatori, made a $10,000 gift (worth approximately $90,000 in 2023) to two ISI scholars to found Thomas Aquinas College in Santa Paula, California, a private Catholic institution modeled on a traditional great books curriculum.[13]

Arranging seasonal lecture circuits and disseminating ideas in print were short-term approaches to combating the persistent faculty indoctrination issue. The problem might finally be solved, however, if the professorate were supplanted with tenured conservatives. Through tactical fellowship programs, ISI and other nonprofits groomed young traditionalists and libertarians to fill tenure-track positions and financed their necessary doctoral credentials. The first of several ISI fellowships began in 1964. The Richard M.

Weaver Fellowship fund was sustained by annual gifts from the Relm Foundation for the cost of ten tuitions plus $15,000 to cover stipends of $1,500 for each fellow.[14] By 1967, seven Weaver fellows were employed as full-time faculty (including at Johns Hopkins and Yale Universities), and twenty-six were completing graduate degrees.[15] Weaver fellowships were awarded to nearly a dozen graduate students each year, guaranteeing a continuous conservative ideological pipeline into the professoriate, however thin its stream.

Were it not for the funding provided by the grants, many students would have never considered teaching and research over opportunities in private industry. As an undergraduate economics major, James Gwartney decided to pursue a faculty career after attending an ISI lecture at the University of Washington by Nobel Prize–winning economist James Buchanan. Buchanan's lecture on public choice theory was the introduction to what would become his own area of scholarship. His doctoral training was funded through a Weaver fellowship, which, he reflected, "would have been the equivalent of $10,000 or $15,000 today [2018], such that if you didn't have anybody else to support, you could get by and it would cover tuition."[16] Gwartney is now emeritus professor of economics at Florida State University and a Cato Institute affiliate. During the Clinton administration, he served as Chief Economist of the Congressional Joint Economic Committee.

Joining Liberty Fund conferences and attending ISI-sponsored lectures gave alumnus Gerald Dwyer of the University of Washington a sense of inclusion on what he perceived to be a radical campus, "more like a Berkeley north." As a graduate student, Dwyer submitted economics textbook reviews to ISI's *Intercollegiate Review.* Through Weaver and Earhart Foundation fellowships, he was able to complete a doctoral degree in economics at the University of Chicago under the direction of famed free-market economists Friedman and Robert E. Lucas, both of whom later received the Nobel Prize. Now a professor of economics at Clemson University and a scholar affiliate of the conservative Cato Institute, he has spent his career in academia and at the Federal Reserve, crediting the success of his tenure as an economist to ISI investments in his training.[17]

Unlike College Republican clubs and the conservative activist Young Americans for Freedom (YAF), ISI did not actively recruit and did not encourage students to use its name. Thus, its membership was never as large, and it has not received the same attention historically. One joined ISI by responding to ads placed in *National Review* or *Modern Age.* Readers often gifted ISI literature subscriptions to their college- or high-school-aged children or relatives. Whereas YAF served as the vanguard group for conservative youth who were developing their campus (and, later, public) activist identities, and College Republicans served as a vehicle for partisan organizing, ISI served an exclusive cohort of students bound for careers in the academy or shaping public policy rather than industry or party politics. Substantial movement investments in individual scholars further set it apart as an elite society.

With respect to the national conservative movement, different student organizations allowed the executives directing them to play the role of *teacher* rather than just advisor. Hosting seminars and overseeing student-produced literature allowed movement elders to play professor as they sidestepped college faculty by creating a parallel structure of pedagogy outside the official classroom. At the same time, the Right's think tanks were being explicitly modeled on academia, with "fellows," "associates," disciplinary departments, and tenure. These adaptations, designed to challenge what the Right perceived as liberal orthodoxy, were akin to its appropriations of New Left political language (discussed in chapter 3).

Speaking Up in Class

Placing conservatives in junior faculty roles was a long-term function of organizations like FEE, ISI, and IHS. In the short term, these organizations made use of crises in the academy to serve the Right's cultural and political goals by arming conservative students with the vocabulary and confidence they needed to challenge their instructors and peers. In the pages of the *Intercollegiate Review*—ISI's magazine for students—elder conservative intellectuals toiled over the nation's moral decay evidenced on campus. These essays were almost entirely in reaction to student unrest, with articles titled "The New Totalitarianism," "The SDS Trip: From Vision to Ego Shriek," "Decadence in the American University," and "Relativism in Higher Learning." While the number of campus radicals was relatively low, ISI writers posited that the general disposition of students was that the American capitalist system was corrupt, because faculty and their teaching assistants were forcing anti-capitalism and anti-patriotism on students in their classrooms. Furnished with this information, college readers were developing intellectual grounds to justify and legitimize resentments they often struggled to articulate.

The Right's organizations thus aimed to protect college learners by providing academic defenses against their professors' supposed brainwashing.

This picture of the YAF book sale shows Richard Roth, President of the YAF, firmly entrenched on the right; as for the man on the left, we don't even know his name, never mind whether or not he bought a book.

Boston College YAF operating a book sale in March 1967. *Heights* (Boston College), March 15, 1967.

"YAF members had the right gut instincts," the group's former executive director Randal Teague explained, "but did not have the intellectual underpinnings."[18] To address this shortcoming, ISI, YAF, and College Republicans sponsored book sales to offer students exposure to what it believed their professors were keeping from them: moral traditionalism and their version of the great books of the Western canon.[19] These books were provided by the Volker Fund's National Book Foundation, which donated bulk purchases of conservative literature annually to thousands of college libraries. The sales also functioned as helpful fundraisers for the clubs.

YAF leadership encouraged members to ready their intellectual defenses by joining ISI, subscribing to national opinion journals, and seeking mentorship from known conservative faculty to develop arguments in anticipation of class discussions. At the direction of their elders, students mined Christian, anticommunist, and free-market classics—so-called debate handbooks—for nuggets of rebuttal to use in class, including works featured at their book sales: William F. Buckley Jr.'s *God and Man at Yale* (1951) and *Up from Liberalism* (1959), Barry Goldwater's *The Conscience of a Conservative* (1960), Russell Kirk's *The Conservative Mind* (1953), Friedrich Hayek's *The Road to Serfdom* (1944), Richard Weaver's *Ideas Have Consequences* (1948), Milton Friedman's *Capitalism and Freedom* (1962), and Whittaker

Chambers's *Witness* (1952). These were the "true classics" of the conservative canon, meant to be "read, studied, memorized, applied, debated, cited, invoked, and quoted persistently."[20] Other works by James Burnham, Ludwig von Mises, Eric Voegelin, Willmoore Kendall, and Leo Strauss were often excellent sources for formulating in-class rebuttals.

Prior to this intervention, being self-conscious about their convictions and unable to voice dissent in class was a common affliction for many conservatives. A University of South Carolina YAF alumna recalled feeling frustrated in the classroom because she could not articulate disagreement with her instructors' politics. She remembered a graduate teaching assistant lecturing at length on civilian casualties in Vietnam, and feeling resentful that he was using her class time to proselytize. "But I couldn't do anything about it," she explained, because "I didn't have the words for what I was feeling."

For students like Gwartney, however, finding the words to speak out in class was less of a problem than the perceived repercussions of doing so. As an undergraduate, "Washington State University was very Keynesian-oriented," he recalled. "If you even asked questions indicating you were a skeptic, you were immediately discriminated against in terms of grades. . . . I would've asked legitimate questions about how things worked, and my macro instructor, who was a very strong Keynesian, perceived that I was a skeptic, and I think it was fair to say that I got a 'B' in that class instead of an 'A' because of it."[21]

It is difficult for a historian today to assess the accuracy of such claims. Were professors in the 1960s biased against their conservative students for comments they made in class, and was that political bias reflected in grade penalties across multiple assignments? It is possible, but other explanations are likely. Another student offered the following interpretation of point deductions: "It's not that professors deliberately persecute conservatives. But if you turn in a conservative analysis, they think you haven't grasped the material and give you a low grade."[22]

Not all students shared the same resentment for faculty with whom they disagreed politically or who they thought graded unfairly. As an undergraduate at the University of North Carolina and in graduate school at Tulane University, Ben C. Toledano recalled both a fascination with and a class-based admiration for openly communist professors:

> The faculty at North Carolina were so elegant. All my professors were
> full professors. They wore three-piece suits, wire-rimmed glasses,
> combed their hair, [were] from nice families. I knew what their

[political] views were. They were so attractive. They were gentlemen. . . . At Tulane my favorite professor was an old communist named Mitchell Franklin, a very intellectual Jew who had given up Judaism, I'm sure. Like so many others of the '20s after strange gods, when they lost their religion, had to find something to replace it. Communism became the strange god they adopted. He was my favorite professor. But I didn't take his views seriously because I knew they wouldn't work. . . . He activated my mind, make me think. When he would talk about a German philosopher, you knew goddamned well he read the philosopher in German, and you'd have to take note. He was openly communist . . . just about every intellectual was a communist.[23]

For students like the YAF alumna, Gwartney, and Toledano, ISI articulated justifications for their intransigence, while references to classical canons and movement writers' polemics provided the language they sought to confidently speak up in class and compose counterarguments in their assignments.

But in seeking intellectual arguments against the New Left's goals of peace and racial equality, students perhaps discovered more rhetorical strategy than substance. Their intellectual mentors often evaded answering such questions directly. By ignoring dissenters' premises and instead focusing on their methods, *Intercollegiate Review* writers reduced student protests to symptoms of decay in cultural morality. There was no need to engage with the Left's objectives of peace and the equal exercise of civil liberties because leftists were nihilists—or worse, communist marionettes—out to destroy the nation. "Problems" of war and racism were just distractions meant to confuse their classmates into thinking that Marxism offered solutions that were somehow not dangerous.

Witnessing the New Left's demands for student and Black power, the Right understood that activists did not simply want to extend higher education to more minority groups and women; rather, the ultimate goal was about "the place that those minoritized people might occupy in the production of university knowledge and the reshaping of American society."[24] Right-wing economist Gordon Tullock derided public universities for churning "a positively dangerous class situation" by educating blue-collar youth who, as historian Nancy MacLean interprets, "might make trouble, having had their sights raised."[25]

ISI writers thus excoriated leftists' tactics of disruption and seemed only to respond to their less palatable ideas, such as moral relativism, using an avowedly Christian framework. The progressive habit of deconstructing language was a path, they claimed, to anarchy.[26] The Left's theories of postmodernism and poststructuralism were easy targets to engage, as they proposed no absolute truth and deeply offended traditionalists whose worldviews were rooted in Christianity and Western tenets of government and philosophy. For some Christian students, this context warranted the creation of anti-leftist spaces where they could seek refuge from liberalism's rampant lawlessness and immorality. Many of these campus groups, especially in the South, were outwardly nationalist and engaged in politically coded messaging through religious lexicon. At the University of Alabama (which appears to have had neither its own YAF nor any College Republican chapters from 1967 to 1970), the University Christian Student Center was created to be "a vital influence" at the Tuscaloosa campus, where it could provide "a wholesome atmosphere" for students "to combat the forces encountered in higher education that tend to usurp Christian ideals." Without making its political or ideological stance known, a student encountering this group would plainly recognize its anti-progressive mission.[27] This demonstrates that the same kinds of anti-leftist ideas were in some cases disseminated through campus groups that were formally unaffiliated with a national organization like YAF.

For the student Left, however, that the relationship between knowledge and power should be suspect stemmed from uncovering deep connections between scientific and social research, universities, and the war in Vietnam. For postmodernists, and the radical students influenced by them, a disenchantment with systems of power (capitalism, colonialism, and patriarchy, for example) provided the foundation for a violent rejection of reigning institutions.[28] But for older conservative thought leaders in the pages of the *Intercollegiate Review*, ideas that hinted at social progressivism needed only to be assessed by the tactics of the youth working to upend tradition to achieve them, without concern for how oppressive such traditions were to certain groups.

Bringing the Conservative Countersphere to the Campus

Throughout the 1950s and 1960s, writers at the conservative journal *National Review* developed the concept of an "American establishment," a reference to apparent liberal control over the media and its attendant propaganda in service of liberal interests.[29] This concept was so ingrained in conservative commentary by the mid-1960s that the terms "liberal media" and "liberal press" had become *Human Events* magazine's staple references to describe other news sources.[30] As Julie B. Lane clarifies, the Right argued that contemporary editorial standards were not a product of "consensus support" but derived from establishment media's "purposeful exclusion of [conservative] expressions of dissent."[31] As such, the raison d'être for right-wing news and opinion outlets was to sow doubt about both the accuracy and the fairness of the pejorative "mainstream media."[32]

Movement leaders on the right thus cultivated a national "conservative countersphere," which Mark Major describes as a protective literary world for "often privileged insiders masquerading as aggrieved outsiders." The conservative countersphere functions as "a contradictory space" that "*assumes* a subordinate status as conservatives are aroused by a sense of loss."[33] This genre was characteristically "antagonistic" toward professional reporting standards. Instead, conservative writers uniquely blended journalism and commentary "from a perspective informed by their ideological commitments, as well as more circumstantial partisan reactions," according to A. J. Bauer and Anthony Nadler.[34]

Countersphere outlets represented by *National Review* and its sister magazines had several functions for the growing conservative movement: they provided a medium for identity formation, places to collaborate on ideas and strategies, and sites to build discursive prose that challenged popular opinion.[35] Editorials triggered affective responses from readers without regard for empiricism. It did not matter whether the reporting that readers received was true, or whether the editorials were based in expert opinion, so long as the content resonated with consumers searching for common cause between the pages. Conservative writings were, as Steven Selden explains, "designed for affiliation, not clarification."[36] Accordingly, the countersphere could be used to "inoculate" consumers "against ideology-contradicting facts and arguments."[37]

Writers building the conservative countersphere directed the students in their charge to follow suit. Because university-sponsored newspapers were perceived as tinged with the common academic and media afflictions of liberalism, the students needed to create alternative periodicals modeled on their national examples. Even more alarming, Morton Blackwell, executive director of the College Republican National Committee (CRNC), was explicit in stating that his students were behind on this critical "technology" that the New Left had already mastered.[38] Moreover, if the Right could figure out how to operate like left-wing groups' "underground" papers, independent of the campus press, then their content would not be beholden to administrative oversight. With this relative subject-matter freedom, ISI supplied students with ideas from the national office and conservative magazines, such as *National Review, Human Events, Modern Age,* and *Public Interest.* As Blackwell recalled, FEE gave a free subscription of its journal, the *Freeman,* to any college student who requested one.[39]

ISI regional directors helped connect students at different campuses within their districts to share publishing resources from the national organization. Student journals included Yale's *Alternative,* the *Harvard Conservative,* the University of Wisconsin's *Insight and Outlook,* the University of Chicago's *New Individualist Review,* and the University of Missouri's *Conservative Digest.*[40] ISI's own publication, the *Intercollegiate Review,* claimed a readership of 45,000 by 1967.[41]

Editorial responsibilities and publication lines also enhanced fellowship students' curricula vitae in preparation for the faculty job market. William Barclay Allen—president of the Pepperdine College Young Republicans, Earhart Foundation fellow, and one of the few active Black conservatives at the time—recalled founding a magazine called *Phalanx* with four other students connected through ISI advisers. One of the four was Peter Schramm, former executive director of the Ashbrook Center for Public Affairs, a right-wing think tank and educational training program at Ashland University in Ohio. After graduation, Allen remained active in ISI's parent group, the Philadelphia Society; became a professor of political philosophy at Michigan State University; served as the Ann and Herbert W. Vaughan Visiting Fellow in the James Madison Program in American Ideals and Institutions at Princeton University; was a member of the National Council on the Humanities; and served as chair of the United States Commission on Civil Rights. He credits ISI for offering classical texts and "meaningful experiences" that helped him "formulate [his] political understandings" for a long career in policy and academia.[42]

Though YAF and College Republican club magazines lacked ISI's intellectual overtones, the intent to interject political conversations on campus remained the same in their publications. The major difference between the clubs' serials was their target readership. ISI and College Republican mentors encouraged students to write for broad audiences—College Republicans were specifically told to be accessible to parents and siblings—whereas YAF's publications appear to be written to build internal camaraderie among their members. Unlike ISI, YAF and College Republican content was mostly written by students rather than faculty, and articles traded ISI's intellectualism for a more extremist punch.

At the University of Mississippi, for example, YAF's *Granite* included a regular feature called Faculty Follies dedicated to exposing errors (or supposedly errant political claims) made by their professors. One section, Words to Remember, offered praise for Chancellor Porter Fortune's harsh condemnation of campus radicals. The column promoted ideas of writer Morrie Ryskind, a member of its national advisory board. An accompanying section, Words Not to Remember, provided disparaging quotes from "Very Liberal Professors." In columns titled Problems on the Left and Answers on the Right, YAFers characterized liberals as unbathed and offered the following solution: "On that feud among our faculty comrades, we suggest an extended field trip to the Sino-Soviet border so they can aid and abet their cause. As for our unwashed stinkers, perhaps they should seek treatment at [Mississippi psychiatric facility] Whitfield."[43]

YAF's bimonthly Free Campus News Service supplied pictures, columns, news releases, cartoons, and other copy to student editors in need of content. YAF's national headquarters disseminated *Do It! On Publishing a Conservative Underground Newspaper,* a how-to manual addressing finances, content creation, hiring staff, and distribution—something start-up underground papers desperately needed. In 1968, Lee and Anne Edwards created a secondary YAF instruction manual for starting a campus magazine called *You Can Make the Difference.* These content supplements and operations manuals helped YAF claim homespun papers at seventy-one campuses.[44] CRNC leaders also produced multiple guides and primers: *Club Newsletters, How to Prepare a Club Newsletter, Communications,* and even an instructional pamphlet titled *Possibilities for Propaganda.*[45] From 1968 onward, YAF and College Republican executives would consistently produce new manuals (and regularly issue updates) on the practical skills they felt the students needed to develop.

When students needed content, editorial advice, or donations, they had a host of mentors in the literary world to turn to: publisher Henry Regnery, YAF founder M. Stanton Evans at the *Indianapolis Star,* and especially the staff at *National Review* and *Human Events.* Often student editors short on ideas penned biographical and political profiles of benefactors and advisory board members like Ryskind and Joseph Coors. In this way, the students could fill editorial space while currying favor with their movement leaders and advertising their donors' businesses.

Not only did they need to promote their sponsors, executives were more concerned with the students' management of their own image. It is striking how often the College Republican newsletter manual directed students to use their writing space to defend themselves from other conservatives' insults and negative characterizations. Regarding content production, the first instruction was that the newsletter provide a record of College Republicans' work. The manual specified that doing so was paramount in "visibly refuting the charge 'The CRs don't do anything.'" It elaborated that such a charge, often leveled by YAF, was "one of the most devastating and dangerous" rumors about the club. The goal was to make the newsletter "an institution" so that College Republican messages would be "respected."[46]

The second instruction was to use the newsletter to push ideology: "It should be a vehicle for waging 'ideological struggle'—that is, a way to make known the Republican stance on important issues . . . to convince the uncommitted."[47] If they needed ideas, students were encouraged to "lift" articles from the Republican National Committee's newsletter *First Monday*, the CRNC's *College Republican*, or the Republican Congressional Committee's *Newsletter*. Editorials should be written on local matters, such as the state education budget, student housing and parking, and any other "good biting topics."[48]

Though CRNC officials directed student writers to use editorials to advance a partisan ideological edge, they differed from YAF elders in cautioning student journalists not to pander too much: "Any attempt at cuteness or an overly 'feature' style . . . is fatal." Campus readers expected a certain mature voice and satisfying that expectation would make the publication more trustworthy and believable.[49] Blackwell underscored that "*students appreciate cleverness but react negatively to unfairness.*"[50] This was a clear distinction from YAF's boorish and antagonistic flair, which its executives condoned. CRNC officers still believed attention to style mattered: "Do not ignore the power of humor. Use cartoons, funny pictures, or anything that cast the opposition in a ludicrous light. Don't get caught taking yourself too seriously."[51]

CRNC executives' formula for distributing club newsletters was very specific: two newsletters for every three students at campuses with up to 3,000 students; one newsletter for every two students up to 5,000; one newsletter for every three students up to 10,000; and one for every four students over 10,000. For a large campus like the University of California at Los Angeles, which had an enrollment of nearly 30,000 students in 1968, the chapter was required to print 7,500 copies of each issue. Ideally, the newsletters were to be sent by post, as "sending things by mail gives them a certain mystic legitimacy." For a $15 application fee, the club could get a $30 annual third-class permit to mail each letter for 4.8 cents each. Printings could be done by Xerox for 25 cents per page.[52] The paper also needed to come out frequently and regularly. Guidance advised that when readers received the third issue, they should still remember the second.[53] Brown University College Republicans, for example, printed twenty-two issues during the 1969–70 year.[54]

When a club's budget did not permit regular mass mailings, members divided up delivery responsibilities to cover residence halls and windshields in the commuter parking lot.[55] However, members' own copies were hand delivered by club officers. In-person delivery offered a unique benefit, in that it "reminds them that you know they are members, and that *you know where they are.* This can be quite terrifying, and especially effective when you go back and ask them to rejoin the CR's at the end of the year."[56] That CRNC executives would use "terrifying" to describe their expected reaction from fellow members is telling of the type of authoritative control they believed leaders should exercise.

As with most conservative youth group efforts, the magazines were largely funded by approving alumni and concerned local business owners. At Indiana University (IU), the *Alternative*'s fundraising letters asked for donations in the name of "the efforts of responsible Indiana University students" working against the "doctrines of anarchy and revolution" on their campus. These funds helped keep subscriptions relatively affordable. The *Alternative* sold its first issue in September 1967 for 15 cents.[57] An annual subscription to the monthly *Carolina Renaissance*, co-published by students at Duke University and the University of North Carolina and subtitled "news and opinions suppressed by the campus press," could be purchased for $2.50.[58]

Publishing expenses for the *True Trojan* by the University of Southern California Young Republicans were paid by certain trustees through coded "alumni subscriptions" or single $200 business advertisements—the total cost of a full printing (worth approximately $1,800 in 2023). The magazine's initial $1,000 start-up budget (approximately $9,000 in 2023) was gifted indirectly by trustee Henry Salvatori—ISI fellowship namesake and patron of Thomas Aquinas College—who further connected students to other wealthy donors. A University of Southern California YAF alumnus who wished to remain anonymous claimed to have received several thousand dollars through legal and indirect means by university trustees.

The *Alternative*, the most successful and long-lasting of these student papers, is still operational today through generous right-wing sponsorship. R. Emmett Tyrrell Jr. and Stephen Davis founded the magazine with a $3,000 donation (worth over $27,000 in 2023) from the Lilly Endowment, a private Christian philanthropy.[59] As Daniel Spillman notes, its writers had "a penchant for cruel, ad hominem attacks" on their campus rivals. The editors refused to capitalize the names of SDS members, especially IU's SDS leader Guy Loftman, whom Tyrrell exhorted to commit suicide in one article.[60] Alongside vicious editorials, the magazine also featured opinion articles from highly regarded conservative scholars like Irving Kristol and Sidney Hook.[61] A $25,000 donation from billionaire Richard Mellon Scaife in 1970 (worth approximately $200,000 in 2023) enabled the campus-based publication to go national. Consistent donations from Scaife and the Lilly Endowment exceeded well over $1 million throughout the 1970s, guaranteeing the paper's legacy among the conservative countersphere.[62] Tyrrell's success inspired the next generation of conservative campus papers, including the *Dartmouth Review*, where writers like Dinesh D'Souza and Laura Ingraham were mentored by Tyrrell, along with advisers Jeffrey Hart, Patrick Buchanan, William Rusher, and Jack Kemp.[63]

Today, the *Alternative* is still in online publication as the *American Spectator*. However, this is an exception. Unlike progressive or radical underground papers, there is little indication that other conservative circulars lasted past their founders' graduations. The only other known campus conservative magazines from the 1960s still in existence are the University of Wisconsin's *Badger Herald* (which is no longer conservative) and the libertarian *Reason*, created by Boston University student Lanny Friedlander from his dorm room in 1968. Today, the right-wing nonprofit Reason Foundation publishes the magazine, its website, and ReasonTV, a media production company that produces provocative videos designed to go viral.

Nixon and Campus Media

During the Nixon administration, College Republican clubs greatly expanded and professionalized conservative campus news and radio with explicit direction from the White House and GOP advisers. A small number of students were doing the lion's share of marketing conservatism on campus to bridge the divide between Nixon's administration and young people. And while Nixon was personally uninterested in courting youth organizers, some among his staff were, including YAF executives Tom Charles Huston and Pat Buchanan. By building close relationships with college editors and radio hosts, Nixon aides ensured that coverage of his administration became less inflammatory.

At the invitation of White House staff, Blackwell and Robert Polack met with Nixon advisers to discuss how the administration could better sell itself on campus. The two CRNC leaders proposed a news service to broadcast updates directly from the White House, bypassing established campus news agencies like the College Press Service (CPS), which was often critical of the administration.[64] Nixon's communications staff provided a list of college newspapers and radio stations and the addresses of current White House interns, noting that they would be "good contacts" for them. They also offered to provide content and financial assistance for the first mailing.[65] Shortly thereafter, the Washington Campus News Service (WCNS) was delivering partisan news releases to the same campus editors and radio broadcasters who received critical pieces from the CPS.[66]

The GOP duplicated this strategy at the state level with its State Campus News Service, designed to "pay big dividends for both the College Republicans and the Republican Party." The operation was "staffed, produced and funded by the College Republican federation," and its goal was to "inundate the campus media with Republican-oriented materials." A group of six students responsible for a state territory "manufactured" news releases (with instructions to "BE BOLD"), radio releases, fact sheets and backgrounders for cover articles, and five-minute taped interviews with GOP members. To build relationships and curry favor, College Republicans were directed to "court" local news stations: "Call them, prod them, be nice to them and ask their advice."[67]

Then, to soften relations with the often critical CPS, Nixon's communications office contacted its editors directly to discuss ways the White House could help provide content through press and radio releases.[68] Though the CPS was opposed to the administration's policies, the liaison benefited Nixon in that his speeches and other messages would be delivered directly to any campus newspaper or radio station whether or not they received CPS or WCNS materials.[69] Nixon staff issued official White House press credentials to both CPS and WCNS student reporters and extended invitations to regular press briefings—privileges denied by prior administrations.[70] Before long, the CPS and the WCNS were receiving exclusive articles by cabinet members and others in the Nixon presidency, with the WCNS distributing biweekly reports directly from the White House.[71]

In its *Possibilities for Propaganda* memo, the CRNC instructed campus chapters to use WCNS releases in their own club newsletters, urging members to create a View from Washington column that summarized several of the WCNS releases in one meaty article. Members needed to reproduce "charts, graphs, quote boxes, filler and other material" from the WCNS. They were also supposed to forward WCNS releases to their own campus newspapers and radio stations in order to reach audiences that did not read College Republican materials. Students kept a file of releases to build a database of details they could use to write counter-editorials in campus and town newspapers, arming themselves with "the facts" to put "a Republican slant on things."[72] Doing so was important, Blackwell urged, not just for building up credibility but to show that "CRs *do* do something!"[73]

Nixon staff directed the WCNS to issue reprints of friendly articles from movement magazines to its college editors and broadcasters, offering to have the Republican National Committee's Communications Division cover the distribution costs, despite the students' $30,000 annual operations budget (equivalent to approximately $270,000 in 2023).[74] By 1972, the WCNS claimed to issue weekly reports to 1,700 campus newspapers, 400 campus radio programs, and 450 College Republican chapters. However, internal CRNC memos show that the WCNS had insufficient funds to continue its operations beyond that point.[75] Nixon and his staff also would not remain in the White House much longer for their propaganda to be necessary.

The short-lived direct-from-the-White-House news service inspired Nixon media consultant Roger Ailes to create a television news version. A memo, "A Plan for Putting the GOP on TV News," circulated between Ailes, H. R. Haldeman, and other staff, outlining a proposal to create pro-Nixon videotapes to distribute to local television news stations as free programming. The estimated $542,000 start-up investment and annual expected operating cost of $167,000 would be covered by the GOP. The plan entailed recording video content (such as a GOP senator's speech), editing out forty-second-to-one-minute clips, and reproducing at least forty copies of the tapes. The videos would be flown from Washington, D.C., and delivered to stations representing the top television markets in the country: New York, Los Angeles, Chicago, Philadelphia, Boston, and thirty-five other cities.[76] Though the Capitol News Service, as it would have been called, never got off the ground, it served as a clear blueprint for the right-wing Television News Inc., founded in 1973 by Paul Weyrich and bankrolled by Coors, and for Ailes's Fox News in 1996.[77]

In the late 1960s, ISI seminars and free access to books and magazines helped equip students on the right with the language they needed to speak up in class and across campus. Strategic fellowships ensured that some stayed on campus for the rest of their careers. From the late 1960s to the early 1970s, student conservatives assembled their own version of the media countersphere to challenge official campus newspapers and radio programs, amplifying the messages of their mentors. During the period when these newspapers and radio programs existed, messages from conservative movement and Republican Party leaders reached a national audience of students directly. Some of these listeners and readers may not have had access to campus conservative clubs or were otherwise unlikely to be exposed to messaging from the GOP. By offering news and radio releases and other content supplements, elders built close working relationships with their college mentees, serving as pedagogical alternatives to their professors. These mentors taught the students practical skills for editorializing, publishing, broadcasting, networking, and fundraising. The students, in turn, practiced projecting their ideas to audiences beyond those they could enlist to join their clubs, a process that reinforced their sense of representing a youth silent majority and one that they would exercise for the rest of their political and professional lives.

3 If You Want to Live Like an American, Act Like One

In the summer before the 1967–68 academic year, racial tensions exploded across the nation, leaving nearly 100 people dead, over 2,000 people injured, and millions of dollars in property damage. In Newark, New Jersey, a week-long July demonstration devolved into mass looting and gun violence as 4,000 National Guardsmen blockaded the city. Twenty-six people were killed and hundreds more were injured. A week later in Detroit, 10,000 troops violently quashed rebellions and arrested over 7,000 people.[1] Though college campuses fared slightly better during the long hot summer of 1967—nationally, only 42 of 249 disturbances, or 17 percent, took place on college campuses—students were active in city streets while class was out of session.[2] The New Left's largest organization, Students for a Democratic Society (SDS), directed thousands of students to canvass neighborhoods spreading antiwar messages in a campaign known as Vietnam Summer.

The summer's 159 racial justice and antiwar protests ignited explosive campus demonstrations that fall, representing a complex mix of student demands for privileges on campus and expanded civil rights with anger over war escalation and the draft. SDS's Vietnam Summer campaign energized returning students to attempt to sever the contributions of their alma maters to government and private war research. Students had already challenged mandatory Reserve Officers' Training Corps (ROTC) programs prior to escalation of the draft within the context of overreaching in loco parentis policies. Following Vietnam Summer, SDS demanded an end to ROTC programs strictly in terms of higher education's service to the "military industrial complex." In addition to mandatory ROTC courses, antiwar students objected to the presence of military and war-affiliated job recruiters from the US armed forces, the Central Intelligence Agency (CIA), General Electric Company, and Dow and DuPont chemical companies.[3]

During the fall of 1967, a burst of no less than sixty antiwar protests at state colleges consumed newspaper headlines, beginning with the University of Wisconsin at Madison (UW-Madison), the University of California at Berkeley (UC-Berkeley), and campus communities surrounding Oakland,

California. The student Right vehemently rebuked their antiwar peers and assembled small reactionary counterdemonstrations to defend not only American involvement in the war against communism but also war-related job recruitment. These pro-recruitment counterdemonstrations received support from faculty, administrators, law enforcement, and local citizens.

The Rules of Gentlemanly Conduct

Chief among the corporations antiwar protesters opposed was Dow Chemical Company. Dow manufactured napalm, a flammable gel that American troops used to deforest Southeast Asian jungles and counter guerilla attacks by North Vietnamese enemies. When brought into contact with skin, napalm inflicted severe chemical burns and often resulted in the disfigurement of unsuspecting villagers and their children.[4] In October 1967, Dow recruiters arrived at the University of Wisconsin to interview prospective new hires.

UW-Madison's SDS chapter planned an anti-Dow protest for October 17 and 18 in anticipation of recruiters and just days before a highly publicized antiwar march on Washington, D.C. On the morning of October 18, nearly 300 demonstrators piled into the Commerce Building for a sit-in, blocking student interviewees from reaching rooms where Dow agents awaited. University police officers arrived to break up the crowd of chanting antiwar activists and were themselves surrounded by demonstrators. Facing an additional 200 protesters outside the hall, campus officers summoned reinforcements from Madison city police. Incoming police dragged dissenters from the building, dodging bricks and other projectiles being thrown by the angry crowd. Officers disbanded the demonstrators with riot sticks, Mace, tear gas, and attack dogs. Dozens of protesters and three police officers were hospitalized. That night, 3,000 students gathered at the Library Mall pledging to boycott classes until administrators agreed to ban city police and grant immunity to demonstrators, beginning what would be a five-day strike.[5]

In addition to police violence, retributive backlash to the Dow strike by administrators and conservative students was immediate. Chancellor William H. Sewell suspended thirteen demonstrators.[6] Young Americans for Freedom's (YAF) David Keene, then a UW law student, reacted to the melee in the campus's conservative alternative magazine *Insight and Outlook* (which he edited), a piece that was reprinted by YAF's nationally distributed *New Guard*. The student Left was completely unconcerned with free speech, he argued, and they used authoritarian tactics to control speech under the guise of progressivism. Despite the chancellor's sanctions, Keene charged administrators with appeasing radical students and their faculty supporters, asserting that "the rules of gentlemanly conduct" were nearly lost. He warned that "if something is not done, the circumstances of an intolerable campus situation might force those students who have been wronged over the years to band together and administer a sound and thorough thrashing to the offending rabble"—a threat that materialized over the next three years.[7]

As police rained tear gas in Madison, conservatives sought to boost approval by highlighting the hypocrisy of peace-promoting students who choked their peers, struck administrators, attacked police, and disrupted university operations. Given the circumstances, the student Right argued that a climate of anti-liberalism had become necessary and was rightly protected through "National Guardsmen, police, and tear gas," which, Keene later recalled, were "de rigueur" on the Madison campus.[8]

During the same week, a more violent protest formed in Oakland, California, as part of the Stop the Draft Week of October 16–20. By the weekend, mayhem had broken out between 10,000 students and Oakland police. At the UC-Berkeley campus, police resorted to mass arrests and the use of force to guarantee that busloads of draftees arrived at the Oakland Army Induction Center.[9] The next weekend, between 70 and 100,000 antiwar protesters, organized by the National Mobilization Committee to End the War in Vietnam (the Mobe), marched on Washington, D.C. Though many of these protesters were not college students, the second half of the protest, aimed at the Pentagon, was student driven. Berkeley's Jerry Rubin and his eccentric comrade Abbie Hoffman promised to entertain and delight youth followers in a march across the Potomac River to the Department of Defense headquarters, which Hoffman threatened to "levitate."[10] Thirty thousand marchers came to witness a promised "exorcism," which would lift the building three hundred feet into the air. Unconventional peace lovers broke through a wall of armed troops and into the building waving the Vietcong flag, while others placed flowers in soldiers' gun barrels. Almost 700 protesters were arrested. As at Madison, order was violently restored with tear gas and clubs.[11]

Violent strikes occurred at campuses across the nation following the precedents set at Madison and Berkeley. In a two-week span, more than twenty anti-recruitment protests were reported. Physical interferences with recruiters occurred at Brown, Harvard, and Stanford Universities; the Universities of Colorado, Connecticut, Illinois, Iowa, and Pennsylvania; and Oberlin and Williams Colleges. Other demonstrations were held at Indiana, Northeastern, and Princeton Universities, and at the Universities of Maryland and Minnesota.[12] Law-and-order responses by administrators and police were swift. At Brooklyn College (now CUNY-Brooklyn), administrators stopped a student from distributing antiwar literature outside an area reserved for navy recruiters. Nearly 1,000 students and 200 police officers clashed in an ensuing riot, with police dragging students from the building by their hair.[13] A strike the next day brought class enrollment down from 10,000 to less than two thousand, and the boycott extended through the weekend.[14] At Oberlin in Ohio, over one hundred students surrounded a navy recruiter in his vehicle for four hours until police disbanded the crowd with tear gas and high-pressure fire hoses.[15] In almost every instance, conservatives assembled counterprotests, praised police, and called on administrators to punish the demonstrators.

Disproportionately punitive backlashes were matched at the federal level just days after the weekend's nationwide demonstrations. On Tuesday, October 24, director of the Selective Service Lewis B. Hershey issued Local Board Memorandum No. 85, or the Hershey Directive, which required all draft-eligible men to carry their conscription cards or risk losing their deferment status. In a subsequent order two days later, Hershey granted local draft boards the authority to revoke deferments from any student who demonstrated against war-related recruitment, claiming that such expressions were in violation of national interest. In November, Congress approved an amendment to the appropriation for the Department of Labor and the Department of Health, Education, and Welfare to revoke grants from students who participated in riots or demonstrations.[16] Conservatives approved of these measures to criminalize the Left's dissent, hoping they would quell campus disturbances and avert interference in war industry employment.

The National Student Association (NSA), a left-leaning conglomeration of college student governments with no sympathies for the war, highlighted police and university officials' retribution. The NSA reported that by the end of the semester, 14,564 students from sixty-two campuses had participated in antiwar or anti-recruitment events, and in response, administrators had enforced punishments. In total, police arrested 477 students, and college officials issued 1,011 disciplinary actions, including 422 probations, 171 conduct admonitions, 60 suspensions, 35 warnings, 32 expulsions, and 10 censures.[17]

National media coverage further helped pro-war counterdemonstrators by creating a public misunderstanding around the degree of destruction stemming from these protests. Coverage of peace demonstrations broadcast by ABC, CBS, NBC, and major newspapers like the *New York Times* and the *Chicago Tribune* focused on violent acts and the size of the crowds they attracted. Sweeping accounts generally failed to clarify that only a small number of radicals were behind instances of actual violence or property destruction. Such generalizations reinforced conservatives' claim that the antiwar Left were nihilists out to destroy the nation. The Right repeatedly insisted that they alone represented the youth silent majority.

Support for Military Research

Demonstrations against military and war-affiliated private companies had an unintended effect: employment application rates increased as reactionary defenses of the corporations showcased their attractive job opportunities. The Department of Defense reported that all branches of the military had met recruitment quotas, and 2,505 college graduates had been admitted to officer training schools. The navy reported a competitive acceptance rate of only 30 percent. The CIA continued its policy of visiting 115 colleges twice a year to recruit researchers in the fields of math, engineering, geography, geology, economics, and political science. In 1967 alone, Dow Chemical hired 1,300 college graduates with degrees in the hard sciences. In 1968, the company hoped to hire a thousand additional graduates to work on its portfolio of 800 products, which, as pro-war counterdemonstrators repeatedly emphasized, included vaccines, antifreeze, and Saran Wrap in addition to napalm.[18]

Conservatives also boasted of the benefits that war research dollars brought to their institutions. This messaging was effective on campuses such as the University of Michigan, where the student government coordinated a vote on the university's association with classified defense research. Confident of popular antiwar support, 300 students staged a sit-in in November to protest Michigan's $10 million in Department of Defense grants (worth over $90 million in 2023). But the antiwar sentiment of activist student government members did not translate to the student body at large. The question of whether the university should cease classified research received 4,787 no votes, constituting a 61 percent majority.[19] Similarly, many Harvard students expressed disapproval after some of their peers imprisoned a Dow recruiter for seven hours in a science lab. Administrators responded by placing 74 men on probation and formally admonishing 171 others. Radcliffe College placed 7 women on probation and admonished

128 others.[20] Students interviewed about the punishments in the wake of the demonstration felt that the captors had been sentenced too *lightly* for interfering with Dow's employment efforts. Most who spoke with a *Boston Globe* reporter said that they expected demonstrators to be expelled.[21]

As the war in Vietnam escalated, students carried the fall antiwar demonstrations into the next semester. By the beginning of the spring 1968 term, the United States had deployed approximately 500,000 troops to Vietnam. Nearly 9,000 men had died in combat. War costs hovered close to $25 billion, and the resulting inflation destabilized the economy. The January 1968 Tet Offensive devastated American domestic morale as 80,000 North Vietnamese troops raided South Vietnam and ransacked the American embassy, exposing the United States' inability to contain communist expansion.[22] Top army officials requested an increase of 206,000 troops in response. In March, American soldiers in search of Vietcong partisans raped, tortured, and murdered over 500 South Vietnamese villagers at My Lai.[23] Human carnage 8,000 miles away polarized the campus and further inspired antiwar activism. A survey by the American Council on Education reported that 60 percent of students were now "violently opposed" to the war, though there is no evidence to support the notion that that percentage of students actually committed violent acts.[24] Radical discontent was nonetheless evidenced by multiple isolated bombings in surrounding campus communities from February to March.[25]

The final two months of the spring 1968 term were especially tumultuous as the antiwar movement grew more popular on college and university campuses. Yale's draft opposition group, RESIST, designated April 15 and 16 as "academic days of conscience," sponsoring strikes at over 400 colleges. SDS labeled the following week through the end of the month "Ten Days to Shake the Empire," in which antiwar strikes would occur daily, while the Mobe pledged to sponsor parades in fourteen major cities.[26] Protests erupted at Louisiana State University, Ohio State University, the University of California at San Diego, and SUNY-Albany, and in Michigan, Georgia, Connecticut, Massachusetts, and New Jersey. In New York City alone, 200,000 students participated in strikes.[27] Abroad, 1,000 students in Prague demonstrated in front of the US embassy building, while Parisians raised the flag of North Vietnam over the Eiffel Tower, Notre Dame Cathedral, and the Arc de Triomphe. Additional demonstrations were held in Tokyo and Mexico City.[28]

Generally, conservative students continued their support for the war in the name of anticommunism despite wide disapproval among their peers, negative economic effects, and the rising death toll of Americans and Vietnamese. Notwithstanding dogmas of peace, even evangelical schools diverged from the national student body's antiwar stance. A 1968 survey of students at Moody Bible Institute in Chicago showed that 54 percent favored escalating bombing campaigns in Vietnam compared to only 21 percent of students nationwide.[29] Students and faculty from the typically progressive Antioch College voted that their Christian institution should not take a public stance on "political" matters.[30]

However, notable exceptions to the conservative pro-war position did exist within a handful of distinctly libertarian YAF chapters. At Pennsylvania State University, which had the nation's largest chapter with 285 members, students of the Libertarian Club cooperated with the Mobe and SDS to demonstrate against the draft and war industries. Penn State YAF even helped pass a measure through the student government to remove the ROTC from campus and worked with SDS to create an "underground railroad" to Canada for men seeking to evade the draft.[31] Aside from these exceptions, students on the right generally argued that the success of the peace movement would all but ensure a communist victory in Vietnam in the immediate, and a global communist victory long-term.

Like an American

Traditionalist conservatives claimed that anyone who opposed the war was necessarily sympathetic to the communist cause, touting the strikes of their leftist peers as antipatriotic at best, treasonous at worst. This attitude was best exemplified by Brooklyn College YAF, whose counterdemonstration banners demanded that others on campus fall in line: "If You Want to Live Like an American, Act Like One."[32] The belief that one should "act like" or embody one's nationality was central to being a traditionalist. In their estimation, Americans acted like heteronormative white Christians. Duty to country was just beneath duty to God.

At southern universities, pro-war counterdemonstrations were highly indicative of what "acting like" an American (and a southerner) during a time of war entailed. At Clemson University and the University of Virginia, for example, all-white pro-war demonstrators sang "Dixie," the Confederate anthem of the American Civil War, to challenge the also all-white peace activists.[33] Because "Dixie" was the hymn of insurrectionist slave owners a century prior, it may seem perplexing that white students used it in defense of American aggression in Vietnam *against* so-called communist slavery as well as against other white students. The Right was reintroducing Confederate emblems, especially the rebel flag, in the 1960s as symbols of resistance to the civil rights movement and integration, which were maligned by segregationists as "un-American." This antagonistic ethos was part of a developing sense of nationalism among the student Right that had less to do with the singular issue of the war than in provoking and intimidating white liberals for their numerous pro-social causes. Thus, nationalists could loudly sing a racist song at an antiwar event because racial justice and peace were entangled in their minds as liberal goals to resist. The point was no longer about the war, but about provoking the left.

And so long as conservatives looked respectable, it did not matter that their provocations were unscrupulous and their beliefs about racial hierarchies were amoral. For example, LSU professor James Hardy Jr. recalled of student and future Ku Klux Klan Grand Wizard David Duke: "When everyone else looked like a shepherd, he wore a coat and tie."[34] In fact simply looking like a respectable square became a chief fundraising strategy of organizations like Campus Crusade for Christ and the College Republicans in these years. A College Republican fundraising manual explicitly stated that "businessmen are very sympathetic to clean cut college students coming before them making constructive presentations. . . . [They] are so susceptible to this presentation that the situation is actually dangerous. There would be little to stop a couple of con-men from pretending to be College Republicans and moving in to loot the business community."[35] There is no evidence that any person ever presented themself as a College Republican in a fraudulent fundraising scheme, but leaders often cautioned their mentees with these seemingly paranoid warnings while encouraging them to dress their best.

Disunity on the Right

As the New Left's antiwar protests became more frequent, the student Right reacted in disjointed ways, which demonstrated an ideological diversity yet to be made uniform by movement leaders. Many of the Right's clubs either supported war industry recruitment or singularly resisted antiwar and racial justice sit-ins, building occupations, and strikes. For example, during the 1967–68 academic year, Columbia University conservatives created three separate anti-SDS clubs, which were made up of athletes, members of the ROTC, and members of groups called Students for a Free Campus and Students for Columbia University.[36] All of these would eventually merge with YAF to form the Majority Coalition (discussed in chapter 4), once movement leaders showed them how their reactions could be coordinated. However, until individual clubs could align their missions under a common denominator—opposing the Left—they acted separately and with distinct missions.

Further, intergroup tiffs over the degree to which others were sufficiently intellectual, activist, or simply "conservative enough" prevented clubs from working together effectively. For example, the George Washington University YAF mocked the GW Young Republicans for being barely indistinguishable from "plainclothes hippies," telling a campus audience that the Young Republicans "wear ties and they wear sportscoats, but they think like liberals. That's the problem."[37] The GW Young Republicans also highlighted the groups' differences, claiming that they were not a YAF "subsidiary:" "the difference[s] between us are far too great for that. The function of YAF is to propagandize and proselytize . . . [whereas we] provide a vehicle for responsible and constructive political activity and social reform."[38]

At the University of Minnesota, the far-right Society for the Preservation of the American Republic (SPAR) derided YAF as "a collection of pitiful do-nothings," to which YAF responded by calling SPAR "all-show-no-brains."[39] The University of Wisconsin's Committee to Defend Individual Rights dismissed YAF as "nonintellectual," while the Young Republicans were too "liberal" and a "do-nothing group."[40] In a jab at YAF, they clarified that they were "not the usual student organization which forms to oppose the left, i.e. non-intellectual and 'status-quo-ish.' We are all interested in ideas."[41] Such insults left College Republican leaders extremely self-conscious of their reputation. In response, College Republican National Committee (CRNC) executives issued a manual called *Up the Hard Core! How Not to Put Your Volunteers to Sleep*, which gave tips on how to combat the image that College Republicans did nothing.[42]

Not only did intergroup rivalries prevent effective mobilization, but an entire campus demographic of conservative women students was generally excluded from their ranks. Because of the "danger involved" in their chapter's counter-resistance activities, women students were not welcome to join the Committee to Defend Individual Rights. Nationally, women members of YAF participated in its founding events, worked as magazine coeditors, and sat on its national and state boards, yet some still reported receiving threats of sexual violence for their club affiliations in these years.[43]

As the Right identified strategies to expand their ranks while refusing to work together, they chanted in unison that liberals were ruining their campus experience and betraying the American pursuit of global hegemony.

Organizing around Anticommunism

It became clear to conservative movement leaders that there was an anti-leftist sentiment among some college students, even if not all of those students would have called themselves conservative. Movement elders had already created three useful vehicles for campus organizing of different purposes: YAF for ideologues, the Intercollegiate Studies Institute (ISI) for intellectuals, and the College Republicans for partisans, in addition to students' own anti-left clubs. To maximize their effectiveness, the three movement-sponsored organizations needed to emphasize their shared grievances, translate them into nonpolitical and nonideological forms, and make common cause with new students they could eventually pull to the right. In the context of disruptive peace and Black Power demonstrations, the Right made communism an issue ripe for exploitation to serve this purpose.

In its mission statement, YAF—the Right's most activist and thus most useful group for gaining attention—branded communism "the single greatest threat" to liberty, emphasized that the United States "should stress victory over, rather than coexistence with, this menace," and endorsed an America first foreign policy.[44] To college conservatives, American intervention to save South Vietnam from North Vietnamese communists was not just heroic but an ordinance of their mission. According to documents circulated by YAF, the ideology that had taken hold in Russia, China, Cuba, and elsewhere had, by 1968, "butchered 100,000,000 men, women and children in the past sixty years and held back the economic development of 1/3 of mankind."[45] By framing efforts to thwart the spread of communism as an urgent matter of human rights, members of YAF, ISI, and College Republicans worked to convince others that communism was not an ideological abstraction but an imminent threat on a global scale—one infiltrating their very campuses through radical peaceniks and civil rights agitators. This understanding made it imperative for students to wage educational campaigns in support of "Americanism" and against anything they felt deviated from it.

According to YAF board member Randal Teague, creating an anticommunist ideological base on American campuses would give the impression that communism was a student concern across the nation. It could also solve another problem. The Right needed to build up its ranks on certain characteristically progressive campuses where organizing proved especially difficult. Those looking to form a Young Republicans chapter at UC-Berkeley, for example, complained that implementing methods from the organizing manual was "almost an impossibility" due to the campus climate. Never mind campus tabling events—the best the young founders could do was to quietly canvass residence halls and gauge the political interests of their peers through conversation.[46] Where conservative clubs were unable to recruit using established protocols, YAF offered a novel solution. Rather than organizing strictly along the principles of conservatism or the GOP platform, the organization began calling for coalition building against "the left,"[47] loosely interpreted as anyone encouraging withdrawal from Vietnam, anyone meeting the demands of the Black Power student movement, and, by extension, anyone vaguely sympathetic to liberal ideas.

In this vein, YAF developed a new strategy to market anticommunist principles without using its own moniker, which had become associated with extremism. Teague instructed members to effectively duplicate themselves by creating auxiliaries with "innocuous" names, such as the National Student Committee on Cold War Education or the Pennsylvania Committee for Improved Schools and Education. The committees presented anticommunist programs, stocked libraries with anticommunist literature and films, and disbursed informational papers. To maintain cost-effectiveness, Teague directed them to congressional committees, such as the House Un-American Activities Committee or the Senate Internal Security Subcommittee, for free literature.

To spread anticommunist messages to new student circles, Teague advised members to schedule anticommunist study groups at regular intervals and include students who were not already affiliated with YAF. The committees were instructed to work in conjunction with other organizations, including the US Junior Chamber of Commerce, the Young Republicans, the Young Democrats "where possible," the ROTC, and local business or civic clubs.[48] As committees got organized, objectives were set, and advisory board members were selected, YAF directed members to contact press outlets to ensure that, like the Left, their activities made headlines.

Guaranteeing proximity to movement conservatives, YAF executives instructed students to invite state legislators as advisory board members to their committees. Members drafted anticommunist bills and located supportive representatives to submit them in legislative sessions, taking care to choose "moderate" lawmakers to introduce the bills. Students would then "assume the responsibility for doing all the work on behalf of the sympathetic legislator" and "make sure that all state laws for lobbying before the legislature [were] complied with fully." Teague stressed the importance of winning public support for the anticipated legislation, even proposals that were underpowered or unfeasible. Practicality was secondary—the importance lay in planting the message and creating a spectacle of patriotism based in anticommunist outrage. Executives directed students to form relationships with sympathetic mayors, council members, and other municipal policy makers to gain legitimacy and favor with local authorities.[49]

The most active of the new auxiliaries was Voices in Vital America (VIVA), initially the Victory in Vietnam Association, at the University of California. VIVA founders Carol Bates, Steve Frank, and Richard Thies kept a list of campus speakers, instituted a mentorship program connecting first-year students with older ones, and instructed constituents to use VIVA as an intermediary when bringing grievances forward to administrators. VIVA's efforts were funded by wealthy Los Angeles members of the Ladies Auxiliary, especially Gloria Wells Choppin, as well as by the Christian Freedom Foundation.[50] Other important auxiliaries were the World Youth Crusade for Freedom and the National Student Committee for Victory in Vietnam.

At Duke University, YAF and College Republican chapters cosponsored lectures from American military generals, members of Congress, and Vietnamese ambassadors.[51] The program of one seminar titled "Vietnam: Past, Present, Prospects" included remarks by a veteran ROTC instructor recently returned from Vietnam and a professor of Asian history.[52] The organization even financed eleven students' travel expenses to South Vietnam to report on local enthusiasm for American intervention.[53] In addition to distributing 1 million position papers in support of the war, the group issued instructions for combating the "Campus Cong."

America First Boycotts

An America first approach to the Cold War ironically brought young conservatives into conflict with a multitude of leading American businesses. While YAF believed in free enterprise as outlined in the Sharon Statement, its commitment to anticommunism superseded all other values but Christianity (of the nationalist, rather than missionary, variety). YAFers were therefore aghast that the US government supported American trade with Soviet-dependent states as part of the Johnson administration's bridge-building policy with the Soviet Union.[54] Conservatives viewed this

Twenty YAF members picketing the St. Louis, Missouri, IBM office in 1968 as part of the STOP-IBM campaign. Bettmann Collection via Getty Images.

trade as a form of "national suicide" because it propped up communism, which they believed was locked in a life-and-death struggle with American capitalism.[55] YAF thus undertook boycotts against several American corporations it suspected of undermining the free-market system by practicing free trade: American Motors Corporation, Firestone Tire and Rubber Company, Ford Motor Company, International Business Machines (IBM), Chase Manhattan Bank (now JPMorgan Chase & Co.), and the Mack Truck manufacturing company.

YAF harnessed its energies against computer giant IBM in a nationwide boycott throughout the late 1960s. YAFers protested outside IBM offices in Massachusetts, Missouri, Texas, and Wisconsin, demanding the corporation cease selling engines, trucks, radar, scrap metal, crude rubber, and other "non-strategic" industrial supplies to friends of the enemy. Picket signs decried IBM customers in Texas as "traitors," while the University of Wisconsin YAF hung a cardboard effigy of a computer outside the company's Madison office. Damning STOP-IBM picket signs read: "Support Your Local

Traitors—Buy IBM," "Support Communism—Buy IBM," and "Work against the Free World—Buy IBM."[56]

The emboldened youth delivered their grievances directly to IBM's corporate leaders at an April 1968 shareholders' meeting. YAF chair Alan MacKay and *New Guard* editor Arnie Steinberg purchased single shares of stock to gain access to the Boston conference, while their cadres distributed flyers outside, exposing the corporation's "suicidal trade with the enemy." The two YAF leaders even secured a perfunctory meeting with IBM chair Thomas Watson.[57] The historical record gives no evidence that the young men's efforts were fruitful in any way, nor does it appear that YAF was able to convince the customers of corporate giants to do business elsewhere. Nonetheless, YAF's noisy boycotts designed to rebalance international Cold War relationships drove Senate Foreign Relations Committee chair J. William Fulbright to label their collective efforts "a nuisance boycott campaign by an extremist political organization."[58] To the conservative YAFers, however, "extremism in defense of liberty" was no vice—it was necessitated by their founding document and encouraged by Fulbright's Senate colleagues, especially movement leader Barry Goldwater.

Despite Fulbright's condemnation and their boycotts' apparent lack of success, conservative students carried on with theatrical demonstrations to bring attention to anticommunist causes. YAF condemned Soviet cultural exchange programs that could "lull Americans into the idea that Russians are good guys," picketing Russian circuses and ballets while claiming that attendance at such events was effectively an endorsement of "slavery."[59] Picket signs outside Russian performances read: "We Won't Co-Exist with Slavery" and "We Get Circuses—the Russians Get Laos, Cuba, and Hungary."[60]

In recognition of the fiftieth anniversary of the Bolshevik Revolution, YAF and Catholic newspaper *Twin Circles* conducted a show trial at Georgetown University. Lev Dobriansky, Georgetown professor of economics and YAF advisory board member, facilitated the production of International Communism on Trial. The mock trial simulated a war crimes tribunal with an indictment brought forth by the extrajudicial World Court of Public Opinion of a conspiracy of communist governments to commit human rights violations resulting in the deaths of 45 to 100 million people. Soviet ambassadors described the show trial as a "vicious kangaroo court," while antiwar protesters disrupted the mock proceedings on three separate occasions.[61]

Appealing their grievances to the highest levels of power, conservative college students briefed party leaders at the Republican and Democratic National Conventions in 1968 on their efforts to stamp out anti-American business and cultural practices. In these meetings, YAF vice chair David Keene of the University of Wisconsin, future chair of the American Conservative Union and president of the National Rifle Association, lobbied both parties to halt US trade of machine tools, data-processing equipment, and other goods with eastern European states, arguing that communist North Vietnam received its military supplies indirectly from Soviet allies.[62] MacKay, Steinberg, Keene, and other college-age conservatives confidently appeared at shareholders' meetings and spoke before members of Congress with the assurance that their objectives were supported by powerful and influential audiences in Congress and on corporate boards.

Blue Buttons

Throughout the late 1960s, peace activists increasingly popularized a black armband as a symbol of war resistance. Black armbands became especially recognized through media coverage of the Supreme Court case *Tinker v. Des Moines,* which upheld students' free speech right to wear political adornments to class. To counter the peace movement's trademark, conservatives adopted a blue lapel button as their own anti-left symbol.[63]

Usually, the campus Right co-opted the New Left's symbols with minor adjustments to fit their own purposes. In this case, conservative elders were clear that the counter to the black armband needed to be a different medium altogether. College Republican manuals explained that buttons were "one of the best types of publicity" because they "connote extraordinary competence." Plus, the design was simply one color without text, so it was cheap enough to mass produce. A CRNC manual directed students to order at least 1,000 buttons at a cost of $56 from Hodges Badge Company in Cambridge, Massachusetts. Chapters that could not spring for the buttons could print tall handbills designed to "stick up visibly in men's pockets," the way leftists fashionably let red communist pamphlets peek conspicuously out of their bell-bottoms.[64]

California YAF distributed over 100,000 blue buttons to college campuses across the state, holding press conferences in Los Angeles, Sacramento, San Diego, and San Francisco.[65] Five thousand blue buttons were distributed at Rutgers University by the Coalition for a Peaceful Campus and at Monmouth University by the Young Republicans and Young Democrats.[66] Blue button events took place at Fresno State College (now California State University, Fresno), Long Beach State College (now California State University, Long Beach), American University, and George Washington University as part of counterprotests against SDS and Black Power demonstrations.[67] Reagan, his staff, and California superintendent of public instruction Max Rafferty all proudly donned blue buttons.[68]

The stated purpose of the blue button campaign was to show support for administrators who used punishment to maintain an orderly campus, but in practical application it mostly just provided the few conservatives on campus a marker of visibility. One of the organizers explained that conservative students "have not been heard because we have been studying" and were finally prepared to make their convictions evident.[69] Donning the button, said one organizer, gives "public notice to would-be revolutionaries" that counteractions aimed at "keeping peace on campus and maintaining academic freedom" were underway.[70]

For students on the right, academic freedom was what afforded them as tuition payers "the right to study, write, and speak according to one's convictions without interference from governments or a mob."[71] This version of academic freedom did not allow for dissent against established political, social, or institutional order. Rather, it guaranteed a transaction: an education for tuition paid. In this framing, the "mob" of war dissidents and civil rights agitators were not exercising academic freedom but infringing on it. When the Right claimed opposition to "interference from governments," they meant democratic actions brought about by popular will. It was not that the Right resisted concentrated power; they simply preferred power to be concentrated in their own hands and were willing to use government force to attain it, as evidenced time and again during conflicts with the student Left.

In addition to the buttons, YAF encouraged its chapters and their auxiliary committees and coalitions to peddle other political kitsch for recruitment and fundraising. The merchandise provided buyers with a public statement of their own resistance to the Left's resistance, which was the point of commonality between all conservative, right-wing, and white evangelical groups.

Some of the most frequently donned buttons, bumper stickers, and signs—many of which were appropriations of New Left slogans—read: "SDS Is Revolting," "SDS = SS," "Up against the Wall Commies," "To Hell with Socialism," "Welfare Is a Right" (with an image of a looted storefront), "I Am a Capitalist," "Eat a Grape for Freedom," "Drop It. Hell Yes" (imposed over an image of a B-52 bomber), "Strike Now, Flunk Later," "Tantrums Are for Kids, Not Students," "Vote with Your Ass, Stay in Class," "Demonstrate against Napalm Today—Right after Burning of Administration Building," "Arson Kills," "Firebombs Now, Firearms Later," "Fight Juvenile Delinquency, Stop SDS," "If You Liked Hitler, You'll Love SDS," "Who Will Be the First Campus Fatality? Think about It," "Ban the SDS Bombers," "LEFT Is a Four Letter Word," "Win: Give Peace a Chance," and "Does NSA Speak for You?"

Chapters were encouraged to place large orders for buttons and stickers so the items could be resold during fundraisers. Bumper stickers and buttons could be ordered for ten cents each, and eleven-by-seventeen-inch posters for twenty-five cents each. As one YAF brochure suggested, "You can buy these items at discount prices and sell them to Leftists at inflated prices!"[72]

Conservative Humor

As they did with symbols and slogans, the student Right often appropriated strategies of their adversaries rather than designing their own. By mimicking and distorting the New Left's techniques, conservatives presented a carnival mirror interpretation of progressive politics to ridicule rather than to engage with. A few popular techniques included creating fictitious New Left groups, penning satirical New Left publications, and staging theatrical counterdemonstrations in mockery of peace or civil rights causes. These activities appropriated the Left's language, slogans, and group names, transforming them into demeaning parodies steeped in ableism, homophobia, and white supremacy. Defensive explanations for these behaviors from former members characterize them as sophomoric fodder.[73] However, their intent was to use satire to communicate disdain and to undermine and embarrass their antiwar and pro–civil rights peers.

Creating spoof clubs with demeaning acronyms was a popular strategy. At Wichita State University, conservatives formed the Society for the Prevention of Asinine Student Movements (SPASM). University of Southern California conservatives formed a World Association of Paisan Students (whose acronym sounds like a slur for Italian Americans), which demanded an Italian studies program to celebrate Al Capone, the culturally sensitive cafeteria option of pizza, and a massive canal project to offer transportation via gondola staffed with mandolin players. The demands were to be met by April 22 to honor the birthday of Italy's fascist dictator, Benito Mussolini.

Other clubs bypassed the acronym and instead mocked the Black Power student movement's demands with their own nonnegotiable versions. From the University of Wisconsin, the Homophiles of Madison satirically demanded a gay studies program and university-sponsored gay social events. At the University of North Carolina (UNC), students demanded reforms for the visually impaired, including hiring blind professors, assigning Braille textbooks, and blinding students without visual limitations so that they would be unable to discriminate by race.[74]

Literary expressions of anti-progressive disdain were best exemplified by YAF's *New Left News*, a parody of SDS's *New Left Notes*. A feature article written by Mark Crudd (referring to Columbia University SDS president Mark Rudd) announced a campaign against on-campus military recruitment by the Girl Scouts of America. Students at North Carolina State University circulated their own version of the *New Left News*, published by the "students for a demented society," edited by one Pat Sturgis and Slightly Frigid, and with editorial staff including Dee Day Jr., Fong Dong Kong, S. Creamcheese, and Zoot Floot Mason. Full of sexual innuendos, drug references, and anti-Asian racism, the magazine featured articles such as "Furniture Stripping" and "Crudd Considers LSD," and an "Atrocity Photo of the Month" section in which readers could submit bloody images of brutalized Vietcong. Membership to the monthly photo club was three dollars or the scalp of a YAF student.[75]

Encouraging readers to mock progressive clubs using their own language, YAF disseminated a memo titled "The New Left Speaks" containing "some of the most revealing and obnoxious quotes from these anarchists and nihilists [that] should be reprinted locally for mass consumption."[76] YAF was proud of its parody, holding it up as an example to other clubs and claiming it had distributed 100,000 copies across a hundred campuses.[77]

Beyond offensive literary satire, some translated their contempt for the Left through theatrical and sarcastic counterdemonstrations. Actress and antiwar celebrity Jane Fonda was perhaps the most prominent personality caught in the crosshairs of the Right's theater. Students attended Fonda events carrying signs that threatened violence while mocking her film titles, such as "They Shoot Traitors, Don't They?" (a reference to 1969's *They Shoot Horses, Don't They?*). YAF hecklers also shouted slogans such as, "Jane's a Pain," "Traitor!" and "Shoot Fonda, Not Film!" and engaged in shoving matches with the actress's bodyguards at her debuts.[78]

A University of Southern California YAF alumnus recalled burning a Fonda effigy along with the North Vietnamese flag: "Frankly, all of us, including me, believed she was a traitor, and should have been tried for treason." When the actress was scheduled to appear at the USC campus shortly after Nixon announced the US bombing campaign in Cambodia, he recalled: "We went to hang a banner from the building behind the stage where she was speaking so any of the television cameras focused on her would show our sign: '*Barbarella* Bombed, Why Can't Nixon?' It illustrated another point that conservatives on campus had an active sense of humor."[79]

Threats of execution, symbolic hangings, the burning of effigies, and literature laden with insults and hate were framed by the perpetrators and those who found comedy in them as harmless jokes. They claimed plausible deniability that they would ever translate these ideas into action by focusing on the implied "humor," hiding their true intent to devalue and delegitimize progressive calls for equality and peace—a tactic still used by far-right youth today.[80]

As Raúl Pérez explains, "Racist humor is not a peripheral, marginal, or harmless form of discourse" but an intentional exercise of social capital that serves to reinforce "boundaries of inclusion, exclusion, and dehumanization."[81] While racist humor is a tool of ostracism, it can also cultivate "affiliation, solidarity, pleasure, and entertainment" among the members of the in-group that use it to denigrate and "other" the targeted out-group.[82] Pérez describes this type of humor as a white schadenfreude that works "to enhance and maintain feelings of racial superiority and amused contempt" among white joke makers.[83] For college conservatives, aggressive humor also functioned to define white liberals apart from whites who were trying to normalize nationalism and racial hierarchies.

As Matt Sienkiewicz and Nick Marx further explain, comedy is extremely effective in bringing together the various "tensions" of the Right's "uneasy conceptual marriage" between traditionalists, libertarians, and white supremacists. Comedy, they clarify, "serves as a lubricant that helps audiences slide among these disparate aspects of right-wing ideology, with a certain gravity pulling them down into the lower, dirtier depths of the complex."[84] Humor serves to "normalize" and even celebrate racism, misogyny, and other "virulent" right-wing principles: "What first breaks through as a joke may well show up later as part of a political platform or a rallying cry among violent extremists." Comedy thus provides "cover and succor to those inclined toward the ugliest of ideologies."[85]

While using comedy to advance white supremacy has a history that extends at least to the era of blackface minstrel shows in the nineteenth century, college campuses circa 1970 functioned as a place where this type of satire developed an extreme hyperbolic and prankish edge, one akin to the supposed humor inherent in fraternal hazing. As they themselves would describe it, many of the young men engaging in this type of banter injected a hypermasculine fraternity culture into their activities, seemingly blending comedy and politics to preserve social hierarchies.

It is important to note that Buckley and other bluestocking elders who were guiding and funding these students remained silent on the matter of crude jokes.[86] Above all, they offered tacit support by continuing to mentor students and fund their expenses, with no evident efforts made to redirect blatantly offensive and sometimes criminal behaviors. This was no oversight, as Buckley, Whittaker Chambers, and other writers constantly policed rhetoric coming from the Right, casting out undesirables (Ayn Rand and Robert Welch, for example) when they saw fit to maintain a standard of respectability within the movement. And every College Republican manual advised students to send in copies of their writings, event advertisements, and other evidence of their activities for inspection.

Evangelical Appropriation of New Left Messages

As College Republican and YAF spoofs co-opted New Left language with harmful intent, a second front of Christian evangelical organizations, such as the Campus Crusade for Christ (now called Cru), adapted radicals' language and tactics for campus ministry. Like New Left demonstrators, Campus Crusaders preached their messages through bullhorns in free speech zones. Their banners adapted the language of antiwar groups: "Boycott Hell! Accept Jesus," "Join a Minority Group (Follow Jesus)," "Prince of PEACE," "Students Denouncing Sin," "Christians Are in the Streets," and "Jesus Is Habit-Forming and Life-Giving." Their literature characterized the life of Jesus as "history's greatest demonstration."[87] Campus Crusade's folk band, the Armageddon Experience, dressed in bell-bottom jeans and sang worship music devoted to the "true revolutionary" Jesus Christ.

The organization marketed its Explo '72, a weekend of evangelical training events in Dallas, as a "happening" and a "Christian Woodstock" featuring folk, country, and rock singers such as Johnny Cash and Kris Kristofferson.[88] At UC-Berkeley, Campus Crusade founded the Christian World Liberation Front (CWLF), co-opting the name of the civil rights organization the Third World Liberation Front. The CWLF created "crash pad" safe houses for addicts, where Christian youth leaders would minister to youth in crisis who needed temporary shelter.[89]

Like YAF, Campus Crusaders performed counteractions directed against New Left events, but to a subtler degree. Rather than stage YAF-style provocations, Crusaders often appeared as participants at New Left events and gently distributed Christian literature among the crowd.[90] At its 1967 Berkeley Blitz—a ministry event that infiltrated a protest against Governor Reagan's dismissal of UC system president Clark Kerr—Crusaders gathered at a sorority house for a mass telephone outreach to nearly 30,000 students.[91] During the Blitz, speakers addressed drug use and premarital sex, advising those in the crowd to "learn how to dress as Godly women so that you will not cause your brother to stumble."[92] Campus Crusade board member evangelist Billy Graham asked students, "Why not experiment with Christ?" as they had with sex and drugs.[93] Crusaders also engaged in these tactics at social gatherings where alcohol or drugs were involved. For example, 500 Crusaders traveled to Daytona Beach, Florida, during spring break of 1967 to execute Operation Sunshine, where they joined their party-loving peers on the beach, at motels, and in restaurants to spread Christian messages.[94]

The incorporation of hippie culture was also a strategy of other Christian clubs, such as the Navigators, Inter-Varsity, and the Jesus Freaks, who gained converts from the so-called average kids disaffected by the New Left.[95] The Jesus Freaks appropriated many of the symbols of the student Left, such as the "one way" gesture—a one-finger adaption of the 'V' peace symbol in which only the index finger pointed upward. They ministered to student radicals, addicts, and others by offering drug counseling, Bible studies, and hostels for people without housing.[96]

Rather than remain silent, as they had with students whose messages threatened violence and whose demonstrations were designed to intimidate, movement elders did express approval of Campus Crusaders and similar organizations by praising their Christian messaging, clean looks, and square demeanors.[97] Yet despite these apparent differences and whatever the Christian groups' intentions may have been, their appropriation of progressive language had the same deleterious effect as the misbehavior of YAF and others: it undermined serious messages of social justice. Evangelical efforts to capitalize on the perceived trend of taking to the streets to win new followers revealed the same shallow and dismissive analysis of New Left demonstrations that movement conservatives betrayed throughout this period: that peace and civil rights activism was fashionable rather than authentic and purposeful. And regardless of whether their tactics were friendly or threatening, each of these campus groups benefited from continuous mentorship and generous financial support from the movement's elders.

Club Takeovers

Students on the Right fought to make themselves seen on campus by staging theatrical counterprotests, wearing blue buttons, and upholding a uniquely square image in the countercultural era. Their most obvious campaigns, however, took the form of club takeovers. M. Stanton Evans, YAF adviser and author of its founding document, the Sharon Statement, gave clear instructions to the conservative students in his charge to "fight the left" by capturing their local organizations and using the momentum of those successes to seek larger targets (the same way they believed communism spread): "First we take over the Young Republicans, then we take over the Republican Party, then we take over the country."[98] In this pursuit, YAFers sought to overtake organizations they believed were illegitimately controlled by liberals and leftists, especially their nearest College Republican club, Young Republicans chapter, and campus student government association (SGA).

Acting in this spirit at the 1967 national convention of the Young Republican National Federation, chair Jack McDonald appointed an absolute majority of thirty-four conservatives to the sixty-seven-person executive committee. Leveraging the authority of his position, McDonald then appointed every conservative to subcommittees to write resolutions that were decidedly anticommunist and opposed to the civil rights movement.[99] Similarly, in an April 1968 meeting of the Columbia University Young Republicans, a tense power struggle occurred between conservatives and other members. The conflict started during a meeting to nominate a liberal student as the new state chair. In what conservatives described as a "liberal coup," twenty members voted in favor of the new liberal chair. Conservatives insisted that since some of the voters' membership cards would expire in the fall, they should not be able to participate. After a heated disagreement, many members left the meeting, while the conservatives lingered. Those who remained amended the constitution in their peers' absence to prevent them from voting on the new state chair.[100]

In instances like these, the student Right embraced winning by technicality over popularity and displayed a dogged commitment to waiting out their opponents in order to achieve these types of victories. There was a clear preference for authoritarianism over coalition building and consensus. By taking over other groups in this way, students on the right had greater power to exert their will, even if that will amounted only to blocking a handful of new reforms. And by occupying representative spaces on

SGAs, they could keep those roles inaccessible to New Left and Black Power activists.

While keeping their sights on College Republican and Young Republican chapters, conservatives next focused on capturing campus SGAs. There were practical reasons for doing so. According to CRNC executive Morton Blackwell, student governments control "surprisingly large budgets." They also "have a significant impact on student opinion" through their ability to operate campus programming and sponsor speakers. Most importantly, they determined whether a campus affiliated "with the faltering, radical National Student Association."[101] YAF and College Republican members claimed that leftists strategically infiltrated SGAs not through winning elections out of popularity (most students, they claimed, ignored student government elections) but by recruiting sufficient masses of voters to secure wins through plurality. At Columbia University, a campaign ad for a prospective student council representative in the *Columbia Spectator* exemplified this grievance: "Is C.U.S.C. democratic? Representative? Relevant? I believe the answer to these questions is NO! The Columbia University Student Council has lost touch with the students and has become in effect a totally autonomous body, representative of nobody and accountable to no one. Unless C.U.S.C. develops a broader base, has its leaders popularly elected, gauges our opinion, and keeps us abreast of what it is doing, it will continue to be a meaningless, irrelevant organization."[102]

It is not clear if the Right appropriated this strategy from the Left, or if the accusation is better understood as a projection. While conservatives complained about the Left's apparent victories by technicality, they frequently employed similar tactics. At Indiana University, R. Emmett Tyrrell Jr. (founder of the *Alternative*) led a campaign to oust progressive student body representatives and replace them with conservatives. Tyrrell's student coalition captured all but one senate seat, including the presidency, which had been held by an SDS member.[103] In addition to YAF, those active in the College Republicans also occupied student body presidencies, including Alabama College Republican chair (and future Trump administration attorney general) Jeff Sessions, then a student at Huntingdon College in Alabama.[104]

Electing conservatives to office was exactly what the College Republicans was designed to do. The organization's executives had already issued multiple training manuals for canvassing and organizing, and by 1970 they released a manual dedicated solely to SGA takeovers. Because justification for the takeovers was rooted in the belief that leftists were using unscrupulous strategies, the Right was paranoid about who had access to these power-gaining secrets, which is evident from the first paragraph in the handbook: "CAUTION: This is a *confidential* manual. It is prepared for *College Republican use only*. Please be sure that no student not a loyal College Republican ever learns of its existence, let alone sees it. Never brag, gloat or let the opposition know anything of your plans. In fact, it is better not to let them know that anything connected with the election is of particular interest to you. A Student Government campaign could be damaged by having word leak out that it was being run by some mysterious 'master plan.'"[105]

According to Blackwell, it was not necessary that every College Republican member run for SGA—that would be too obvious. In fact, having most of its members involved in other organizations could take away from the group's most important responsibility: serving the GOP. And it was not necessary that SGA representatives be "Red Hot Republicans" either: "You may be better off electing good allies rather than good club members," Blackwell clarified. That way, trusted College Republicans could keep their eyes on their own duties and not "stop to kick every barking dog."[106]

Instead, chapter chairs assigned a few "bright freshman and sophomores" to serve on SGA "subcommittees and important lower echelons." This was the best course of action, Blackwell suggested, since "a term or two of hewing wood and drawing water" could build their credentials and prepare them as "our potential leaders." Blackwell showed the students how to strategically run a few members on a coalition ticket rather than running members as individuals. They chose party names (such as Impact, Student Action, Reform, and Challenge) and referred to their coalition as a team, a ticket, or an alliance. The coalitions duplicated themselves across ad hoc committees with creative acronyms, like Students Wanting Election Activities Reform (SWEAR), to create the appearance of widespread support.[107]

A finance chair handled the coalition's fundraising from local business owners, but Blackwell warned that fundraising was potentially "an explosive" matter. "*Only*" the finance chairs should know the details. Students could appoint other committee chairs from social, religious, professional, interest, or recreational clubs. Chair names were written on a large organizational chart placed somewhere with lots of visibility so that each person would "be impressed by seeing his name" on the board. College Republican candidates did not expect these chairs to do much, but the flattery of a title guaranteed that they would at least show up with their group members to vote.[108]

Special advantages were to be had during a campaign by advertising the opposition's failures. Blackwell reminded College Republicans to issue press releases when the other candidate "lose[s] his temper or make[s] a faux pas, play up this issue in flyers, statements to the press, letters to the editor, etc. Consider ways to engender such situations. Try to set up situations which demoralize the opposition." They could even "save up a few of their mistakes for a combined release." And if the challengers were "extremists," College Republicans needed to "hammer away on this issue. Pin them down, for instance, on whether or not they think any students should have the right to prevent other students from attending classes or from expressing opinions on which they disagree." They could also develop concerns over unrepresentative campus newspapers and mismanaged student fees into campaign issues.[109]

When it came to promoting themselves rather than discrediting their opponents, chapters with tight budgets needed to get creative. Some members walked around campus and attended classes wearing sandwich board advertisements over their shoulders. One student candidate appeared at every town event that drew police and local reporters, such as traffic accidents and fires, where the student knew he could be featured in city news ("the station thought it was a clever gimmick; the candidate became the talk of the town," noted Blackwell). In other instances, College Republicans washed car windshields in commuter parking lots and left notes under the wipers: "Now that you can see clearly, we hope you will vote for Smith." Public endorsements from campus "football heroes" and the homecoming queen were also free and effective.[110]

All hands were on deck during SGA election day. Blackwell told the students not to bother making a time chart for members working the polls— they needed to spend "*as much time as possible, preferably all day*" gathering voters. Assigned times would only discourage members from serving full-day shifts. They needed to call friends, acquaintances, even classmates whose names they did not know "out of the passing throngs," and tell those students that as a favor to the College Republican member making the request, they had "to go over and vote for our man (or team)." College Republicans needed to win the election, and "[win] it big," in order to "give a clear mandate to the new student leadership" that conservatives were taking over.[111]

In order to win it big, there could not be any "hanky panky" from the opposition at the ballot box. Blackwell was extremely concerned about campus SGA voter fraud. College Republicans had to station "security" personnel around the box at all times—"every minute" from the time voting began until the final ballot was counted. Someone needed to be there to confirm the box was empty before the polls opened. Be on the lookout for students trying to vote more than once, Blackwell warned. Have multiple representatives there when the ballots are counted. Check the total ballots against the total votes cast. And if anything suspicious were to happen, they needed to "get names of witnesses, signed statements, physical evidence . . . [and to] be prepared to appeal the election if opposition abuses" occur.[112]

Beyond a perceived progressive overrepresentation in student leadership, another major grievance of conservatives was their campus governing bodies' affiliation with the National Student Association (NSA), a confederation of college student governments. The NSA's antiwar stance and its other progressive platforms placed it at odds with nearly all conservative, and many moderate, student organizations. For example, in August 1967, after the NSA hosted a draft card burning at Kansas State University, students overwhelmingly withdrew their membership in a vote of 3,731 to 943.[113]

During a STOP-NSA campaign, the UNC YAF and the Young Republicans joined forces to have their campus government disaffiliate from NSA after it formed an alliance with the Southern Student Organizing Committee (SSOC), a regional sister to the national SDS with its own dedicated civil rights mission.[114] However pro–civil rights the group's mission may have been, as historian Joy Ann Williamson-Lott details, the SSOC still embraced white supremacist icons and rhetoric, as exemplified by the Confederate flag in its logo and the title of its newsletter, the *New Rebel*.[115] Despite SSOC's nods to its southern legacy and the fact that UNC students were among the national officers in the NSA, the UNC student body ultimately voted to disaffiliate.[116]

When the NSA admitted to receiving covert funding from the CIA for international events, YAF widely circulated the news across campuses. Boston College YAF accused the organization of engaging "in rabble-rousing political activities" and functioning "as an adjunct of the left-wing of American parties." Its pamphlets further suggested that the NSA should have its tax-exempt status revoked for "flagrant violations" of the 501(c)(3) tax code.[117]

These negative campaigns appear to have been successful. By the late 1960s, it was harder for the NSA to maintain its membership as chapters disaffiliated or joined its conservative equivalent, the Associated Student Government (ASG). A splinter organization from the NSA, the founding members of ASG were NSA defectors who described their group as a "neutral" option to the "political" NSA that would provide "a constructive alternative to the disruptive approach." They purported to offer a forum for SGA leaders to share ideas on campus governance without the overtly political agenda they sensed from progressive leaders hailing from New England or California. The founders mostly came from southern and midwestern institutions: Auburn, Louisiana State, Purdue, Tulane, and Vanderbilt Universities, as well as the University of Oklahoma.[118] In the NSA-ASG saga, when conservatives were unsuccessful in subverting existing governing bodies, they pivoted to establishing their own alternative organizations, which they categorized as unbiased or politically "neutral."[119] Creating this type of alternative club was in the same spirit that had justified the campus Right's alternative newspapers and magazines (discussed in chapter 2).

Changes in Mobilization by 1968

From 1967 to 1968, students on the right rapidly enhanced their messaging and recruitment efforts. The strategy of duplicating themselves across multiple club rosters and creating secondary organizations gave the illusory public impression that college conservatives were more widespread than they truly were. Often a YAF student would have dual membership in ISI, College Republicans, Young Republicans, or another campus club where they could contribute a conservative perspective. In class, they openly challenged their professors to debates about the benefits of capitalism over other types of planned economies (with information provided by donated books from right-wing benefactors and found in movement magazines). On campus, they became readily identifiable by their blue buttons and other antagonistic accoutrements, which displayed New Left slogans co-opted to fit the Right's messages. The right led national boycotts against corporate giants, picketed theaters, interrupted shareholder meetings, and spoke at both Republican and Democrat conventions to loudly endorse their America first brand of patriotic economics. This increasing visibility was deliberate and formulaic and forcefully encouraged by conservative elders. The trend toward outward visibility also signified a transition from semesters past, when students on the right had been primarily concerned with outreach through messaging via print and radio.

At this point in the campus wars, there was a clear transition from the student Right's focused anticommunism, as outlined in YAF's Sharon Statement, to a much broader fixation with anything they perceived to be anti-American, even Russian ballet performances. College conservatives aimed to promote conformity defined along traditionalist standards—"acting like" an American or, within and between their own groups, a "true" conservative. It started to become apparent to organizers that, for the sake of generating new members, their branding would be more effective if it promoted a shared aggrieved *attitude* rather than a coherent set of principles.

Even with the guidance of mentors, the general culture of students on the right was reactionary and largely devoid of unique ideas. Ideologically fickle, conservatism as executed by students seemed fixated on themes such as tradition, war, and punishment. While unifying against radical violence on their own campuses, conservatives took no issue with violence executed in Vietnam, especially if they did not have to participate. Students on the right often acted on conflicting impulses, supporting the war while personally evading enlistment or supporting capitalism while organizing boycotts against some of the nation's largest businesses. The only evident principle that guided these distinct groups, and which would shortly unify them, was a reflexive anti-liberalism.

It was clear to older leaders that when left to their own devices, students with pro-war or anti–civil rights attitudes were less effective because of their fractionalization and intergroup tiffs. In the context of this revelation, CRNC and YAF executives armed their students with guidebooks and instruction kits to illuminate shared cultural objections and unite previously disparate groups. This better-organized iteration of the conservative student movement was thus not entirely grassroots, even if the spirit and determination of students on the right were indisputably organic. Instead, organizing on a practical level was driven by formulaic directives from national leaders that accelerated after notorious antiwar demonstrations, such as those in Madison, Oakland, and Washington, D.C., which opened the discussion in this chapter.

This activity exploded in frequency and intensity after demonstrations at Columbia in 1968 (discussed in chapter 4) and would reach a fever pitch after the Kent State massacre in 1970 (discussed in chapter 9). It also at times became more aggressive, as David Keene anticipated in the spring of 1968, when he threatened that "those students who have been wronged over the years [may] band together and administer a sound and thorough thrashing to the offending rabble"[120] if the understood "rules of gentlemanly conduct" were not obeyed. Such sentiments foreshadowed the increasingly authoritarian, and at times militant, turn in the demeanor of conservative students after 1968.

4 No Amnesty

· ·

In the spring of 1968, a devastating combination of domestic and international events left the nation and its college students in a state of political turmoil, including news of massive American casualties from the North Vietnamese Tet Offensive, Lyndon Johnson's announcement that he would not pursue presidential reelection, and Martin Luther King Jr.'s assassination. The spring semester was ripe for a "perfect storm."[1] Columbia University would become the site of the New Left's most infamous antiwar protests and one of the Black Power student movement's most important civil rights demonstrations. For the Right, events at Columbia provided a case study in reactive combat, helping them substantially refine their model for campus mobilization.

The Columbia Majority Coalition

Columbia's Institute of Defense Analysis (IDA), one of a dozen research affiliates of the Department of Defense (DOD) located at the university, was developing war weapons and researching riot control, which some students argued was intended to suppress their own antiwar organizations.[2] Members of Columbia's Students for a Democratic Society (SDS) and the Student Afro-American Society (SAS) planned a joint rally on April 23 to demand an open hearing for the "IDA Six"—students who, one month prior, had violated an indoor protest ban when demonstrating against the university's DOD partnership. An additional point of contention for the SDS demonstrators, and the central issue for local activists representing the nearby majority-Black community of Harlem, was the construction of a new campus gymnasium.[3] Community organizers had long opposed the gym project— the latest university "space invasion" following decades of encroachment into the neighborhood. Columbia's SAS was willing to lend its support to the Harlem community directly from the campus. While white SDS students centered their demonstration interests on the university's complicity in war research, Black students of the SAS and their community partners focused on the "Gym Crow" athletic facility.[4]

For Black Harlemites, Columbia's urban renewal expansion would effectively colonize their living area and the Morningside Park green space where their children played.[5] As it was originally designed, the gymnasium would also block the college's view of the Black community below. Though Harlem residents would have access to some parts of—but not the entire—gym, opponents argued that the building's design was itself racist by enforcing segregation. The plain-front Harlem entrance, located on a lower level, would be separate from the attractive upper-level main entrance intended for Columbia's mostly white students. Because Harlem residents lived 200 feet below the hilltop on which the top part of the gym would be situated, conservatives smugly defended the dual-entrance design as "not one of bigotry but geography."[6] Conservatives viewed the response from Black Harlemites as yet another example of outside agitators inciting disruption on their campus.

SDS, under the leadership of Mark Rudd and others, united against the gym expansion alongside the SAS at the Tuesday, April 23, rally. At noon, approximately 500 students arrived at a popular gathering point located in the center of the campus, a stone platform known as the Sundial, to hear speeches from SDS and SAS members.[7] Approximately fifty counterdemonstrators from Columbia's conservative Students for a Free Campus (SFC) were among the crowd.[8] According to the SFC's idiosyncratic interpretation of events, conservatives intercepted an SDS leaflet outlining plans for the joint demonstration, which then allowed them to organize a preemptive counter-rally of 200 people to block SDS and SAS members from entering the building they intended to occupy.[9] In reality, SDS and SAS demonstrators were denied entry into Low Memorial Library—Columbia's main administrative building, which included the president's office—by campus police or administrators inside the building, though it is possible that authorities were alerted in advance by SFC members.

Undeterred, SDS and SAS protesters carried their cause to the proposed site of the new gym at Morningside Park, where some participants tore down the chain fence surrounding the construction zone. Once police arrived, SDS engaged in fistfights with officers. One white student was arrested. When the crowd of demonstrators returned to the Sundial, leaders from the SAS encouraged SDS to continue taking action.[10]

The two groups decided to begin a sit-in in the Hamilton Hall lobby. SDS and SAS demonstrators recalled that the then acting dean of Columbia College, Henry S. Coleman, emerged from his office, calmly walked to the center of the lobby to address the group, and asked if he should assume that he was being taken hostage. SDS and SAS witnesses maintained that members gave the dean mixed answers. Coleman then elected to return to his office and, without force or coercion, shut the door. Protesters who were present for Coleman's interaction with the group have insisted that it was clear he was free to leave if he chose and would not have been stopped.[11] A group of SFC students nevertheless declared that Coleman "was being held prisoner," appointed themselves as his sentinels, and stood guard outside the office.[12] SFC students were horrified that protesters had erected giant portraits of Vladimir Lenin, Che Guevara, and Malcolm X under a banner reading, "In Revolution One Wins or Dies."[13] They were further enraged by demonstrators' promise that the sit-in would endure until Columbia administrators agreed to meet several nonnegotiable demands, including ending the gym construction, dissolving the university's partnership with the DOD, and granting amnesty to the IDA Six students and all those currently protesting.

Black nationalist groups, including the Student Nonviolent Coordinating Committee (SNCC), the Congress of Racial Equality (CORE), and the Mau Mau Society, joined hundreds of SDS and SAS occupiers during the evening and night. The additional demonstrators included influential leaders Stokely Carmichael and H. Rap Brown, who were advocates of Black separatism. Despite their common cause, Carmichael and Brown were unwilling to fight alongside white organizers, who appeared to be at the helm of the demonstration.[14]

According to both SDS and SAS participants, the two groups had incompatible organizational structures and ideas on how to carry out the sit-in moving forward. Specifically, SDS wanted the building to remain open so that demonstrators could come and go. Its leadership was disorganized and appeared to be making decisions on impulse. The SAS had a power structure that was tightly defined. Its leaders' decision-making was extremely careful due to the potentially severe consequences Black youth faced during confrontations with authority. After lengthy deliberation, SAS leaders decided to secure the building and closely monitor those entering and leaving. White SDS students who presumed they should lead both the antiwar and the antiracism campaigns were upset that Black SAS students and Harlem community members wanted to chart their own course over the gym matter.[15] At approximately 5:30 A.M. the day after the occupation started, white SDS protesters began leaving the building until only seventy-five occupants remained in Hamilton Hall, half of whom were not students.[16] Once the sit-in had become mostly composed of Black students and Harlem residents, Coleman and two other staff members constructed a furniture barricade inside his office.[17]

After leaving Hamilton Hall in the early morning hours, white SDS members expanded their protest to include Low Memorial Library, where they established communes throughout its rooms, including in President Grayson Kirk's office. Once inside the president's office, SDS occupiers indulged in Kirk's cigars and sherry, relieved themselves in his trash can, and threw trash bags from the windows onto faculty members below, who were present as both observers and supporters. Others photocopied Kirk's papers, which they believed contained damning evidence of a relationship between the university and the federal government. The occupiers used Kirk's telephone to call in reinforcements, who wheeled in grocery carts full of food and other supplies. Commanding the main campus switchboard, SDS members playfully fielded calls from the press and concerned parents, declaring that the university might not survive the takeover. With the help of the university chaplain, students even staged a marriage between two demonstrators. The newlyweds spent their honeymoon night in a faculty office, which they described as "holy ground." Outside the occupied administrative office hung a sign reading "LIBERATED AREA, BE FREE TO JOIN US."[18]

Reports of antics inside the occupied buildings infuriated administrators, local politicians, and many working-class New Yorkers, who did not disguise their contempt. To remove the reveling "nihilists," President Kirk summoned the New York City Police Department.[19] Over 500 officers swarmed the campus in the middle of the night, stationing guards in front of every building that had not been occupied by strikers and sealing off all but two entrances to campus.[20] Some Columbia faculty and SFC members, acting a second time as self-appointed deputies, helped police screen students entering campus during the lockdown, donning white armbands and using the code word "freedom" to identify themselves as officer aides.[21]

Over the weekend, an ad hoc umbrella group led by SFC and Young Americans for Freedom (YAF) assembled a "majority coalition" of antiradicals to hold a silent vigil for the self-imprisoned dean. The group—dubbed "the jocks" by SDS—consisted of white participants from SFC, YAF, the College Republicans, various fraternities, and the university's sports teams and clubs. Flyers asked participants to wear coats and ties to reflect the seriousness of their counteraction, attempting to create an air of respectability by differentiating themselves from the demonstrators.[22] But before the group of jocks and other conservatives could hold the vigil, Dean Coleman anticlimactically left his office after twenty-six hours.[23]

The next afternoon, Thursday, April 25, the majority coalition met and made plans to invade Fayerweather Hall, one of several other buildings that SDS had newly begun to "liberate." It does not appear that the planned intrusion was successful, nor were there any other impactful majority coalition efforts until Sunday, April 28.

Columbia student and host of the WKCR campus radio station, Vaud Massarsky, claims to have inspired the Right's next counteractions.[24] Contemporary newspaper and witness accounts credit the idea to Columbia's football coaches, which would follow the pattern of conservative youth taking instruction from older authorities.[25] More likely, the following idea was conceived independently by several people and spread through rumor.

In a speech on April 28, Massarsky recommended locking demonstrators in the buildings they occupied via a blockade of men around the exterior "to place the occupiers under siege and starve them out." Central to the cruel counteraction was maintaining a dignified image so that the young, square, athletic white men could contrast with the white hippie SDS, the Black SAS, and the less affluent Black Harlem residents they planned to hold captive. The men needed to be distinguishable from the "disheveled adversary" they would trap inside.[26]

In the history of American higher education, white people using their bodies to create physical barriers for Black students was not a unique idea. This had already been done multiple times (white governors Ross Barnett and George Wallace blocking Black students from entering public universities in Mississippi and Alabama, for example). Surely the symbolism was not lost on the Black students and Harlem residents, only this time, white conservatives would be locking Black and white liberal protesters *in*.

There were not enough conservative counterprotesters to cordon off every building with a sit-in; thus, a coalition of 250 white men sporting coats and ties formed a human chain around Low Memorial Library, between the building and its hedges, to prevent food and supplies from reaching the SDS occupiers inside.[27] In response, about thirty faculty members formed an interior ring on the building's ledge to separate demonstrators from coalition students and police, suffering abuse from each side. John Thoms, a graduate student, recalled the "furious" jock line of athletes "who had been massing, with some menace," and who were finding it difficult "for them to hold themselves back."[28] When several majority coalition students broke through the faculty line and appeared on the ledge, professors physically removed them.[29]

The next afternoon, Monday, April 29, a second skirmish took place at the coalition line, this time between the jocks and "phalanxes" of about fifty protesters trying to break through to deliver supplies.[30] After a five-minute fistfight, protesters were unable to break the line of football players and other white men, including later George H. W. Bush and Trump administration attorney general William Barr. Demonstrators then began throwing the supplies of "fruit, salami and Wonder Bread" over the athlete cordon into the building's windows.[31] Majority coalition members attempted to knock the items out of the air using blankets and trays.

On Tuesday, April 30, one week after the demonstration's inception, 1,000 New York City police officers entered the occupied buildings to end the strike at the university administration's request.[32] Officers peacefully escorted the Black protesters out of Hamilton Hall. White SDS students in other buildings were expelled by force with tear gas, clubs, and fists, as students fought back with office supplies and furniture. Police indiscriminately beat demonstrators and observers alike. In total, 148 students and spectators were injured by police, and 712 people were arrested (80 percent of whom were Columbia and Barnard students).[33]

Expressing contempt for the privileged college radicals, one officer determined that the students' demonstration was an excess of their affluence: "Everything I got I worked for. It gets me sore when I see these kids, who have been handed everything, pissing it away, talking like bums."[34] In this case, of course, the affluent white students were not wasting their privilege but exercising it. Of the estimated 800 students who participated in the occupation of five campus buildings over an eight-day span, only seventy-three were suspended temporarily from their coursework.[35] None were expelled. Anticipating this outcome (and able to seek education elsewhere if their estimation had been wrong), elite white Columbia students had little to lose by protesting institutional injustice. Conservatives, too, had little to lose by trying to punish them for it.

Backlash to the Columbia Demonstration

Conservative students were shocked by the administration's penalties, which they considered far too lenient. SDS's demands for amnesty further enraged the Right, who decried the strikers as spineless.[36] To show that SDS's exoneration countered the wishes of an implied student silent majority, the majority coalition students gathered 2,600 signatures on a petition opposing amnesty.[37] Regarding the amnesty demand, an SDS member reported to the *Chronicle of Higher Education*: "It's the perfect issue for us. We win either way. If you give us amnesty, we go back to our classes and

Conservative student protesting against SDS demands for amnesty, 1968.
Photograph by Manny Warman, Office of Public Affairs Protest and Activism
Photograph Collection, Columbia University Archives.

prepare another confrontation. And we inspire students at other universities to revolt. With Columbia's precedent, they too can demand amnesty. If you don't grant it, you have to call in the police to clear the buildings, and that will be bloody and bring many of the moderate students to our side. We win either way."[38]

The demonstration did inspire sit-ins at other institutions, as well as a second demonstration at Columbia in May. A global rallying cry for student activists became "Two, three, many Columbias!"[39] But the young SDS member may have been too confident in his prediction that subsequent sit-ins would prove popular among moderate observers. A survey of 2,000 faculty members and 3,400 students conducted by Columbia's Bureau of Applied Social Research shortly after the demonstrations revealed that while sympathy for the demonstrators had doubled from 14 percent to 31 percent after the police resorted to force, only 22 percent of faculty and 30 percent of students favored amnesty for the brutalized rebels.[40] New Yorkers were even less sympathetic. A *New York Times* opinion poll showed that 83 percent of readers believed police intervention was appropriate.[41] Several politicians shamed Columbia administrators for allowing the episode to endure for longer than a week.[42]

To understand why the student Right at Columbia were willing to intervene as a third party and physically confront the Left in its protest against the administration, it is helpful to examine how the Right understood SDS and SAS aims. According to Fred Lowell, a majority coalition student: "[SDS's] vision of Columbia was an institution at odds with the principles of academic freedom. The radicals felt that the university should become a political weapon to be wielded by them in support of a 'just' or 'socialist' society; this was justified by their view that the American university already was politicized because of its ties to the government. They sought to change its politics to make it an effective tool for their 'revolution,' and they were willing to use force, which made universities like Columbia a soft target."[43]

It is telling that those representing the majority coalition framed the SDS and SAS demonstration as part of a larger national conspiracy by leftists to use the academy as a political tool. They did not engage the specific issues raised by the SAS and the Harlem community against Columbia's encroachment into the Black neighborhood to build a gymnasium that residents had unequal access to and that would intrude into their living and recreational spaces. Conservative students thus did not (or felt they did not need to) come to terms with the actual matters at hand. Animated by the imagined threat of a nationwide conspiracy, they were bizarrely confident that they needed to physically intervene on behalf of powerful university authorities, who had visibly been deploying police since the initial April 23 rally.

Regardless, counterprotesting at the SDS-SAS Columbia demonstration was "galvanizing" for the conservative students who participated.[44] Students on the right, similar to the SDS student previously quoted, imagined that the strike would inspire duplicate demonstrations that they needed to be prepared for. Columbia conservatives forecasted that their "extortionist" "hoodlum" peers would soon appear in local city halls, state capitol buildings, and Washington, D.C., pointing to SDS's plans to disrupt the Chicago Democratic National Convention in the coming summer. They called for "intelligent counter-action" via the restriction of financial support for universities that did not respond harshly to radicals, and for alumni to pressure trustees and administrators to expel and prosecute demonstrators.[45]

Though their fears of copycat instances were technically realized, the overwhelming public and campus backlash to subsequent sit-ins was likely much greater than conservative students anticipated. The University of Denver expelled thirty-nine SDS members for attempting to take over an administration building in a manner similar to the Columbia occupation. Chancellor Maurice Mitchell boasted that the university had received over

1,000 letters of support for his hardened stance.[46] At Northwestern University, white students harassed more than one hundred Black students of For Members Only and the Afro-American Student Union who had peacefully occupied the bursar's office. When administrators agreed to many of the Black students' demands, faculty and alumni responses ranged from disapproval to outrage. Of the faculty, only a third supported the outcome, and over 600 alumni letters out of the 900 sent to the president expressed disapproval.[47]

Matching campus-level and local backlash, New York's state legislature overwhelmingly approved a measure to revoke financial aid from students convicted of violent acts during a demonstration.[48] US representative Louis C. Wyman (R-NH) proposed an amendment to the National Defense Education Act that would revoke a student's federal aid for misdemeanors or felonies resulting from participation in demonstrations or riots.[49] Two weeks before the Columbia event, Congress passed an interstate riot act that federally criminalized any interstate method (including the use of mail, radio, or telephone) to orchestrate or participate in a riot. The penalty carried a fine and a five-year prison sentence.[50] To pursue potential offenders of the new law, FBI director J. Edgar Hoover ordered a covert FBI counterintelligence program, COINTELPRO-New Left, to investigate SDS and other peace and civil rights activists.[51]

Despite this mounting public opposition to amnesty for the rebels, Columbia SDS did sponsor a second strike in May that lasted until the end of the spring semester. During the monthlong strike, SDS attempted two additional building takeovers, which resulted in an accompanying 148 arrests. Nearly 300 students staged a commencement walkout. The second round of demonstrations garnered less sympathy than the first. A Columbia faculty member expressed that the strikes "were as much about finding ways to allow privileged students at universities to fulfill themselves as they were to fight particular social injustices."[52]

Providing credence to the conservative charge that campus revolts were self-serving rather than a genuine pursuit of peace and civil rights, the next fall, SDS president and IDA Six leader Mark Rudd remarked, "We manufactured the issues. The Institute for Defense Analysis is nothing at Columbia. Just three professors. And the gym issue is bull. It doesn't mean anything to anybody. I had never been to the gym site before the demonstrations began. I didn't even know how to get there."[53]

Harlem residents did not think the gym matter was "bull," and it certainly *did* mean a great deal to them and their children. Rudd's confession that his own chapter's actions at this particular event were inspired by a less-than-authentic belief in antiwar and civil rights causes was a point that conservatives, as well as prominent media outlets such as the *Boston Globe*, readily exploited. The Right used Rudd's confession about this particular event as a charge against the Left writ large. Conservatives were further satisfied with and emboldened by public outrage against the perceived nihilism at Columbia and the wave of retributive state and federal legislation that followed, even if they thought the Columbia demonstrators themselves were insufficiently punished.

Majority Coalitions as a National Strategy

Prior to the initial Columbia incident, YAF had created a model of organizing through student committees that established campus-based anticommunist front organizations (discussed in chapter 3). These YAF auxiliaries were given new names, but their rosters were made up almost entirely of YAF members and College Republicans. The presence of so many committees was meant to create a false public image about the popularity of student conservatism and a youth silent majority. The apparent success those on the right felt about the majority coalition at Columbia led them to refine and enhance the model for nationwide application. To be clear, the Columbia coalition was not successful in ending the multi-building sit-ins that had persisted for a week, nor did they actually capture the majority approval of their peers. But YAF leaders celebrated the coalition for the group's ability to weld together multiple anti-leftists who had previously worked independently of, and were frequently antagonistic toward, one another (see chapter 3).

In that sense, the majority coalition model was a success. As Lee Bebout explains, weaponized victimhood is an excellent mobilization strategy for "otherwise potentially disparate groups." Because they "are asked to see themselves as victims under siege, their shared logic makes mobilization and coalition based on perceived grievances possible."[54] Thus, community can develop among those who determine that their shared privileges are under threat (similar to how in-group and out-group humor can serve as a community building force, as discussed in chapter 3). By experiencing "a common affective state of aggrieved entitlement," Bebout explains, "discrete political concerns become legible across other differences and coalitions become possible."[55] In this spirit, YAF executives hastily issued a majority coalition instruction manual and several action kits inspired by the field-tested

Columbia model. Students were instructed to start forming coalitions as early as the upcoming fall.[56]

By design, majority coalitions included a range of white students: fraternity and sorority members, student government representatives, Young Republicans and conservative Young Democrats, athletes, technical and science majors, and a few concerned liberals. YAF urged that majority coalitions be large, even if intolerance for violence was members' only unifying factor. This was a key change in strategy that solved factional infighting among different conservative groups on the same campus. Because majority coalition organizers sought to maximize followers, coalitions were politically mixed (yet still demographically identical) and included those singularly interested in shutting down antiwar and civil rights demonstrations.

Majority coalition leaders encouraged members to adopt an attitude of complete intolerance toward any act of campus violence. Similar to its strategy in creating anticommunist shell organizations, coalition founders were encouraged to choose a neutral group name that communicated maturity or peace, such as Students for a Responsible University. Any anti-radical action should be conducted under the auspices of the coalition group to signify a majority consensus against demonstrators (though these groups did not, in reality, represent majorities). Coalitions could circulate literature defending the rights of students to pursue their education and generally serve as a nexus of anti-left activity on campus.[57]

The action manuals offered practical tips on how to react to events such as anti-military recruitment sit-ins. Coalition members were instructed to form a line in front of the recruiter's office to maintain access, suggesting that "the alternate spacing of girls and athletes often proves the most effective arrangement."[58] As part of its contingency plan to surround occupied buildings, YAF called for implementing tactics such as cutting off essentials like electricity, plumbing, and food (or allowing food contaminated with a stimulant laxative).[59] The action manuals also provided lessons on satire, sign making, slogan creation, recruitment, confronting leftist groups, occupying New Left spaces, and taking legal action against demonstrators and acquiescent administrators.

The new coalitions undertook counterdemonstrations, circulated punishment petitions, and sought support from alumni, administrators, politicians, police, and others in power. To fundraise, they began reaching beyond the typical sources of conservative support (such as corporations and churches) to those broadly interested in the good reputation of their alma mater. Those invested in campus stability included local constituents: Main Street business owners; members of the Chamber of Commerce; civic and social organizations such as Kiwanis, Rotary, and Lions Clubs; alumni associations; and women's groups.[60]

Adapting the Intercollegiate Studies Institute's (ISI) efforts to inject conservative ideology into the classroom, the majority coalition manual encouraged readers to capitalize on a perceived imbalance of thought in their curriculums. Coalition members denounced liberal bias in their textbooks and reading assignments. They circulated comparative lists of liberal versus conservative faculty and liberal versus conservative campus speakers. Students delivered these reports to the boards of trustees at state schools, demanding that regents explain why their tax dollars were being used for indoctrination. To correct the perceived instructional imbalance, coalition members devised Free University teach-ins (another appropriation of the Left), which included lessons on capitalism, Christianity, and other areas of conservative interest. The program offered student-run libraries of paperbacks to serve multiple campuses. The manual encouraged the well-exercised habit of appropriating New Left expressions, reminding members that, if framed correctly, "All of the liberal slogans about academic freedom and the marketplace of ideas can be used to your advantage."[61]

One popular Free University project involved distributing issue papers to students entering class before a lecture predetermined to be politically biased. Supposedly, the issue paper would force the professor to acknowledge and respond to conservative positions on the topic.[62] At the University of Pittsburgh School of Law, for example, students circulated an issue paper before a lecture on judicial activism. One alumnus, who was a founding member of the YAF chapter at the University of Pittsburgh and who later joined the national staff, recalled creating a paper against judicial activism and in favor of the founders' interpretations of the law (what we would now call originalism) for his courses.

Appeals to Power for Punishment

YAF used its majority coalitions to romanticize their crusade against the Left. Coalition leaders characterized stalwart support of the military as patriotic and condemned the peace movement as anti-American. In the semester following the Columbia demonstration, there were over forty instances of bombings and arson on college campuses, which students on the right continually highlighted as evidence of the peace movement's radicalism.[63] Throughout the months of September and October 1968, activists bombed war-related spaces at or near universities on a near-daily basis. These acts of arson and property destruction were committed by only a few radical activists, but the inordinate amount of physical and financial damage wrought superseded this fact in headlines. Most protesters were nonviolent when they appeared at demonstrations, but because antiwar event participation often numbered in the hundreds (these tallies, of course, included many onlookers), conservatives could extend blame for enormous property destruction to the sensationalized number of attendees and assail the peace movement as a whole as inherently destructive.

Conservative students not only supported harsh penalties from administrators but expected them. So did legislators, especially in the South. Historian Joy Ann Williamson-Lott explains that "as the federal government loosened the grip that white elected officials maintained on the higher educational institutions in the region, those officials looked to campus administrators to take up the mantle."[64] Students on the right began to indirectly assert greater power against antiwar and civil rights demonstrators by pressuring authorities to enforce punishments. A popular student tactic modeled after Columbia's majority coalition was to collect signatures on a punishment petition urging administrators to expel radical dissenters. A sample petition was worded: "We, the undersigned, believe that change in the university structure should come about through peaceful means, not by sit-ins, blockades, or any other use of force. Those who initiate force should be expelled."[65]

Following the guidance of YAF executives, coalition leaders published the numbers of signatures they received in campus and local news outlets and wrote to legislators serving on state education committees, trustees, and prominent alumni to publicize a given petition's popularity with an implied student silent majority. Punishment petitions strategically signaled to administrators the apparent existence of wide student and public support for penalizing demonstrators. The student Right often flaunted the fact that the number of demonstrators always seemed less than the number of signatures they were able to secure for punishment petitions, which at some campuses in the South and Midwest numbered in the thousands—6,000 signatures at Colorado State University, 4,000 signatures at the University of Tennessee, 3,300 signatures at the University of Georgia, and 1,000 signatures at Cornell University, according to conservatives.[66] Beyond expulsion, the University of Wisconsin's Committee to Defend Individual Rights called for the arrest of campus rioters and the abolition of student organizations advocating violence to bring about social or political change.[67] Students donned blue buttons as an outward symbol of support for authoritarian administrators.

To the same end, movement leaders urged the student Right to build relationships with deans, faculty, and other sources of power on campus who could serve as "valuable allies."[68] But in the event that "indecisive and gutless" administrators were unimpressed by punishment petitions, a more powerful authority was needed to keep campuses open through strikes: the courts.[69] Members threatened to sue not only demonstrating students but also administrators and trustees who were ineffective at preventing strikes from "interfering with the civil rights of conscientious students to pursue their academic careers" and for "breach of fiduciary responsibility."[70] According to Columbia student Fred Lowell, the SDS and SAS demonstration resulted in "the complete deprivation of the civil rights of the vast majority of students and faculty by mostly middle-class students playing at 'revolution.'"[71]

For conservatives, there were plenty of reasons students and university employees across the board should fight administrative tolerance of the sit-ins. Delayed graduations meant delayed employment for students and delayed salaries for faculty and personnel. It was also a First Amendment violation, according to those on the right: "By shuttering the university and its classrooms, and instilling fear of increasing violence, the natural forums for debate and discussion—those hundreds of classrooms and related informal venues—were eliminated, and only the occupiers' message was broadcast."[72]

To counter the amplification of leftist demands for justice, freedom, and peace, YAF students took to newspapers to publicize that they had preemptively secured legal counsel and listed the names of young attorneys (who were YAF members themselves), including Alan MacKay, the organization's national president, and J. Lawrence McCarthy.[73] As they awaited a ruling in the Columbia lawsuit, which would set a legal precedent for breach of contract, YAF issued a legal action kit for members to file subsequent suits at their own institutions. The kit provided students with a legal warning to threaten their president and trustees if a shutdown seemed imminent: "By accepting our tuition, this university has entered into a contract with us. . . . If the actions of a belligerent minority deny us our rights by interrupting classes, we will bring suit, if necessary to have the university live up to its contractual obligations."[74] Students used the script to threaten lawsuits at several campuses in Texas, New York, and California.[75] At Boston College, students insisted that if the university took a political stance, it would risk the institution's tax-exempt status. The YAF chapter warned that the university "will not long exist" if administrators continued to condone "radical acts of terrorism."[76]

Investigating Radicals

Between the academic semesters of fall 1967 and spring 1970, instances of on-campus bombings or arson typically declined during the summer months and over winter breaks. During the summer lull, lawmakers often increased punitive antiwar legislation to address the spring events. Authority figures continued to call for investigations of campus radicals at the federal, state, and campus levels. Following the Columbia demonstration, the state of Oklahoma created an Office of Interagency Coordination, known as the Sooner CIA, a "uniquely military" surveillance department with a special interest in antiwar and pro–civil rights college students. It was funded by almost half of the state's National Guard budget.[77] The FBI had already been collecting surveillance data on antiwar demonstrators, and for more than three years US attorneys general Ramsay Clark and John Mitchell received requests from university presidents to investigate campus radicals, especially the SDS.[78]

In this context, conservative students reached out to law enforcement offices to ensure them that their presence was supported on campus. Coalition members attended antiwar demonstrations to potentially catch radicals on camera in illegal acts and volunteered to serve as witnesses in police investigations. They supplied local newspapers with photographs taken at antiwar events and personal testimonies as to the radical nature of the protesters.[79] This practice further helped members establish working relationships with local media and police.

The White House also received an influx of requests from alumni associations and private citizens to investigate the radicals behind campus disturbances. Punting the inquiries, Nixon staff replied that campus disorders were exclusively under the control of state and local authorities. However, they stated that the federal government did have some discretion "in appropriate cases" to withhold federal financial aid from students.[80] In other instances, Attorney General Mitchell strictly enforced the new criminal laws against interstate travel to commit a riot, as many SDS and Black Power events drew participants from multiple states.

Two House investigative committees, the Special Education Subcommittee and the Internal Security Committee, had already begun holding hearings regarding campus demonstrations. Testimony was taken from police, reporters, members of the House Un-American Activities Committee, and college administrators. Donald Meinshausen, an alumnus of Teen Age Republicans and YAF, agreed to be an informant for the House Internal Security Committee, going so far as to establish an original SDS chapter at the Essex County College in Newark, New Jersey. Meinshausen claimed to have received expenses and a $100 payment from the House committee.[81] The Senate Permanent Subcommittee on Investigations also debated an anti-riot clause to revoke higher education funds if administrators did not comply with federal investigations.[82]

Of the nineteen organizations under investigation, the three groups under the most intense scrutiny were antiwar and civil rights college and youth clubs: SDS, SNCC, and the Black Panther Party. Nixon himself requested that the congressional hearings be televised to the public. Given national interest in campus radicalism and the federal response to it, Senator Lamar Alexander (R-TN) promised that the investigations were "sure to be a blockbuster."[83]

Lasting Significance of the Columbia Event

The events at Columbia and other universities involving students reveling in occupied administrative offices, smoking cigars with their feet on presidents' desks, and indulging in general administrative disrespect did little to bring real reform to campus. Rather, backlash within and outside the academy eroded public sympathy for legitimate demands for peace and racial justice.[84] The New Left's negative publicity empowered the student Right to challenge the Left's claim of majority representation and create new tactics to spoil progressive advances.

Defenders of campus order learned a critical lesson from the Columbia incident—that even at a liberal Ivy League institution, forming an anti-radical coalition was a successful strategy for bringing unaffiliated students into the conservative fold. In the wake of the Left's "vigilante action," YAF capitalized on an opportunity to convince more students that revolution was neither necessary nor desirable. Building "neutral" majority coalitions of square white students dressed in suits cast the student Right as leaders of a respectable and responsible youth silent majority—bystanders frustrated with Black and white leftists' strikes and building occupations—even if the organizers of these coalitions were motivated largely by ideology. And despite the sometimes outright antagonistic relationship between conservative groups, the coalition model was able to mobilize students so quickly because of the infrastructure movement leaders had already been helping them build: the ability to rush out a majority coalition handbook, the availability of YAF lawyers offering pro bono legal services, interlocking front groups with identical memberships, and so on. These tools from recent semesters were already familiar to campus activists.

Through these coalitions, YAF deepened its commitment to promoting what it described as ideological diversity in the classroom to the new audiences it was now able to influence (athletes, student sports fans, and others). YAF elders directed students to become assertive in exposing liberal bias in the classroom and reporting it to trustees. Most importantly, conservatives confirmed from the backlash of the Columbia events that off-campus support from locals, business leaders, and lawmakers was assured. Where alliances with on-campus authorities were not guaranteed, students on the right, by the fall of 1968, were emboldened enough to threaten their institutions with lawsuits to ensure that their minoritarian will was enforced through the courts.

Though student conservatives of the late 1960s demanded punishment against peers with whom they disagreed, they did not yet broadly assert violence themselves (with notable exceptions such as at Columbia), as they were confident that state violence was on their side in the form of the police and the National Guard. As discussed in part 2, however, that reticence would change beginning in the fall of 1969.

Part II Law, Order, and Punishment

....

By 1968, the conservative student movement was well underway in its efforts to gain new recruits and build coalitions with various other political and religious student organizations. Anticommunist and anti-leftist clubs appeared to bloom as students on the right, following explicit guidance from their mentors, tactically founded new groups, outwardly identified themselves with blue buttons, and increasingly added theatrical elements to their counterprotests to draw attention. Having secured new message platforms in campus print and radio—a campus adaption of the larger postwar conservative countersphere—the student Right extended their coalition-building efforts off campus to leverage support from anti-leftist Republican Party members, key administrators and alumni, influential community and business leaders, and corporate and religious philanthropists. As described in part 1, leaders of the student Right claimed to represent a youth silent majority by consolidating various conservative missions into a singular opposition of the Left.

After 1968, the student Right's anti-leftist attitude accelerated into punitive action using appeals to authority figures and, in some instances, violence. Part 2 explains the student Right's support of law-and-order political candidates, calls for increased police presence on campus and in nearby communities, demands for political leaders to impose national order through force, and insistence on carceral punishment for peace and civil rights demonstrators. Assistance from on- and off-campus authorities in investigating, delegitimizing, and punishing student demonstrators reinforced the anti-leftist attitudes conservative students sought to cultivate. Court injunctions (or even the threat to pursue them) forced reluctant administrators to keep campuses open during violent strikes of record-breaking magnitude. This pivot toward punishment and violence signifies the height of conservative and right-wing resistance during the campus wars.

5 Apple Pie, Mother, and Nixon

. . . .

Throughout the summer of 1968, college conservatives served as campaign volunteers to help their favorite right-wing politician become the official Republican Party nominee for president. The major groups on the right formed new auxiliaries, such as Young Voters for Nixon, Students for Reagan, and Youth for Wallace, to promote the candidate of their choice. College conservatives learned from their mentors about the political value of primaries and caucuses, which tended to attract partisan and ideological voters, thus affording an opportunity to nominate an extreme candidate as the party's official representative.

For students on the right, hardliner candidates like George Wallace were attractive for their ability to pull the party further toward the right, even if it were unlikely that Wallace would ever receive the actual nomination. The popularity he garnered would send a message, just as Barry Goldwater's nomination did in the previous election. Because College and Young Republicans, YAF, and white supremacist groups each supported different politicians ahead of GOP primaries, the story of college conservatives in the summer of 1968 is one of internal differences and rivalries in the weeks leading up to the Republican National Convention, even as movement leaders were trying to unite the youth Right under a majority coalition tent.[1]

Most college students of the late 1960s were too young to cast ballots until 1971, when the Twenty-Sixth Amendment extended the franchise to eighteen-year-old voters. For those eligible, the Republican Party's turn toward conservatism in candidate Goldwater during the previous presidential election was an unattractive pivot by a party founded on the progressive ideas of abolition and civil rights. Absent Lyndon Johnson on the presidential ticket and regardless of the new nominee, the Democratic Party's liberal platform was poised to attract young voters in 1968. Robert Kennedy's progressive campaign plan targeted young and poor voters (both Black and white), but college students polled stronger still for antiwar candidate and senator from Minnesota, Eugene McCarthy.[2]

Republicans were far less interested in seeking the youth vote, which party leaders equated to "pandering."[3] But campus conservatives who counted on GOP candidates to attack the countercultural Left nonetheless campaigned to get their desired candidate elected in the primary. Students on the right appeared unbothered that the candidates they supported were generally apathetic to the extra assistance from vote-ineligible college kids.

More than any other youth organization, the College Republican National Committee (CRNC), then a college affiliate of the Young Republican National Federation, led the charge to campaign in communities surrounding universities. CRNC executive director Morton Blackwell implemented Project Target, a program "designed to locate, recruit, and train full-time student coordinators" for GOP campaigns nationwide. Student workers were paid from campaign funds supporting twenty-six GOP Senate races in thirteen states (Alabama, Arkansas, Florida, Illinois, Kentucky, Louisiana, Maryland, New Jersey, New York, Oklahoma, Oregon, South Carolina, and Utah), four congressional races (in Louisiana, Maryland, Tennessee, and Virginia), four gubernatorial races (in Illinois, Indiana, Texas, and West Virginia), and the Nixon presidential campaign.[4]

Youth coordinators appointed by CRNC executives ran club membership drives at every campus within their district, registering new members to vote in the process. The coordinator assigned participants election-day duties for their respective areas, arranging for absentee ballots to guarantee their organizers' votes. Campaign projects, such as mock elections and voter registration drives, were designed to recruit not only new students but also their families, friends, and neighbors.

CRNC leaders Colleen Conway McAndrews and Gary L. Fairchild planned intensive district-based training programs for the summer before the election. At one such seminar, chapter representatives gathered at the University of Louisiana at Lafayette over a weekend. They learned about financing, canvassing and precinct work, and interacting with local news media; took workshops on writing press releases; and discussed new ideas for fall programs in their district. Chapter leaders left this and other summer training schools with an arsenal of manuals and workbooks to bring back to their campuses.[5] Sending one representative from each chapter was mandatory, but the CRNC enticed additional members to sign up for the trainings by pointing to former students who had been hired based on the skills the conference afforded them. Some were even relocated to other states "as full-time, salaried youth campaign fieldmen."[6]

Being able to recite from the 1968 *Campus Voters Manual* was so important that members were tested on its contents. The manual directed College

Republicans to do extensive digging in order to locate people who were newly qualified to register to vote. They were instructed to mine campus registries and assume that all undergraduate seniors and graduate students were twenty-one years old. They should then ask the registrar's office "if their I.B.M. print-out or the like" containing addresses was available for copying so that they could create a mailing list.[7] (Mining public records to create mailing lists was a technique perfected and encouraged by conservative fundraiser and YAF advisor Richard Viguerie.[8]) Other members canvassed residence halls asking for twenty-one-year-olds. The manual reminded canvassers that "there are many methods. Use them all." Once a list of eligible voters was created, College Republicans were directed to cull it to eliminate Democrats, "since we are not in the business of building the number of Democrat-leaning voters."[9]

CNRC executives encouraged chapters to canvass their college precincts and make personal connections with known Republican and conservative voters they could visit for multiple campaigns. Keeping a file on each voter was a handy strategy with expected gains over several election cycles. Members were encouraged to remember the favorite activities of voters' children and their pets' names so that the student "will no longer be a stranger to the family. You will be a friend—a Republican friend." With this friendship, voters would trust the student to arrange a ride to the polls and even childcare services on election day. Further, members should not waste time visiting known Democratic voters in their precinct. Students were left with the warning that in registering two Republicans and two Democrats "YOU DO TWICE AS MUCH WORK . . . as it gets you ABSOLUTELY NOWHERE!"[10] On election day, College Republicans were to call those they were responsible for registering and remind them that they could arrange rides to the polls and childcare if needed. They were also to identify weeks in advance if an absentee ballot was necessary and to follow up to make sure it was submitted.[11]

The CRNC provided its College Republican chapters with literature to memorize and then distribute, such as a brochure called *You Are America's Future* about why the reader should vote Republican and join the College Republicans, and an index card of voter registration requirements. CRNC headquarters sold these materials to their own chapters for three cents per copy with the expectation that the materials would circulate among hundreds of prospective new voters.[12] This contrasts with YAF and ISI, whose leaders often provided bulk materials for their members or connected them with ways to receive free literature.

Beyond getting new Republican voters registered, CRNC insisted that its students practice the nominations and voting processes by setting up mock conventions and elections. Knowing how these procedures worked—not just conceptually, but by physically enacting them—was a "learning experience" and a fundamental part of their role on college campuses.

Executive director and future George W. Bush senior advisor Karl Rove's *Mock Convention Guide* was a detailed manual for organizing such experiences. According to Rove, getting the dress rehearsal right was critical: "The mock convention must seek to re-create the atmosphere of the gathering. Role playing, a hall with all the trappings, procedures imitative of the real National Convention—these are bits of realism that will make the mock convention a learning experience with lasting impact." To reproduce the atmosphere precisely, students should arrange "suitable trappings, such as large campaign signs and pictures of the candidates, balloons falling from the ceiling, and placards for demonstrations." Rove placed much emphasis on getting students to accurately play the role of the politicians they were to represent: "Imitation of personality and position will draw out the realistic, ideological, sectional, and personal loyalties which are so vital to an exciting Convention." According to Rove, "Southern dialects, string ties, boots, [and] Palm Beach shirts" would help to correctly capture the "flair" of particular regions. College Republicans conducted interviews to match student actors to their most fitting state. Unlike YAF, College Republican leaders sought out women and minority student participation (even if not minority student membership—yearbook photos commonly depict all-white chapters). The mock convention manual stressed that women and at least "one minority ethnic group member" participate as representatives on mock steering committees, following examples set by the Republican National Convention.[13]

When it came to funding mock elections, Rove suggested to College Republicans that "imagination and hard work [would] go a long way." This is also in contrast with YAF and ISI, whose members were somewhat encouraged to do their own fundraising but who were told they could ultimately rely on gifts from regular financiers. The CRNC's Speaker Assistance Program furnished recognizable keynote speakers for the mock events. Beyond that, College Republicans were told to get creative: forgo honorariums, charge a fee to delegates, partner with university symposia committees or the student government, solicit trustees, and use family connections with local businesses. The manual cautioned: "If the Mock Convention does not end up in the black, the college administration may bail it out . . . once. Next time around, there probably won't be a Mock Convention."[14]

Students for Law and Order

Throughout the campaign season, elder Republican Party strategists exploited older Americans' longing for social order. To translate feelings of fear into votes, conservative rhetoric equated youth liberalism with oppressive communist regimes in eastern Europe and Asia. Nixon, popular within the larger Republican Party but not among the most hardened conservatives, specialized in converting feelings of anticommunism into antiliberalism to promote himself as a law-and-order candidate the right could support. On the campaign trail, Nixon ads blended urban civil rights violence with campus rebellions, demonizing both middle-class white students of the antiwar counterculture and members of the Black Power student movement.[15] California governor and presidential candidate Ronald Reagan likened campus radicals to Vietcong partisans.[16] Wallace pushed the conflation of liberalism and communism to an even further extreme while trying to distinguish himself from the two major parties, about which he stated, "There's not a dime's worth of difference."[17] The rhetorical association of youth violence with progressivism boded well for conservative candidates by creating a false dilemma for voters choosing between Democrats and Republicans during an era in which the parties were not yet ideologically defined along liberal and conservative lines.

Despite Nixon's overall popularity in the GOP, many students on the right endorsed the more conservative Reagan as a challenge to the former vice president, who, until that campaign season, had a political reputation as a moderate. YAF had supported Reagan's political endeavors since his contributions to the Goldwater campaign in 1964. Reagan's youth supporters were enamored by his charisma and seemingly natural ability to communicate free-market principals and anticommunism to large audiences. The best example of this was "A Time for Choosing," the speech he gave in support of Goldwater, which was so iconic to movement conservatives of this era that many remembered it simply as "the speech."[18] To these supporters, Reagan was a made-for-office upgrade of Goldwater. He had a Hollywood polish and a friendliness the Arizona cowboy lacked.

Students for Reagan clubs built momentum for the California governor by arranging a showing of a CBS News debate between Reagan and popular

Democratic hopeful Robert Kennedy. Students for Reagan traveled to different campuses to meet with chapters of the College Republicans, YAF, the Young Republicans, and other clubs willing to host a showing of the debate tape to make Reagan more credible among young people, whose knowledge of the actor was limited to his Hollywood career.

Though YAF was a project of William F. Buckley Jr., some students flexed their independence through ardent support of Reagan even as Buckley's own *National Review* threw its support behind Nixon. Some YAF leaders, such as national chair Tom Charles Huston, endorsed Nixon over Reagan and attempted to get club members to fall in line. Huston believed that Nixon was more qualified to deal with Soviet aggression and the threat of nuclear war, since Nixon had served as vice president to Dwight Eisenhower in the early Cold War years. And while Huston was a self-declared "conservative hard-liner" who "didn't work [his] way up to be national chairman [of YAF] by being often moderate," he was also a political pragmatist.[19] Huston explained that after the 1964 election defeat of Goldwater, "it struck [me] that [we] had basically undertaken a kamikaze mission": "It was fine to say that it's better to be right than president. My notion was you ought to strive to be right and president. And so what I was looking for in '68 was somebody who could head the ticket and do credibly well."[20] The only option for Huston was Nixon.

In exchange for their votes, Huston promised reliable YAF members jobs in the Nixon administration, which he was ultimately able to deliver.[21] Once in the White House, Huston and fellow YAFer Pat Buchanan worked closely with younger YAF men, who later became politicians or political advisers themselves (many during the Reagan administration): Frank Donatelli, David Keene, Ron Robinson, Dana Rohrabacher, Chris Cox, Phil Crane, and others.[22]

By the end of September 1968, 80 percent of Americans agreed that the nation was experiencing a breakdown of public order.[23] With just over a month left until the election, the national political landscape was ripe for law-and-order campaign approaches, especially as they related to higher education. Along the fall campaign trail, Nixon and Wallace were both directly confronted by college demonstrators. When challenged at the University of Akron, Nixon belted into the microphone, "Unlike Hubert Humphrey, we shout down the hecklers," to the roaring approval of the 5,000-member audience.[24] Nixon encouraged administrators to adopt policies to expel protesters immediately, suggesting that discussions with radicals only encouraged bad behavior.[25] Wallace similarly responded to hostile campus audiences with threats: "You anarchists are what this country is getting sick and tired of. . . . I say to you when a professor at Rutgers rises on the floor and says, 'I long for a Communist victory [in Vietnam],' we're going to have our Attorney General indict him and put him in a good jail."[26]

Despite regular encounters with student opposition, both Nixon and Wallace enjoyed various degrees of admiration from the collegiate Right. The Student Coalition for Nixon-Agnew, a research group led by students at the Georgia Institute of Technology and the University of Pennsylvania, surveyed campuses to devise ways to enhance Nixon-Agnew support among college youth. By October, Youth for Nixon-Agnew director Mort Allin claimed that his group's membership had topped 30,000. John Acord, head of Youth for Wallace, made wild claims that the club had grown to 12,000 students and was welcoming an additional 500 new members daily.[27] Even at its height, the entire YAF organization never surpassed 20,000 members.

For all their efforts to assemble and proselytize, active youth on the right were still a clear minority. In the previous 1964 presidential election, just 36 percent of voters under thirty years of age favored the conservative candidate Goldwater despite the measures YAF had taken to inject a youthful image into the senator's campaign. Goldwater Girls dressed as cowgirls, YAFettes dressed in bikinis, and the folk band the Goldwaters were the youth Right's attempts to lure their countercultural peers. The same techniques were updated for 1968, with the Nixonettes appearing at rallies in dresses, sashes, and hats, carrying signs that read, "Nixon Is Groovy," "Bring Us Together," and "Apple Pie, Mother, and Nixon."[28] A reluctant Nixon eventually recruited YAF's Buchanan to his campaign as an opposition research assistant and partisan speechwriter to better market the moderate candidate to young conservatives with whom Nixon "welcomed a loose relationship."[29] Together, Buchanan and Huston functioned as liaisons between the hard-line conservatives in YAF and the administration.

Right-Wing White Supremacy

While right-leaning student activists purposefully failed to distinguish radicals and communists from pluralist liberals, it became necessary for them to defend their own association with right-wing extremism, specifically with segregationist Wallace and the white nationalists from whom he drew support. YAF historian and former executive Wayne Thorburn insists that among YAF members, support for Wallace for president in 1968 never reached above 4 percent nationally and was nonexistent among its leadership.[30]

Based on a likely peak membership of 20,000, this indicates that approximately 800 members were Wallace supporters. Out of sync with the larger organization's support for Reagan, three YAF members created their own Youth for Wallace campaign club. When YAF leaders refused to support Youth for Wallace's main fundraising initiative by denying them editorial space in *New Guard* magazine, the three Youth for Wallace founders disaffiliated from YAF. "Thousands" of YAFers also quit the club to join the Wallace group, which claimed that its membership grew to 15,000 by 1968.[31]

YAF issued defensive news releases clarifying that it had no affiliation with the segregationist group, though Youth for Wallace participated in YAF's majority coalition at Columbia's April counterdemonstration (covered in chapter 4) even after the split.[32] YAF's board of advisers also included segregationist congressmen Strom Thurmond (R-SC), L. Mendel Rivers (D-SC), and William Colmer (D-MS).[33] Exactly how large Youth for Wallace was, and exactly how many YAF members defected to join the club, is difficult to assess. The numbers are self-reported from two organizations known for misrepresenting their sizes to appear more influential than they truly were. The Wallace group likely did have a few hundred college supporters (including YAF turncoats), indicating that among the nation's white college youth in the late 1960s, support for a segregationist as president came from a minority that was affluent, educated, and nationally dispursed. YAF nonetheless attempted to make its division with Wallace supporters clear following mandates from its executives.

Conservative movement elders despised Wallace. Frank Meyer considered him a radical and not an actual conservative. Buckley dubbed him "Mr. Evil" and described him as racist and autocratic.[34] According to YAF's national chair, Wallace was the "Pied Piper of pseudo-conservatism . . . [and] based on his record as Governor, he simply does not qualify as a conservative but rather as a populist-segregationist who wants massive government spending."[35] In the fall of 1968, YAF issued *A Conservative's Guide to George Corley Wallace*, outlining criticisms for students to use when discussing Wallace's candidacy.

Efforts by traditionalist conservatives to distance themselves from the Far Right were sometimes reciprocated. Pro-Wallace and other white supremacist student groups struggled with whether the label "conservative" was sufficient for capturing their position on the extreme right. One such student, James, a member of the University of Minnesota's National Socialist Liberation Front (a Nazi college division of the larger National Socialist

White People's Party), was unsure whether he identified as conservative: "I'm a racist. . . . I'm for a new type of revolution; not economic, but racial." The student explained his racial outlook in objectively violent terms: "There are only two realistic solutions: separation or extermination. I would prefer to see separation. . . . The whole race question could lead to open warfare, with millions of blacks being shot in the streets by outraged whites, if it's not handled properly. If we're elected to office, we will offer the other alternative."[36]

White supremacist student groups, such as James's, typically organized in small numbers (though their clubs were often larger in membership than some campus radio stations or literary societies). One example is the eight-member Nazi paramilitary group, the Minute Men, which appeared at the University of Minnesota "armed to the teeth" with automatic weapons.[37] At Louisiana State University, future grand wizard of the Ku Klux Klan and Louisiana state representative David Duke was able to organize at least three different white supremacist clubs from 1968 to 1971, though it is unclear (and unlikely) whether membership in each group was entirely unique.

Youth for Wallace made no effort to conceal its commitment to using violence to maintain white supremacy. Its vice president, Dennis C. McMahon, claimed that the organization's aim was "to liquidate the enemies of the American people on the campus and in the community." Under this guidance, members understood their mission in terms of explicit political violence. They described themselves as "ready to fight, and die if necessary," to "eliminate" campus liberals.[38] In this pursuit, the president of Youth for Wallace, thirty-six-year-old Louis T. Byers, advocated for continuous campus surveillance by right-wing youth trained in martial arts.[39]

The blatantly racist club was clear about its insistence on social order in the hierarchical sense. Its slogan explained, "Free Men are not equal, Equal Men are not free."[40] The club adopted the mathematical symbol of inequality as its logo. Members antagonistically advocated for white studies programs, which would include courses in eugenics, ethnology, biology, and anthropology to ensure that "the equality myth will be exploded forever." Out of step with the stances of YAF and other members of the student Right who were against socialism and in favor of a hawkish foreign policy, Wallace followers promoted planned economies over the free-market system and were opposed to international wars, which they believed would necessarily result in miscegenation. Wallace youth described liberals and their other enemies as "animals," including communists, Black Americans, Jewish

Americans, Native Americans, and other American minorities.[41] In other words, those who were Americans but who did not look or act within the parameters of the traditionalist conception of one.

The theme of "acting like" an American (discussed in chapter 3) was as pronounced among white supremacists as it was among traditionalists. A letter from the Los Angeles Youth for Wallace chapter promised the candidate unwavering adulation using terms of coded white supremacy cloaked in patriotism: "You can count on our club to support you and any other conservative person we feal [sic] will give America back to Americans. . . . We must not let America be run by certain people without your direct supervision."[42] Similarly, Kansas City Youth for Wallace promised to provide unconditional support in the "never ending fight against 'ones' who would destroy our country," understood to mean Black and Jewish revolutionaries.[43]

Though divorced from YAF, young Wallace supporters continued to share the club's fixation with membership size and publicity, as well as its ability to fundraise. Ousted YAFer and Youth for Wallace leader John Acord encouraged members to keep growing their ranks by inviting three new recruits to each meeting.[44] Acord made several claims about the success of his organization, including that the group had fundraised between $28,000 and $35,000 from "anonymous rightwing angels"; placed Youth for Wallace editorials in 400–500 college newspapers; inducted 6,322 new members; and established Youth for Wallace chapters at Baylor, Creighton, Dartmouth, St. John's, North Carolina State, Ohio State, West Virginia, and New York Universities, in addition to the University of California at Los Angeles, the University of Kentucky, and Columbus College in Georgia (only three members were required for a club charter).[45] After Wallace addressed a crowd of 20,000 at the John Birch Society's annual New England Rally for God, Family, and Country in Boston, Youth for Wallace claimed to have enlisted one hundred new members.[46]

Pledges from Arkansas, California, Idaho, Kentucky, and Montana helped the Wallace effort by typing, speaking, placing phone calls, walking precincts, demonstrating, passing out handbills and petitions, and driving voters to polls.[47] The organization even considered a Youth for Wallace caravan that would travel across the country beginning in a large southern city—such as Miami or New Orleans—encouraging busloads and individual cars of students to follow, ideally creating a "bandwagon effect" that would capture additional youth support.[48]

Youth for Wallace's mantra commanded, "Be thou an example in word, in charity, in spirit, in faith, in purity."[49] However, the organization's leadership seemed principally interested in unsanctioned fundraising. Youth for Wallace solicited donations to its unendorsed headquarters at 1629 K Street NW in Washington, D.C., rather than to Wallace's official campaign headquarters in Montgomery, Alabama.[50] (Duke similarly requested his various clubs' dues be sent to his personal address.) Wallace youth mailed solicitations advertising campaign materials at special rates to major companies, such as the Gulf Oil Corporation, and sold Wallace "victory" bonds to supporters.[51] Throughout the summer, Acord constantly wrote to the Montgomery office requesting Wallace's campaign itinerary, most likely so he could appear at events to establish his own legitimacy. His requests appear to have gone unanswered, and Wallace staff seem to have become suspicious of Youth for Wallace's unapproved fundraising.[52]

It is unclear how much money was raised through the sale of Youth for Wallace campaign materials and bonds, though if Acord's claim to have raised $35,000 in a few weeks were true, that total would be worth approximately $315,000 in 2023. It is also unclear how the funds were spent. William Luther Pierce and Willis Carto, two of the youth organization's leaders, each accused the other of fraud, theft, and libel, and ended their working relationship in a civil suit over financial matters.[53]

As for Wallace, he personally distanced himself from Acord and his student followers. He refused to recognize the youth organization, firmly stating that "no Youth for Wallace has any authority from my headquarters."[54] But even without Wallace's endorsement, his college youth followers still benefited from the guidance of white nationalist academics who shared his political views, such as William Luther Pierce, former physics professor at Oregon State University and ideological head of the National Socialist White People's Party, and Revilo Oliver, classics and languages professor at the University of Illinois.

Compared to his friends Bill Buckley, who recruited him as a contributor to the *National Review*, and Robert Welch, with whom he cofounded the John Birch Society, Oliver was a lesser known but no less important mentor of the youth Right. Historian Damon Berry describes Oliver as "one of the most important figures in the development of American white nationalism . . . [for] defining white nationalist ideas concerning conservative politics and Christianity."[55] Oliver endorsed the "elite of young Americans" within the Wallace youth movement and attacked the perceived indoctrination of students navigating "the subtle and devious hostility of the whole Establishment." He insisted that professors and the media were to blame for a generation of corrupted youth. Educators, Oliver claimed, "try to trap them in an endless net of ambiguous rules and pettifogging regulations. Great idealists, who beam benignly when young Americans are beaten or knifed on the campus, will turn purple with rage at the slightest slight to the fauna of their academic jungles. And, of course, the press will bark 'Fasheest,' 'Natsee,' and 'Aunt-eye-Seemeetic!' [*sic*]."[56]

Oliver spent his academic career as a tenured neo-Nazi advocate. And despite exaggerated membership numbers, the historical record reflects that Youth for Wallace represented a sizable and energetic cadre of collegiate white supremacists, with an academic mentorship that included faculty like Oliver and Pierce. Their inconvenient existence could not be denied no matter how hard George Wallace or YAF tried to discredit or distance themselves from them.

Nixon's the One

Following Nixon's nomination as the GOP candidate, the student Right mostly realigned to support him, though the white nationalist wing of students remained faithful to Wallace. College Republicans had long backed Nixon as the GOP hopeful. YAF and Students for Reagan members were amenable to taking the governor's advice to support the candidate, as YAF firmly believed the rumor that Nixon had a "secret plan" to win the Vietnam War quickly.[57] Generally, the student right carried on in service to Nixon's campaign despite the nominee himself being unreceptive of their work on his behalf.

Nixon's half-hearted attempts to capture the enthusiasm of students and his failure to address important youth issues was generally met with a lackluster response. As Seth Blumenthal explains, Nixon was plainly not interested in accommodating young voters. The best Nixon's youth campaign organizers could muster was to create a poster series announcing that "Nixon's the One" and outfitting college campaigners with signs reading "Student Coalition," "18 Year Old Vote," and "Dick Wants Volunteer Army" printed on a psychedelic backdrop.[58]

As Nixon learned, campaigning *against* the media conception of young radicals served as a greater boon than embracing them as supporters. Almost 75 percent of Americans, including the half of the nation that was opposed to the war, disapproved of disruptive protests. Nixon could not make sweeping generalizations about college students everywhere, as many of them—protesters and pot smokers included—were the children of his supporters. Complicating matters, college students overall tended to identify with their own age group regardless of political differences. Attacking baby boomers as a disruptive generation risked alienating otherwise sympathetic voters who would be of age in time for his reelection. This strategy of restraint played especially well with blue-collar urban whites and religious southern conservatives. After all, working-class students tended not to be part of the most egregious campus offenses in national headlines.[59]

The most right-wing students lacked confidence that Nixon would use state force to remedy the problem of "un-American" college protesters, no matter how often he promised to enforce law and order.[60] For these students, Wallace was the candidate they trusted to assert state violence against the campus Left. Nevertheless, immediately following the nomination, Youth for Wallace reorganized as the National Youth Alliance (NYA) to support Wallace's run as an independent, even though they still lacked the candidate's actual endorsement. The NYA operated under the leadership of Pierce, Louis T. Byers, Willis Carto, and Dennis C. McMahon. While George Wallace himself campaigned on a nationwide populist, law-and-order platform, the NYA was specifically interested in achieving white supremacist goals for higher education. Acord promised that even after the 1968 election, the NYA would remain a permanent organization pledged to upholding order on college campuses.[61]

Democratic National Convention, 1968

As the student Right rallied behind their favorite conservative candidates, the student New Left criticized the American political system itself. In the weeks leading up to the August 1968 Democratic National Convention (DNC) in Chicago, the city received riot threats from several youth groups, including the National Mobilization Committee to End the War in Vietnam (the Mobe) and Students for a Democratic Society (SDS). Hundreds of students from both groups planned to march together to the convention amphitheater to demonstrate against the war. Anarchist founder of the Youth International Party (the Yippies) Abbie Hoffman and comrade Rennie Davis threatened to contaminate city water with LSD and sewer lines with gasoline, detonate smoke bombs on the convention floor, and unleash thousands of nudists to float in Lake Michigan and embark on sexual escapades on its beaches.[62]

While the threats seemed facetious, Yippie founders Abbie and Anita Hoffman and their friends Jerry Rubin and Paul Krassner spent eight months formulating a bizarre intervention outside the DNC.[63] After several chaotic precursors, such as the October 1967 March on the Pentagon and the March 1968 Yip-In at Grand Central Station, the Yippies vowed that their earlier radical exploits were mild previews of an upcoming explosion in Chicago. Hoffman promised to corral a group of anarchic young people seeking "risk, drama, excitement, and bullshit."[64]

The flippant promises riled Chicago and Democratic Party leaders, who called for mobilization in defense of the convention. Mayor Richard Daley assembled an infantry numbering over 25,000, including 12,000 city police, 6,000 National Guard members, 1,000 FBI and Secret Service agents, and 6,000 US Army riot troops, as well as a backup force of over 5,000 trained military personnel from various parts of Texas, Oklahoma, and Colorado.[65] In defense of police brutality, Daley infamously remarked to the press, "The policeman isn't there to create disorder, the policeman is there to preserve disorder."[66]

Over four days, 5,000 protesters gathered at the convention arena for a Festival of Life celebration.[67] Tom Hayden of SDS estimated participation from his organization to have been between 1,500 and 2,500 people; Rennie Davis of the Mobe estimated that his group contributed 2,500 people.[68] The demonstrators were well outnumbered by city and state law enforcement, though it made little difference in their efforts to carry out the fantastical demonstration they had planned for months. Outside the convention, entertainment-seeking Yippies mocked politicians and police by nominating a pig they named Pigasus for president, setting it loose in Chicago's Grant Park before the swine was confiscated by officers. Student participants carried signs urging spectators to "Vote Pig in '68" and "Live High on the Hog."[69]

That night, police, youth activists, and curious bystanders clashed in a battle of swinging nightsticks and flying rocks and soda cans. Police and National Guards outfitted with bayonets, plexiglass shields, and gas masks assembled in a phalanx to disperse the crowd with tear gas. Youths responded to the state's overt use of force by asking, "Is this Czechoslovakia?"[70] Military forces smashed the bodies and cameras of journalists and beat or pepper-sprayed thousands of others. From the Hilton Hotel, convention delegates and media correspondents gazed down in shock at the violence overtaking Lincoln Park. News stations broadcasted the chaos live for seventeen minutes to viewers at home.[71]

Most Americans who witnessed mayhem unfold on television were unsympathetic to the injured. Placing blame for the police riot on youth demonstrators, Americans sided with Mayor Daley and the Chicago police by a large margin. National polls reported that 71.4 percent of Americans felt police action in Chicago was justified, and only 21.3 percent felt the officers had used excessive force.[72] Police officers themselves expressed contempt for the youth anarchists, asserting that they could not distinguish the men from the women because they wore their hair in similar styles and used the same profanities.[73] YAF described police violence as "justifiable" because officers had suffered "days of terrible abuse."[74]

Following the turmoil, the convention ended with the nomination of incumbent vice president Hubert Humphrey, alienating the liberal wing of the party, whose support was behind antiwar candidate Eugene McGovern. Undergraduates had thrown their support behind both McGovern and Robert Kennedy, but after Kennedy's assassination in June and McGovern's clear defeat at the DNC, they were left without a standard-bearer. Draft calls continued, and campus unrest intensified. As for the Republican nominee, Nixon's campaign capitalized on the youth violence outside the DNC to stimulate and exploit white working-class hysteria against college and youth dissenters.

Presidential Election, 1968

On October 31, within a week of the election, outgoing president Lyndon Johnson announced an end to air, naval, and artillery bombing against North Vietnam. Despite the promised bombing relief, New Left protesters were concerned that the war would potentially endure under new leadership. In anticipation of the November 5 election, SDS declared plans for a two-day strike on November 4 and 5 to demonstrate that "all elections under the present system are fraudulent." Michael Klonsky, SDS national secretary, explained, "Elections in America are not relevant; we have three racists running, three warmongers, three fascists."[75] A young protester in Washington, D.C., expressed displeasure with the presidential options by hoisting a banner with images of Nixon, Wallace, and Humphrey captioned, "Are you kidding me?"[76]

Several conservative groups reacted to the election strike using majority coalition techniques. At George Washington University, a coalition group created signs and circulated flyers and other literature to build support against class cancellation.[77] The coalition produced a satirical pamphlet, authored by the Sandbox Dictatorship Society, insisting that the inclement weather that had canceled their rally was part of a larger conspiracy by the military-industrial complex.[78] At American University, the Conservative Union student group circulated a petition to censure the student government association for its support of the election-day strike. Pennsylvania State University YAF threatened President Eric Walker with a lawsuit if he allowed the campus to shut down.[79]

While YAF was focused on keeping campuses open during election strikes, College Republicans were gravely worried about voter fraud in the national election. CRNC materials distributed to College Republican chapters warned that "this problem . . . does exist" and that "several thousand illegally cast votes may determine the outcome of an election." The best way to combat voter fraud was by positioning their own loyalists as poll watchers. One of the biggest threats was "the deliberate spoiling of opposition party ballots by a dishonest judge," presumed to be a Democrat, "who may either tear a ballot, erase on it or disfigure it with a piece of graphite under the fingernail." A second major concern was poll crowding by "political stooges" who could discourage end-of-the-day votes. The students were instructed to be present at the polls, prepared to shout "time" at anyone taking too long in the voting booth. They should especially be on the lookout for "chain balloting" (known also as chain voting), by which a subversive voter hands a counterfeit ballot to a judge, takes a legal ballot out of the polling place, and continues "a steady succession of stooge voters" who mark their ballots "as their leaders wish."[80] (It is interesting to note that there was no legitimate contesting of the 1968 presidential election, which resulted in the Republican candidate's election. However, there is evidence that in the 1960 presidential election, the same GOP candidate, Richard Nixon, was the beneficiary of an illegal voting scheme.)[81]

As New Left strikes and right-wing election fraud paranoia overtook campuses on November 5, the GOP's law-and-order candidate Nixon was declared the next president of the United States. Pundits attributed the victory to his capture of the resentful white silent majority. His success divided the two major political parties along economic and racial lines. Most blue-collar workers voted Democrat in 1960, but in the 1968 election, that majority had fallen to a one-third share. Throughout Nixon's first term, political partisanship and economic inequality would increase for the first time in decades.[82]

To explain the youth voting trend, contemporary political sociologists Seymore Martin Lipset and Earl Raab posited that young people were interested in candidates who would "resolve basic problems quickly and in an absolute fashion." Lipset and Raab used this rationale to explain why voters aged twenty-one to twenty-nine supported George Wallace more than those in any other age group. Among college students, Wallace received

7 percent of the vote. Employed youth voted for conservative candidates Wallace and Nixon at 25 percent and 31 percent, respectively, while only 23 percent voted for the Democrat Humphrey. Poll results showed that working-class youth voted for conservative candidates, while upper middle-class youth—those least likely to be called to war in Vietnam—supported the antiwar candidate.[83]

The NYA insisted that their candidate's loss was owed to biased liberal television, news, and radio coverage, and that Wallace remained the strongest anticommunist contender—a claim further evidenced by his wide support from far-right conspiratorial groups, such as the John Birch Society.[84] Following the election, financial benefactor Willis Carto, head of the neo-Nazi Liberty Lobby, assumed control of the NYA after a legal battle with William Luther Pierce.[85] With Carto's financial power, the NYA remained active in its crusade for white supremacy on campus and across the nation. In June 1969, a Montclair, California, GOP group passed a resolution to support the NYA for its endorsement of California educational code 7851: to "teach the principles of morality, truth, justice, patriotism, and dignity."[86] By September 1969, nearly a year after Wallace's election loss, the NYA still claimed 3,000 active members and pledged to campaign for the ex-governor in the 1972 election.[87] In 1974, professors Pierce and Oliver established the white supremacist National Alliance, which still exists as a neo-Nazi political organization today.[88]

An Ally in Nixon?

Once elected, the reluctant YAFers who supported Nixon's campaign were willing to allow the new president time to put his policies into place. In a gesture of support, some mailed letters of affirmation to the White House regarding his promised proposals.[89] To their shock, Nixon announced a withdrawal of American troops from Vietnam once in office. Promising that 65,000 soldiers would return by the end of 1970, a total withdrawal would not be complete until the end of the following year.[90] Nevertheless, on-campus violence directed at ROTC and war-research centers persisted, as neither of the new president's promises were kept. In the first year of his presidency, the FBI recorded as many as eighty bombings at ROTC centers and draft boards.[91]

Bolstered by the presidential election results, state and federal lawmakers continued to crack down on campus violence. By February, state legislatures in California, Colorado, Iowa, Kansas, New York, Washington, and

Wisconsin passed bills to punish student demonstrators through expulsion, revocation of financial assistance, and legal action.[92] In 1969 alone, the California legislature produced more than seventy bills sanctioning unruly campus activists.[93] At the federal level, Republican congressmen proposed bills that would revoke university funds if college administrators failed to punish peacebreakers.[94] The Department of Justice requested an FBI investigation of Ford Foundation grant recipients.[95] Following the wave of legislation, Nixon delivered a statement on campus disorders, reminding university presidents of the effectiveness of expulsion threats, which carried implications for the draft.[96]

The election of a law-and-order president intensified conservatives' pressure on administrators and legislators to gain control of the campus. In support of military and industry recruiters who were the target of antiwar demonstrators, YAF demanded that administrators guarantee adequate "facilities and protection" to potential employers. The national organization preemptively contacted attorneys in over one hundred cities where campus disruptions had already taken place with requests for injunctions to keep colleges open.[97] To gain publicity for YAF-backed counterpickets against peace and anti-recruitment demonstrations, majority coalition organizers issued press releases and wrote to national and state leaders for support.[98] Newspaper editorials requesting financial support for anti-left youth groups used racial red-baiting to create a sense of urgency among local constituents, declaring, "Youths are the only ones who can stop campus trouble from the minority backed by the Communists and Black Power."[99] If administrators were unwilling or unable to get a handle on disruptions, conservatives needed funds to stop the Left themselves.

But in the wake of Nixon's inauguration and the rush of nationwide legislation punishing campus demonstrators and permissive administrators, the student Right may have miscalculated its own degree of approval among authority figures. To its dismay, requesting Nixon's support was a fruitless pursuit. The new president described youth in YAF as "about as nutty . . . as the militants."[100] Nixon, continuously distancing himself from ultraconservative and right-wing groups, ignored their requests.[101] In March, the White House contacted YAF, ordering it to discontinue a fundraiser mailing that had used the president's name without authorization.[102]

To soften the strained relationship between the administration and students who relied on its help, Nixon aide and YAF's recent chair Tom Huston suggested it would be beneficial for the president to publicly endorse the student groups helping to combat radicalism.[103] Nixon ultimately indulged another of Huston's requests to have the White House distribute pro-war propaganda to YAF, the College Republicans, the Young Republicans, the Freedom Leadership Foundation, the Association of Student Governments, and the United Student Alliance. As discussed in chapter 2, the Nixon administration was also successful in reaching campuses through the College Press Service (CPS) news agency, which delivered copies of Nixon's speeches and other messages directly to college newspapers and radio stations, despite the fact that the CPS was antagonistic toward his policies. White House staff also built close relationships with CPS writers, ensuring that rhetoric toward the administration became less inflammatory.[104]

By the end of the spring 1969 semester, Nixon's popularity among youth was stunningly high (especially given how low his approval rating would eventually fall). An early June Gallup poll revealed a 57 percent approval rating among college students and a 68 percent approval rating among adults under the age of thirty.[105] But just six months into the new administration, YAF members were already becoming disenchanted with the compromise candidate. The patience they had extended him was quickly running out, as evidenced by a summer poll asking members to identify the politician that best represented their ideology: 39 percent chose Goldwater as their ideological favorite, followed by 37 percent for Reagan, 9 percent for Nixon, 6 percent for Wallace (up slightly from 4 percent before the 1968 election), and the remaining 9 percent split among others.[106]

Conservative youth activists who relied on leveraging power through authority figures were now finding it difficult to establish a meaningful relationship with the new president. When unable to count on authorities to do their bidding, students of the Right ambitiously and extrajudicially took matters into their own hands. Racial resentments and calls for white nationalism that informed the 1968 presidential campaign—and continued to animate supporters of these politicians after the election—were increasingly apparent through white supremacist violence on campus in the years that followed.

The first Black Studies programs were soon created in 1969, early in Nixon's presidency. Disenchanted with the administration's ability to stop the student Black Power movement, white nationalists forged ahead in parading their racial contempt across the campus. The college-based white supremacy movement was about to reach its fever pitch.

6 The Black Studies Thing

· ·

Throughout the 1960s, most instances of campus protest took place at predominately white institutions (PWIs); however, at historically Black colleges and universities (HBCUs), several events evidenced antiwar and civil rights discontent. As at many PWIs, HBCU student strikers demanded that administrators revoke mandatory Reserve Officers' Training Corps (ROTC) participation, allow greater student involvement in discipline issues, and create Black studies programs. Beyond diversifying the classroom, Black women students were central in demanding greater institutional diversification and student support by calling for a more representative administrative staff.[1] In pursuit of these demands, Black students organized demonstrations on as many as 200 campuses.[2]

Disruptions at both PWIs and HBCUs intensified in April 1968 following Martin Luther King Jr.'s assassination. Absent the nation's most recognized civil rights leader, activists were gridlocked along generational lines in their approach to demands for equality. Older Black activists continued to promote nonviolent civil disobedience in the spirit of Dr. King, while a younger generation, inspired by Malcolm X and the Black Panther Party, were increasingly intrigued by separatism and self-defense. As historian Stefan Bradley explains, "Young learners understood that the beloved leader's peaceful approach to fighting racial bigotry did not work to spare his life. At that moment, for many of them, using love to persuade the enemies of freedom was no longer an option."[3] Historian Joy Ann Williamson-Lott notes that "many blacks began to identify integration as a philosophy that ignored questions of power and drained the black community of its most productive members. Instead . . . [Black Power] would build cultural, political, and economic institutions that advanced their collective interests."[4] The Student Nonviolent Coordinating Committee's (SNCC) Stokely Carmichael, among the nation's most prominent youth leaders, urged Black Americans to take up arms as a means of self-protection against police and white supremacists. For marginalized students who increasingly expressed powerlessness within the existing political system, radical demonstrations attracted attention—and offered solutions—to long-ignored problems.

Of course, the degrees of difference between King's nonviolent civil disobedience and the younger Black Power brand of militant direct action did not matter to the most influential leaders of the conservative movement, nor did it matter at the highest levels of federal power. In 1967, future Supreme Court justice Lewis Powell Jr., then serving on the Johnson administration's National Commission on Law Enforcement, grouped King along with Carmichael, SNCC chair H. Rap Brown, and other leaders of the Congress of Racial Equality (CORE) as "men determined to remake America" through "coercion." Warning that society was being actively "destroyed" by communists, Powell advocated for an end to "toleration of civil disobedience" and that those inspiring "riots and rebellion" be "relentlessly prosecuted."[5]

In this spirit, the FBI created a special counterintelligence division specifically to monitor and disrupt the activities of Black civil rights groups in August.[6] The Johnson administration further subsidized municipal police and state National Guard forces with millions of dollars in cash and surplus military-grade weapons used in Vietnam as part of its domestic War on Crime. Historian Elizabeth Hinton explains that these weapons, especially tear gas, were as effective in "pursuing the Vietcong" as they were "in putting down so-called riots in Black American neighborhoods."[7]

Addressing educational inequality was a key concern of the Black Power liberators who were under the federal government's watch. Black leaders argued that simply admitting more Black students into PWIs was not achieving true educational justice. In addition to having a racially diverse student corps, American universities needed to diversify the faculty, offer curricula that acknowledged the Black experience, and empower Black communities off campus. Even at HBCUs, as Williamson-Lott explains, student leaders determined that their institutions would be most effective by "keeping the student body exclusively black and hiring more black professors—black professors with an orientation towards Black Power principles."[8] Where administrative resistance to such changes was the norm, student Black Power leaders used strikes to advance their demands for autonomy.[9] Initial calls to increase Black student enrollment and diversify faculty were restructured as militant demands for bona fide Black studies departments. At PWIs, white conservatives felt provoked by the increasing visibility of Black separatist leaders and their calls for representation, reform, and resistance.

Black Power strikers faced intense backlash at nearly every institution that would create a Black studies program in this era.[10] Exemplary of this is San Francisco State University, where protests from 1968 to 1969 for the first Black studies program were met with "a punitive response, an unsympathetic media, and external political pressure to reject negotiation in favor of bringing in the police."[11] Such backlashes were not spontaneous or organic; they represented a broader and deliberate strategy on the part of white reactionaries mobilizing on campus during these years. The vengeance conservatives unleashed against Black studies strikers mirrored the tactics they applied against the peace movement (as they often blended the memberships between the distinct groups): starting information wars, threatening authority figures to enforce punishment, and condoning or even executing violence against strikers to uphold the academy's existing hierarchy.

The Right's information wars aimed to delegitimize strikers' demands and were usually performed through countermessaging, argument reframing, or visceral displays of negative support via theatrical counterdemonstrations in favor of order (defined as Black acquiescence to the racial status quo). Depending on an administration's reaction to strikes, conservatives pressured authorities through their overt support or condemnation and threats to sue. As a last but not entirely rare resort, they used personal violence against strikers and their supporters, or called on law enforcement to do it for them.

As administrators proposed measured solutions to stall or alleviate issues of campus civil rights unrest, the reaction from leading conservative figures was outright condemnation. As they did with the white New Left, conservatives redirected focus from Black protesters' objectives to their methods, arguing that protecting civil order against an anti-American cadre of youth agitators was the nation's paramount domestic issue in the war against communism. By stripping away the dual contexts of social oppression and the need for educational representation, leading figures on the right, such as William F. Buckley Jr. and California governor Ronald Reagan, frequently reduced demonstrations for civil equity and educational justice to criminal breakdowns of law and order. Even liberal social scientists and policy makers diagnosed rebellions as a pathological symptom of a "culture of poverty."[12]

As Nancy Bristow explains, "Those wielding power in the community possessed an overwhelming advantage in the fight not only to control events but also their meaning, as they routinely do in cases of state violence committed against people of color."[13] Despite the fact that most radical campus demonstrations post-1968 focused on the United States' involvement in Vietnam's civil war, conservatives tactically recast unique issues of domestic civil injustice and international war opposition as a leftist monolith to attack. This framing informed public and administrative understandings of unique and specific instances of student dissent as simply part of a sweeping fad of disruption and lawlessness by the campus counterculture.

While instances of violence involving the Black Power movement did occur, students on the right condemned both militants and nonviolent activists indiscriminately for lawbreaking (and regularly misattributed urban racial unrest in response to police brutality as conspiracies of Black Power masterminds). The argument was that one should work through proper channels to correct unjust laws. But this viewpoint, according to student Black Power leaders, failed to acknowledge that legal procedures themselves were often insufficient, and legal assistance not always accessible, thus creating a need for more direct action.[14] Students on the right were nevertheless unconvinced and inconvenienced by civil rights activities. They therefore amplified instances of disorder or violence, allowing them to both ridicule and condemn the methods Black agitators as criminal without ever having to meaningfully engage with real goals of equity and justice.

One exemplary case is the 1968 student protest for a new course at the University of California, Social Analysis 139X, to be taught by Black Panther leader Eldridge Cleaver. UC regents, citing Cleaver's pending trial for assault with intent to commit murder and subsequent parole violations, refused to endorse the course's credit option. Throughout the semester, Governor Reagan issued inflammatory statements decrying the idea of a felon lecturing in the UC system.[15] With frustration against administrators culminating over the course of several months, Black Power and antiwar agitators carried their dissent off-campus to nearby People's Park the following spring. When the field became occupied by radical students in a "full-scale riot," Reagan sent in police, who fired among the crowd, killing white observer James Rector and injuring hundreds of others.[16]

Black Educational Justice as Oppressive to Whites

In the wake of chaotic and deadly episodes such as the People's Park protest, conservatives argued that the cost of educational and civil equality was simply too high, as it came at the expense of white students' peace and safety. The student editor of Cornell's *Daily Sun* denounced his institution's permissiveness toward protesters, writing, "A lot of people here feel that the university is disregarding white students in its dealings with the blacks, and that much of what it does is being done under an implicit threat by the black students."[17] In this way, conservatives weaponized their own supposed victimhood in a "discursive maneuver," which Lee Bebout explains is used to uphold privilege "in the guise of powerlessness and justice."[18]

In other instances, students on the right were straightforward in their racism. The Campus Conservative Club at the University of Georgia touted the "racial inferiority of blacks" and "warned of the repression of conservative students" as administrators sided with "hip degenerates against normal people."[19] *New Guard* magazine, produced by Young Americans for Freedom (YAF), echoed white supremacist victimization: "The n——s at Stanford are no longer black students, they're conservatives. The administration doesn't give a damn about the moderates or the conservatives on campus because they know that we're not going to sit in the Old Union or try to burn down Encina Hall. . . . You think having blck [*sic*] skin is some kind of a drawback here? Try wearing a Nixon button to class."[20] Other *New Guard* editorials claimed that white students were victims of reverse oppression, declaring that "the SNCC people talk like black-sheeted Klaners" or, as in San Francisco State's *Daily Gater*, describing the boxer Muhammed Ali as "a clown . . . hysterian [*sic*] . . . and a front man for a hate group as vicious as any Ku Klux Klan ever was."[21]

In further instances, conservatives terrorized Black and Jewish students with promises to put activists to death. Members of the "silent majority of Cal State Long Beach and the surrounding cities" addressed a letter to "the N——," threatening that "if this verbal harassment of white people does not stop, the B.S.U. . . . will be exterminated."[22] Louisiana State University student David Duke appeared at the Tulane University campus in 1970 wearing a Nazi stormtrooper uniform with a swastika on his left arm, hoisting a sign that read "Gas the Chicago 7," a reference to the New Left demonstrators (some of whom were Jewish) who were awaiting trial for disrupting the 1968 Democratic Convention. The reverse of the poster read "Kunstler is a Communist Jew," referring to the group's lawyer, William Kunstler.[23] To those of the self-proclaimed silent majority, Black and Jewish student agitators were part of one conglomeration of agitators bent on destroying the campus and nation.

In addition to using a rhetoric of victimization and justified vengeance, conservatives reacted with mockery to minority student calls for equity. UC-Berkeley YAF ridiculed Black Power demands with sardonic calls for a college of conservative studies, preferential seating on administrative committees, mandatory hiring of conservative faculty, and holidays to commemorate the birthdays of Buckley, Nixon, and Barry Goldwater.[24] The most overt white supremacists called for white studies programs and courses in eugenics and ethnology, which they believed would scientifically demonstrate the superiority of the white race.[25]

Outside the realm of outspoken white supremacists, most conservatives generally denied not only their own internalized racism but also the existence of institutional racism, and they interpreted Black separatism as a contrarian exercise meant to divide campus and country. Dick Lindmark, a member of YAF and the Intercollegiate Studies Institute (ISI) at the University of St. Thomas in St. Paul, Minnesota, explained, "I don't think it's a question of physical or mental superiority. I think the attitudes are different. The breakdown of the Negro family, so well documented by Daniel Moynihan, is the root of the problem. It stems from historical problems—too rapid emancipation with no preparation for it. . . . I agree with Eric Hoffer about the [Black] inferiority complex. All doors are open to them now, but they're afraid to walk through. That's why they're turning to separatism now. They were given the opportunities and they couldn't hack it."[26]

Underlying these claims is the culture-of-poverty framework conceived by liberals Moynihan, Nathan Glazer, Seymour Martin Lipset, Daniel Bell, and other contemporary political scientists and commentators. As noted by Robin Marie Averbeck, their scholarly and policy contributions were "ensconced in universities," designed to reach "a white and liberal audience."[27] Their work has resulted in decades of perhaps well-intended but harmful policy programs lauded by Lindmark and others on the right.

Civil Rights Activism as Communism

The Right's opposition to equality was further extended through conflation of civil rights activism with communism. Demonstrations against the Vietnam War and for racial justice were chiefly organized by progressive student clubs, such as Students for a Democratic Society (SDS) and SNCC.[28] These organizations had already been the ire of students on the right due to their interest in ideologies perceived as anti-American. According to YAF mentor and chief fundraiser Marvin Liebman, "The civil rights thing became a demon, became a left operation which had to be fought."[29] YAF leadership remained especially skeptical of Black campus initiatives, insinuating connections between Marxism and student civil rights organizations, such as SNCC, CORE, and W. E. B. Du Bois Clubs.

These beliefs were amplified by the students' movement leaders, state legislators, and federal agencies. Speaking before the Virginia Association of Colleges in 1966, Lewis Powell explained that New Left communists were strategically branding the Vietnam War as racist "to coalesce" the campus civil rights and peace movements.[30] For years the FBI's domestic intelligence program, COINTELPRO, surveyed Black civil rights leaders it suspected of having communist or militant associations. FBI director J. Edgar Hoover publicly branded the Black Panthers as "the greatest threat to the internal security of the country."[31] Members of Congress similarly used hysterical red-baiting language to incite suspicion around Black Power organizers and their social justice goals. Senator Robert Byrd (D-WV), for example, described Howard University as "infiltrated, infested, and contaminated with black power."[32]

Some students on the right cited these statements from the highest levels of government as their organization's raison d'être. Two weeks after Indiana University approved a W. E. B. Du Bois Club in 1966, seniors Gayle Faunce, Carol Child, and fifteen others founded Students for an Orderly Society (SOS). The presence of the socialist club left Faunce "particularly appalled" and inspired to counteraction, with support from the local John Birch Society chapter. As Faunce explained, she and other members identified "a need for a conservative, anti-Communist organization, and it is our purpose to conduct an educational program to combat the distortions and falsehoods perpetrated by those whose intention it is to undermine our Republic and hence our orderly society." Plans for its first semester included meeting with the Bloomington Committee to Support Your Local Police to watch films of campus "riots" across the country.[33] In a letter to the editor of the *Indiana Daily Student*, Faunce explained that her opposition to the W. E. B. Du Bois Club stemmed from the FBI's public condemnation of the club, citing King's advisers, who were members of the American Communist Party. For Faunce and others like her, pedantic concerns about Marxism were more important than their own association with the conspiratorial Far Right. The op-ed offered a lengthy defense of the Bircher conspiracists who supported her and her classmates.[34]

The added tendency of news media to amplify the federal government's characterization of nonviolent civil rights activists as agents of a radical communist conspiracy further exacerbated the problems Black students faced. On campus, the effects of these negative depictions had consequences for civil rights initiatives, from the firing of Black faculty to a ban on assembly for Black Greek organizations, Black Student Unions (BSUs), and other student clubs. In southern states like North Carolina and Mississippi, anticommunist speaker bans were effective in keeping the messages of civil rights activists from reaching collegians on their campuses.[35] The president of the University of Illinois explained that granting a Du Bois Club access to its facilities would be "widely misunderstood and misinterpreted by the general public, and the university program would significantly suffer as a consequence."[36]

Communist associations were further used to attach the Black Power student movement to violence, such as the Panthers' practice of funding the organization's arsenal of guns and ammunition by selling copies of Mao Tse-tung's "little red book" on campus.[37] Historian Stefan Bradley explains that for many young Black men, arming themselves was not just a method of self-defense, but a show of protection for Black womanhood against white men.[38] To conservatives and many others, these romantic symbols were perceived as dangerous and inflammatory, and the Right used them to justify its charge that Black Power anarchists aimed to destroy the campus and society.

Administrative and Legal Resistance to Educational Reform

The relationship between conservative students and the authorities of their institutions was usually symbiotic when it came to taking action against "the Black studies thing."[39] In one instance, Columbia University's YAF chair became a self-appointed bodyguard for a faculty member serving as a jurist during a Black Panther trial.[40] Conservative students showered praise over administrators whose postures against strikers they approved of, such as S. I. Hayakawa of San Francisco State University. Hayakawa fired dozens of sympathetic faculty members, stripped funding from student clubs, frightened students with threats to revoke their financial aid, and allowed the police—who made close to 800 arrests—to occupy the campus for months.[41] Students on the right flaunted support for Hayakawa's "hardnosed" stance by donning blue buttons—a reactionary symbol created to rebuke the black armbands associated with antiwar and civil-rights-adjacent New Left groups (discussed in chapter 3).[42] Students at the University of Hawaii delivered a lei to the president, formed an honorary Hayakawa Society, and circulated petitions of support endorsing his firm position against student "storm troopers."[43]

Among administrators resistant to educational justice efforts was the conservative argument that admitting more students of color for the sake of diversity would decrease program rigor and institutional cachet. Exemplary of this was the Pennsylvania State University president's reaction to the Frederick Douglass Association's demands for a minimum enrollment of 1,000 Black students (then a fivefold increase of its Black population), greater Black representation among faculty, and a Black studies program with a dedicated new building. To appreciate the magnitude of these demands, at nearby Ivy League Cornell, Black students numbered just 250 out of several thousand.[44]

Contemporary with demands for Black studies programs, colleges in the late 1960s—especially in the South—were just barely beginning to integrate. Even though legal desegregation for K–12 schools had already been required for well over a decade, flagship PWIs had vanishingly small numbers of Black students. As recently as 1962 and 1963, white governors had physically "stood in the schoolhouse door" to block the entrance of the first Black students at the University of Mississippi and the University of Alabama. A US Census Bureau report reflects that nationwide, only 5,220 Black students were enrolled in college during the fall of 1970 (just .07 percent of the national total college enrollment of 7.4 million).[45]

In this context, Penn State president Eric Walker claimed that the admission of a flood of students on the basis of race rather than achievement would diminish the institution's prestige. He expressed that Black faculty were in extremely high demand throughout the nation and that nothing could be done to meet the demands in such a short time. Unsatisfied with the president's rebuke, SDS and the Douglass Association occupied the administration building. A crowd of 1,500 hostile counterprotesters led by the white student government president demanded that the building be released. The demonstration ended when police were summoned. One faculty member, incredulous that the police response had been insufficient, remarked that the demonstrators "can get away with just about anything. If they were treated like adults, most of them would be in jail." A campuswide poll immediately following the demonstration revealed that only 25 percent of students approved of the Douglass Association's demands.[46]

Regarding President Walker's concerns, it was true that Black faculty were in short supply. That year, there were fewer than 200 Black doctorates qualified in the social sciences, and fewer than a hundred actively teaching.[47] Compounding the problem, public land grant institutions, such as Penn State, were competing with the Ivy League, where the student and faculty diversity problem existed as well.[48] At Cornell, for example, there were less than a dozen Black faculty members out of a total of 2,200 in 1969.[49] The problem was extremely apparent in the South, where flagship colleges in Alabama, Mississippi, Louisiana, and South Carolina did not hire a single Black professor until after 1970, and where no PWI had "more than a handful" of Black faculty by the middle of the 1970s.[50]

Speaking to a small college audience in rural South Dakota, President Nixon reinforced the Right's charge that admissions concessions for students of color were cheapening institutional prestige: "Our colleges are under pressure to collapse their educational standards in the misguided belief that this would promote 'opportunity.' Instead of seeking to raise lagging students up to meet the college standards, the cry now is to lower the standards to meet the students. This is the old, familiar, self-indulgent cry for the easy way. It debases the integrity of the educational process."[51]

Beyond the hurdles of accepting more minority students and hiring more diverse faculty, civil rights educators and activists were also forced to defend the legitimacy and necessity of Black studies programs to those who would see the curriculum as "an academically suspect, antiwhite, emotional intrusion into a landscape of rigor and reason."[52] Martin Kilson, a Black faculty member who voted to create Harvard's Afro-American program, cautioned that "students must be trained by people who are [intellectually disciplined]. Otherwise these black studies programs will be just a kind of revivalist situation where the repetition of the experience that each black kid has had will give him a sense of cathartic gain or of therapeutic value, but this will not be an intellectual process. It'll really be a kind of group therapy."[53]

After justifying why Black studies courses were necessary, criticisms of implementation still abounded. Even among administrators who were willing to institute the reforms, adherence to the traditional procedures for curricular modification slowed the pace of attaining students' demands. And because the programs were new, no standard curriculum or textbooks existed to provide a framework for faculty eager to take on the challenge of creating the first courses. The faculty diversity problem meant that most of the instructors available to teach were white and disconnected from the actual Black communities their stated missions were meant to uplift.[54] This further led to PWIs, especially those outside the south, poaching Black professors from HBCUs. Eddie R. Cole explains how white researchers went on to create programs and centers without the expertise of Black faculty, a practice rooted in "one of the most prevalent white supremacist beliefs: that whites were best at advising Black colleges, and Black people generally, about how to rectify societal racial inequalities. In short, Blackness was valued as long as it was under white control."[55]

Demands for Punishment against the Black Power Student Movement

Even before the success of the first Black studies programs, the most hardened conservatives sought punishment against student agitators who drew attention to the need for them and administrators who approved of them. From students and their parents to federal agencies, calls for retribution included fines, jail time, and civil suits. At the highest level of government, the Department of Health, Education, and Welfare (HEW) threatened to revoke federal funds from any institution that created Black studies programs that discriminated against whites by enrolling only Black students or hiring only Black faculty. HEW officials required Antioch College in Ohio to submit a "desegregation plan" for its Afro-American Studies Institute on such a basis, threatening to withdraw $1 million in federal funding for violations of the 1964 Civil Rights Act.[56] At the institutional level, clubs like LSU YAF threatened to sue if the university invested in a Black cultural center on campus.[57] As Bebout explains, such "assertions of victimhood function to flatten out or invert social hierarchies and make them illegible." By claiming that Black studies programs discriminated against white students, they were knowingly weaponizing "victimization and fairness to secure inequality."[58]

Conservative students took it upon themselves to report their institution's civil rights initiatives, though not all their petitions bore results. Dick Lindmark's complaint with the state human rights department against the University of Minnesota for allowing the all-Black Afro-American Action Committee to participate in a Morrill Hall sit-in was apparently ignored.[59] While the complaint proved inconsequential, the effort to punish the institution for creating an educational justice committee was revealing.

Other students on the right were outspoken in calls for violence against Black activists, issuing disturbing literature at institutions such as the University of Minnesota. One self-declared neo-Nazi group passed around advertisements for tear gas as "Negro control equipment, guaranteed to drop the most vicious buck in his tracks." The ad was originally from a 1969 issue of the *Liberator*, the magazine of the National Socialist White Peoples' Party. Duke shared copies of the same issue on the LSU campus.[60] Other materials from the University of Minnesota group characterized white men as "gutless creeps" for condoning interracial relationships between "your women" and animals, and encouraged white men to execute Black campus demonstrators en masse.[61]

The president of the Society for the Preservation of the American Republic at the University of Minnesota explained, "Perhaps I have a good deal of racist tendencies in me. I can't help it, it's just the way I was brought up. . . . When a black person walks up to me and says that I have him in slavery and my forefathers were raping his in the backyard—well, I know for a fact my forefathers didn't own slaves and chances are yours didn't and anyone else's in Minneapolis, for that matter. Gross generalization makes me sick. They condemn the entire white society for what only a few whites did."[62]

While the overt white supremacy paraded by neo-Nazi groups did not characterize conservative students as a whole, certainly implicit bias, microaggressions, and a reflexive defense of institutional racism were characteristic of the Right and white college students generally. The rhetorical argument posed by conservative resisters against Black educational equity essentially reduced student protesters to violent anti-American criminal agitators who, at the very least, sought to diminish the rigor of the nation's educational institutions. To some, demonstrators were nothing more than "people who couldn't read, write, compute—people who . . . just came up and raised a lot of hell and took stuff over and then left."[63] This characterization was widely accepted by the national media who benefitted from sensationalized coverage of Black power groups (often citing stories fabricated by the FBI).[64] Aggrandized media coverage provided the Right some credence with the public for their damning accusations about Black educational justice efforts.

Calls for punishment were also aimed at campus presidents and faculty directly. Conservative student groups threatened a range of lawsuits and violent retaliation if administrators failed to protect white student interests when Black Power strikes occurred, though typically administrators did not need the threat to act. Chancellor William McGill forbade faculty from canceling class at UC-Berkeley amid student calls for strikes in support of the Cleaver course. McGill explained his position to student protesters: "I understand what you are trying to do and I do not question your good intentions, but I cannot permit you to influence the rest of the campus to this extent. . . . There are thousands of other students here who do not feel your depth of commitment [to civil rights] and who want to be left alone so that they can go to school. They have rights too and I am obliged to keep the campus open."[65]

After the president of San Jose State College vowed to dedicate a section of the library to Black authors, suspend fraternities or sororities who refused to accept Black pledges, and create an ombudsperson to hear minority student complaints, an immediate backlash ensued against the president and sympathetic faculty.[66] Reagan responded that faculty who endorsed the protests that led to those reforms should be fired, while Max Rafferty, the state superintendent of public instruction, insisted that a football game that had been canceled due to demonstrations should have carried on under the watch of the Marine Corps.[67]

At California State University–Northridge, known as Valley State, the president declared a state of emergency during a joint BSU-SDS strike. After the police were summoned, twenty-four students were arrested on charges of false imprisonment, burglary, and assault and sentenced to between one and twenty-five years in prison.[68] Police arrested an additional 286 students and faculty who surrounded the administration building. Though Valley State administrators ultimately agreed to create Afro-American and Chicano studies departments, President Delmar Oviatt placed a ban on all further demonstrations under threat of arrest in response to the pressure he faced by the governor and his constituents.[69]

When students on the right felt that the police had not reacted sufficiently, they sometimes attempted to administer punishment themselves, as was the case against Cornell students who demonstrated for an Afro-American Studies Center in 1969. Once a budget was approved to fund the program, opponents threatened the institution—and specifically its Black students—with a burning cross outside of the Wari Cooperative House, a student residence for Black women. Some members of the Afro-American Society (AAS) armed themselves and occupied Willard Straight Hall, where visiting parents were residing for the weekend. Incensed white parents and students demanded a court order to remove Black students. Eleven white students from the Delta Upsilon fraternity broke through a window and, acting in place of police, engaged in a physical fight with the AAS in an attempt to eject them from the building.

No physical harm was inflicted on the AAS by university officials or police, only by their white classmates. In the aftermath, students, alumni, and faculty expressed outrage that the AAS members had not been disciplined; they were furious that the AAS members had entered and left the building with rifles and not been arrested by supervising police forces. Several faculty members pledged to strike, threatening to stop their teaching duties if the students went unpunished. Conservatives reacted in fury that the president seemingly appeased the rebelling students' demands, with strikers evading legal charges and the plans for the Afro-American Studies Center continuing. The Right delighted in supporting Thomas Sowell, one of the nation's few Black professors of economics (and an Earhart Foundation fellow), who resigned in response. President James Perkins, too, ultimately resigned.[70]

Many students on the right also unequivocally defended police brutality against demonstrators as part of their defense of institutionalized white supremacy. After police fired on South Carolina State College students during a demonstration against the 1968 Orangeburg murders of three young Black men as well as the injuries of thirty-four others, Duke University YAF invited the Durham police chief to campus to defend "the other side of riots."[71] Flyers advertising the event asked, "Are they really Brutal Stormtroopers and Bent on Genocide???"[72] Some hung Confederate flags in dormitory windows and sang the Confederate anthem, "Dixie."[73] Here, as was often the case, white alumni and campus locals "clamored for" police to intervene in Black student demonstrations.[74] Signaling police to target students of color routinely resulted in arrest, physical harm, or death. Compared to student protests at PWIs, demonstrators at HBCUs, such as South Carolina State, were more likely to be brutalized by police during protests and face fabricated criminal charges in their aftermath.

Perhaps the most pervasive form of resistance against the student Black Power movement was the passive acceptance of brutality against students and young people of color, as evidenced by national apathy in response to the infamous police shootings of Black Panther youth organizers Fred Hampton and Mark Clark in December 1969. Only months later, police again made headlines for a mass shooting of Black students at Jackson State University on May 15, 1970. At this Mississippi HBCU, police fired 469 bullets for nearly thirty seconds into a dormitory in retaliation for being "cursed by blacks."[75] Phillip Lafayette Gibbs and James Earl Green were killed, and twelve others, mostly Black women, were injured. The common historical explanation is that exhaustion following the Kent State massacre, which had occurred just days prior, in combination with tacit acceptance of Black deaths at the hands of police, led to a nationwide silence. But as is documented in chapter 9, white students' antiwar demonstrations continued well into May beyond the Jackson State murders, and outrage against the use of force against white students by the police and National Guard was nowhere near exhausted. White students devoted little or no space to the Jackson State murders in campus editorials and declined to organize any major protests in response.[76] The few commemorative events honoring the students' deaths were organized by the Black community, with little recognition of the event in the broader press then or since. As for the Black Panther assassinations, the FBI and Chicago police raid that led to the murder of Fred Hampton and Mark Clark *did* further radicalize a handful of white SDS members to become more militant, but their response is exceptional of white students generally.[77]

Bristow highlights the effect of the Right's countermessaging on the legacy of the Jackson State slain: "This unwillingness of white Americans to look squarely at the racial hatred at the center of the shootings was facilitated by the misleading student and law and order narratives that emerged in the aftermath."[78] Mississippi's white governor, John Bell Williams, blamed the Black student deaths and injuries on "disrespect of law, and contempt for all duly constituted authority, and total disregard of the rights and property of others," falsely implying that the victims were protestors (and amplifying conservative stereotypes about Black criminality) to justify police retribution.[79]

Resistance from HBCUs, Black Faculty, and the White New Left

Demands for Black student rights were concurrent with those made by the mostly white antiwar movement. The peace movement efforts tended to garner more attention and at times were directly at odds with the demands of the student Black Power movement. With anti-draft events in frequent occurrence toward the end of the 1968 fall semester, discontent over student civil rights began to disappear from the national headlines. Martha Biondi claims that "the most prevalent demand in the hundreds of campus protests in 1968–1969 was African American inclusion, not opposition to the Vietnam War," but contemporary evidence suggests otherwise.[80] A November 1968 survey of 859 colleges by Educational Testing Services reported that the primary instigator of student disruptions was the war in Vietnam, followed by in loco parentis policies, and then civil rights demands. Civil rights had alternated between the first- and second-most important issue to student demonstrators throughout the decade but had by then fallen to third priority.[81] Majority white students were more concerned with rules that determined coed visiting hours in men's and women's dormitories than in continuing to acknowledge the academy's racial injustices.[82]

Though conservatives often attacked the student antiwar and civil rights movements as a monolith, the two causes were distinct and often at odds. This could be partially explained as a consequence of white radical antiwar violence in northern, western, and elite universities, which created strain on nonviolent Black student civil rights leaders in the South. By 1968, SDS antiwar radicals and Black nationalists had tired of southern Black students' nonviolence. Even in the rural New England setting of Brown University, the most dramatic display of disruption consisted of sixty-five of the university's eighty-five Black students staging a walkout to demand a more representative student body and faculty. The students had chosen "nonviolent militant action" as their primary method of attaining Black Power.[83] SDS leaders assessed the demonstrations at Brown as "insufficiently militant."[84]

But even peaceful protests and strikes were by no means safe tactics for first-generation students at HBCUs or southern flagship institutions with overwhelming conservative majorities. Black presidents, such as Jacob Reddix at Jackson State, were still beholden to an all-white board of governors, which undoubtedly influenced his decisions to expel students and dissolve the student government to "[keep] a tight lid" on dissent.[85] Black presidents who could be counted on to preserve order, such as Howard University's James E. Cheek, received praise from conservative politicians and renewed institutional funding. Cheek himself enjoyed positive working relationships with Republican presidents Nixon, Reagan, George H. W. Bush, and the latter two's GOP adviser, Lee Atwater, whom Cheek appointed to Howard's board of trustees.[86]

Cole further explains how Black university presidents carefully navigated demands for justice while under the watch of white legislators, often having to "sacrifice their public reputations because they only fought privately for Black liberation behind the scenes."[87] At HBCUs in particular, disruptive tactics and demands for Black Power were risky for several reasons: actions toward separatism ran counter to federal regulations and thus threatened funding; students' calls to revolutionize colleges into "movement centers" threatened institutional academic missions and thus challenged their intellectualism (or so conservative resisters claimed); and, to compete for Black student enrollment, administrators strived to make their institutions viable alternatives to the PWI mainstream.[88]

Additionally, Bradley explains that educated students of the Black bourgeoisie faced a double marginalization. While their Blackness barred them from accessing the full civil benefits of society, their economic privilege also denied them, at times, acceptance by other Black Americans. Black student agitators experienced some success with disruptive campaigns, but they came at the cost of infuriating some whites and disillusioning other Blacks.[89] For Black faculty, becoming an activist or a mentor to student activists "was dangerous for any number of reasons."[90] As James Turner, the first director of Cornell's Africana Studies and Research Center, explained, "The Negro universities are controlled by conservative whites or by Negroes who think like them. Thus Harvard can readily come out for black studies but Howard can't. Yale can mount an Afro-American studies course but North Carolina A&T can't. Duke University can but Shaw University can't."[91] Indeed, most HBCUs still had all-white trustees directed by all-white legislatures, who preferred that their state institutions of higher learning remain segregated, to say nothing of instituting Black Power curriculums.[92]

In this context, Professor Myrna Bain—Black Panther activist, advocate for LGBTQ women of color, Black studies professor at CUNY, and unlikely voice in YAF's *New Guard* magazine early in her academic career—predicted that the violent campus response would soon lapse, as the overwhelming majority of Black Americans were completely unconnected to the "third world revolutionary *zeitgeist* of white and black SDS." Black Americans' goals were to join the middle class, afford suburban homes and cars, be hired in corporate occupations, and obtain "savings accounts, stocks and bonds and other manifestations of the 'decadent capitalist structure.'" As Bain explained, "When you have never had, you usually cannot afford the luxury beforehand of rejection."[93] For middle-class and elite Black students faced with the double marginalization of race and economic status, the call to choose between self-segregation and inclusion was difficult, as they faced being "shamed or shunned" by radical factions of the Black Power movement in addition to the Right's massive resistance.[94]

Legacy of Conservative Resistance

The Black Power student movement was ultimately successful in achieving several of its goals, including increasing nationwide Black student enrollment, accelerating Black faculty hiring, and diversifying curricula. The students' activism was largely victorious against counterweights hurled by white reactionaries. However, conservative resistance no doubt impeded the breadth of and pace at which progressive goals were attained, especially considering the power of its various sources: administrators, leading politicians, police, and anticommunist and overtly racist citizen constituents. These sources were informed by rhetoric from conservative movement leaders and their student protégés. Impediments generally took the form of broadscale campaigns to delegitimize Black and minority studies programs and to thwart student organizing. Conservative attempts to focus on student activists' methods over the merits of their causes effectively stymied support for educational justice initiatives, complicating and prolonging their realization.

Rallying around a shared resistance to Black justice was also energizing for the various white reactionaries who absorbed and amplified misinformation surrounding the civil rights movement. For the small but growing campus conservative movement, the caricature of the Black Power radical became yet another useful recruitment tool.

7 Mickey Mouse William Buckleys

. . . .

Since 1967, Young Americans for Freedom (YAF), the vanguard group for students on the activist right, had begun to build a model for organizing that maximized membership by reducing its mission to one simple principle: rebuking the Left. While the student Right never represented a campus majority, YAF leaders understood that appearing popular was important for disguising its minoritarian aims. Given this understanding and its obsession with appearing to represent a campus silent majority, it is a curiosity that in the summer of 1969, YAF would expel approximately a quarter of its members.

Traditionalism and libertarianism were (and continue to be) two major ideological strains within the Right. Traditionalists, the larger group of the two, stressed social conservatism, while libertarians were more concerned with promoting free-market economics. Libertarians' laissez-faire approach to certain cultural matters at times drew them ideologically nearer to the New Left—far closer than traditionalist hardliners were willing to tolerate. Traditionalists considered it objectionable that libertarians would partner with New Left groups when their goals aligned, such as at Pennsylvania State University, where YAF and Students for a Democratic Society (SDS) united to create an "underground railroad" to Canada for young men evading the draft.[1] Sometimes libertarian principles so thoroughly overlapped with the New Left's values that, as one former SDS member recalled, at Dartmouth College, the University of Kansas, and Furman University, the YAF president was also the SDS president.[2]

Since its founding in 1960, YAF had supported American intervention in Southeast Asia to thwart the expansion of communism. However, as the draft was instituted and the Vietnam War raged on without an apparent end, libertarians questioned the legitimacy of America's "imperialist invasion" into another nation's civil war.[3] The draft, which libertarians referred to as the "Selective Slavery System," became the litmus test for traditionalist and libertarian students, though there were other points of contention, including the propriety of burning American flags or draft cards and police brutality against demonstrators. Libertarians justified flag and draft card burning as an expression of free speech. To traditionalists, such actions equated to treason. Many libertarian students who had attended antiwar rallies experienced police brutality firsthand in the form of baton lashes and tear gas and were thus more antagonistic toward police. Traditionalists, always in support of social order, frequently defended and encouraged police officers' use of force against disruptive protesters as a legitimate way to restore that order.

Libertarians had other grievances with traditionalists who controlled YAF. Many felt the organization was not actually interested in student issues but instead existed to pander to "middle-aged businessmen who support law and order." They criticized YAF as "too old-fashioned to appeal to today's college students, too authoritarian and too aligned with elements of American society seeking to suppress civil liberties."[4] At the same time, traditionalist elders warned young libertarians that, fully expressed, their ideology would ultimately lead to anarchy. For some libertarians, however, intellectual anarchism was in fact the goal.

Sharp distinctions between the "lib" and "trad" factions within YAF became magnified as the decade waned, finally developing into a schism during the summer of 1969. In the context of these fundamental disputes, libertarians and anarchists assembled three separate caucuses in advance of the group's August national convention to voice frustration about their underrepresentation on YAF's traditionalist board. Penn State YAF, the nation's largest chapter, assembled a caucus of 300 libertarians under the direction of Don Ernsberger.[5] Within the libertarian sect were smaller splinter groups with approximately thirty to fifty members each. These included the Radical Libertarian Alliance (organized by mentors Murray Rothbard and Karl Hess III, a former speechwriter for Barry Goldwater) and the Anarcho-Libertarian Alliance (organized by Karl Hess IV, son of the elder Hess). When YAF executives became aware of the intention to disrupt the summer conference, they responded preemptively by revoking the charters of twenty-six libertarian-dominated YAF chapters in Pennsylvania and California, preventing members from attending the conference by invalidating their credentials.[6] In their judgement, libertarian contradictions to the group's dominant anti-left norms had metastasized into a threat serious enough to risk the movement's cohesion. For traditionalists in the process of perfecting their organizing techniques, adherence to orders from leadership superseded the need for longer club rosters.

The August 1969 YAF National Convention was held in St. Louis, Missouri, at the Stouffers Riverfront Inn. Predictably, the conference theme was

"Sock It to the Left." During the convocation, leaders announced a fall Freedom Offensive campaign designed to meet radicals with violence, bring lawsuits against university officials who did not react to campus rebellions with sufficient punishment, and abolish student fees that benefited clubs the Right considered "political" (meaning liberal).[7] Among the sea of white men and women students, only two Black faces dotted the crowd.[8] One of the two was Jay Parker, a Black traditionalist who had just been appointed the state chair of Pennsylvania to replace the ousted Penn State libertarian. An attendee who wished to remain anonymous recalled looking around the arena and easily identifying the square "trads" from the "libs" and "rads" (radical anarchists).

On the first night of the convention, some libertarian attendees declined to participate in the opening prayer and the Pledge of Allegiance. As headlining speaker William F. Buckley Jr. ascended to the microphone, a letter by anarchist mentor Murray Rothbard began circulating through the crowd, encouraging libertarians to defect from YAF and join forces with the New Left. If they abandoned their "false friends," Rothbard wrote, the "F" in YAF would "stand then for what it has secretly stood for all along—fascism."[9] Giving their standard refrain, YAF executives suggested that the letter was planted by radical "outsiders bent on destroying" the organization.[10] Indeed, they were radical, but they were not outsiders.

During his opening remarks, Buckley condemned Rothbard and the elder Hess, who were among the audience before him. Buckley, regarded as an almost divine mentor by the traditionalist majority, was met with boos from students representing California and Pennsylvania, who waved black flags and screamed "Fuck the draft!" "No more Vietnams!" and "I am an enemy of the state!" While most libertarian students remained until the end of the speech, a cadre of approximately fifty followed Rothbard and Hess out of the convocation after Buckley's scolding.[11]

Once the sessions began, libertarian and anarchist groups expressed frustration that the traditionalist majority appeared to have abandoned the group's dedication to freedom and liberty as defined in the Sharon Statement. In their preoccupation with "socking it to the Left," traditionalists were violating what were, in libertarians' estimation, their original commitments to free thought and debate. Traditionalists were likewise horrified when libertarians proposed support for the legalization of prostitution and drug use and an end to morality laws against homosexuality.[12]

At the heart of the various disputes was a disagreement over the concept of freedom. Libertarians applied a literal and universal meaning to the word. For traditionalists, freedom was simply a coded reference to their conception of Americanism. Freedom, then, was the opposite of communism: it meant an America first brand of protectionist capitalism and a nationalist approach to Christianity.

The factional disputes came to a head when traditionalists proposed a resolution to condemn draft resistance. University of Virginia law student Lee Houffman approached the microphone during the general session to declare that every citizen had a right to object to state violence. Donning a green army jacket, he lifted a photocopy of a draft card and touched the flame of a cigarette lighter to its corner, symbolically taking the torch of liberty, YAF's emblem, to the conscription notice.[13] Traditionalists responded by shouting in mockery at the draft-resisting "lazy fairies" (a play on the supreme libertarian tenet of laissez-faire). A fight soon broke out on the convention floor among college libs, trads, and rads, who pushed and shoved one another in the name of freedom.[14]

Late that night, the elder Hess delivered a speech under the Gateway Arch to a group of approximately 300 students, mostly libertarians and anarchists, and other scandalized onlookers. Hess urged libertarians to abandon YAF and align themselves with the more welcoming SDS. After midnight, hundreds of competing traditionalists, libertarians, and radical anarchists, incited by the contentious events of the day, marched around the Gateway Arch, burning the flags of both the United States and North Vietnam. One faction of the crowd cheered, "Ho, Ho, Ho Chi Mihn, B-52s are going to win!" as others retorted, "Sock it to the Left!"[15] In the early morning hours, libertarian and traditionalist students provoked one another from their hotel rooms, each calling for the execution of the other group's members.[16]

At the opening of the conference meeting the next morning, many of the remaining libertarian students were turned away over credential disputes. A new national board made up entirely of traditionalists was elected with support from 60 percent of the 723 delegates. The recently appointed Black representative from Pennsylvania, Jay Parker, took credit for arranging the traditionalist takeover. This new board resolved to adopt "a policy of active resistance to the efforts of radical groups to disrupt and destroy our nation's educational institutions" and endorsed lawsuits, court injunctions, and physical altercations as solutions.[17] None of the libertarian motions for marijuana legalization, withdrawal from Vietnam, or a revision to the Sharon Statement to include "domestic statism" as a threat to individual freedom were accepted. Executive board members also passed a resolution to revoke the membership of any YAFer who burned his draft card or sought dual membership with SDS. David Keene, the new national chair who warned of coming violent clashes between the Right and the Left (discussed in chapter 3), advised libertarians to commit unconditionally to one side.

After the conference, few libertarians remained in YAF, rendering it an almost entirely socially conservative student group as it entered the fall of 1969. Libertarian defectors began creating their own chapters at Temple University, Wesleyan University, and throughout California, Arizona, Pennsylvania, and New Jersey. Stanford University YAF rebranded themselves as the Free Campus Movement. The group was still conservative, but it was now anti-YAF and self-consciously using a majority coalition title. Others joined the Society for Individual Liberty (SIL), a libertarian-anarchist group that included members of SDS. In September 1969, SIL claimed an official membership of 2,500 after absorbing YAF turncoats. Within a year, the organization grew to over one hundred chapters, including international ones based in Australia, Canada, India, and Sweden.[18]

From their time in YAF, libertarians learned techniques of political organizing, event hosting, writing press releases, and creating student news and radio programs—all of which required considerable financial capital. YAF's traditionalist donors happily wrote checks to sponsor clean-cut, orderly squares, but they were unwilling to support marijuana-smoking draft card burners whose long hair rendered them indistinguishable from the New Left. Libertarians also had difficulty recruiting members to their cause, as efforts to form a mass coalition ran counter to the philosophy of individualism. Indeed, several members were unaffiliated with any actual campus chapters, and chapters that did exist often preferred to maintain autonomy from the national organization (a practice that was, ironically, encouraged). The national arm of SIL merely served as a conduit for exchanging ideas and sometimes made suggestions for national projects.[19]

As the new academic year approached, YAF's clubs became avowedly socially conservative. Now it was possible to retaliate against the Left without the influence of exiled libertarians, whose squishy politics they found insufferable. This represented an important point in the trajectory of conservative organizing. That YAF was willing to disaffiliate over two dozen chapters and expel hundreds of members—even with its strong commitment to gaining membership (or at least to its perception of itself as a youth silent majority)—puts into stark relief the fact that the leaders of the campus Right became increasingly puritanical and were willing to terminate dissenters within their own ranks who demonstrated sympathy for the peace or civil rights movements. As libertarians highlighted at the 1969 national convention, it had become clear that dedication to the cause of resisting the New Left superseded all other goals, including those outlined in YAF's own mission statement.

In some ways, the trad-lib breakup represents the general attitude of conservatism all along: to split between in-groups and out-groups and to build negative affinities in opposition to their "enemies" instead of building on their shared values. The split may have been inevitable under the logic that had brought the differing ideologies together through YAF in the first place. The timing of the fissure, the summer of 1969, is also more than coincidental, coming after the 1968 majority coalition surge and different student factions on the right coming together to back the Nixon candidacy that fall. These unions had always been a bit ideologically uneasy, as they were mandated by elders in attempt to minimize latent differences among the students whose true commonality was merely in being suspicious of nonwhites and liberals.

How to Be a Conservative

With libertarians purged from their ranks, the student Right had an iron-clad definition of campus conservatism: no overlap with or sympathy for the Left. But after three years of continually escalating campus demonstrations from the New Left, a George Washington University student complained in the campus newspaper of simultaneously having "to endure the spectacle of a group of Mickey Mouse William Buckleys speaking the loudest and carrying the biggest stick."[20] The observation was likely written in jest, but this student was describing—perhaps unknowingly—a deliberate phenomenon. Regarding technique and style, activist and partisan student affiliates of YAF, the College Republicans, and other conservative campus clubs closely followed prescribed guidelines from their national advisers, and none was more influential than Buckley. And while the two major groups, College Republicans and YAF, still retained their partisan and ideological roles, the actual differences mattered less post-1969, as both groups were dominated by student trads.

In its plans for the fall 1969 semester, YAF urged students to be "more missionary in nature" and "make greater attempts to romanticize our movement." Noting that New Left organizations had done a better job of messaging to their peers, columns in the *New Guard* explained, "SDS has been saying the *wrong* things in the *right* way, while we have been doing the opposite."[21] As part of this guidance, the student right's mentors continued to produce extremely detailed instruction manuals for the students in their charge to reference. These how-to handbooks, which were updated and reissued annually, made a science of churning out rubber-stamped college Buckleys. The manuals instructed students on club organizing, event programming, fundraising, newsletter crafting, recruitment, canvassing, and nearly every conceivable activity they needed to perform.

The College Republican organizing manual, issued by national chair Joseph Abate, is exemplary of the explicit guidance officials issued. It also exemplifies the national GOP's expectations that its subsidiaries be interconnected and mutually reinforcing. To form a College Republican club, interested members first needed to assemble a "core group" of six to ten insiders, no larger. They were then supposed to contact their local GOP office and the state Young Republican Federation to let them know which campus they should expect to find the new club operating at, join their mailing lists, and agree to provide help whenever summoned. Known Republican faculty members from political science departments made ideal sponsors; however, if they had trouble tracking down a faculty sponsor, they were to call the College Republican National Committee (CRNC) headquarters for the contact information of campus employees whose names appeared on GOP voter lists.[22]

College Republican leaders issued chapter quotas, challenging members to recruit 10 percent of their campus student bodies and ensure that all members were paying dues.[23] Careful attention was paid to appearances. Instructions for staffing membership booths were to "look sharp, have pretty girls, and some handsome guys."[24] Students placed sign-up notepads on their tables with a list of the current members already written in to give the impression that several people had just joined that day. Recruiters strategically placed their tables to block foot traffic. They did not waste time with Democrats and completely ignored radicals. Instructions were clear: "Do not spend five minutes arguing with a McGovern supporter. Fifty people could have walked by and one of them could have been David Eisenhower."[25]

Regular, well-attended chapter meetings were a must. College Republicans were to advertise their meetings and events widely, so that "everyone on campus" knew when and where they were being held. The meetings were supposed to be lively. Core group members were advised to stick to their scripts and keep discussions interesting and well-paced. At the end of every meeting, core members were to discuss which practices worked and which did not, decide what to continue or improve on, and share their good or cautionary examples with other chapters.[26]

One advantage of well-advertised and well-attended meetings and projects, Abate noted, was that they squashed any rumors (from YAF) that the College Republicans were a do-nothing group. CRNC executive director Morton Blackwell called such a "misimpression" the "greatest threat a CR group faces."[27] So as not to seem "stodgy," student squares carefully curated their social calendars, hoping to make group events seem fun and engaging. Directors urged members to go camping together, take trips to the beach, and organize events such as dances, cocktail parties, and dinners.[28] Blackwell encouraged them to hold their meetings at venues where young people were guaranteed to be present, including beer and pizza dives.[29] When clubs were having a hard time getting members to show up, they hosted meetings at midnight, offered refreshments and fifty-cent mixed drinks, and "put out a tremendous hoopla about it on campus." This was an especially good tactic for ensuring quorums during business meetings.[30]

Aside from midnight mixers, College Republican clubs focused heavily on inviting speakers to campus. These were highly curated events. Speakers usually included GOP politicians, columnists, businesspeople, and "academicians" interested in appearing before college audiences. But College Republican chapters often lacked the funding advantages of groups like the Intercollegiate Studies Institute (ISI) or YAF, which did not have as much competition for donors. College Republicans were seeking funds from patrons equally likely to support their local Young Republicans chapter, individual GOP candidates, and the state and national Republican Party. CRNC leaders thus cautioned their chapters against turning to speakers' bureaus to find headlining guests—they simply could not afford them. They were better off finding local people, those "extremely happy" to do the "favor" of speaking on campus—alumni, parents, or trustees, for example. Alternatively, they could partner with YAF, ISI, or the student government, provided their chapter was not footing the bill. College Republicans' contribution to the cosponsorship of such events usually involved taking care of "publicity and arrangements." They could also contribute by leaning on their connections to the larger Republican Party to secure secondment letters needed to entice speakers expecting "first-class treatment."[31]

When well-known speakers agreed to address College Republican events, the students booked the speaker's flight, picked them up with a convoy of officers (and select "freshmen and sophomores with leadership potential") at the airport, and delivered them to a desirable hotel, such as a St. Regis. The students designed full itineraries for their guests, which included lunches and dinners at university clubs with faculty from the political science and economics departments, exclusive interview tapings for the campus radio station, guest lectures in undergraduate government courses, photography sessions, and cocktail receptions.[32]

Blackwell's "only rule" for students when choosing venues for their events was that "the room *must* be too small. . . . First make a realistic, hard-nosed conservative count of exactly how many people you expect to come to the event. Do *not* be optimistic. Then reduce this number by 20% and plan for a room that will hold that number of people." A packed room created excitement. After all, "a crowd of 75 in a room that holds 65 will *seem* larger than a crowd of 150 in an auditorium that seats 600." Students needed to consider potential headlines that might follow their events. Did they want coverage that read "Sparse Turnout for Campus GOP" or "Republican Speaks to Overflow Crowd"?[33]

Removing chairs was a good way to create the appearance of overflow attendance. Crowds were drawn more easily if the event was marketed as "controversial" or a "social necessity." To boost turnout, Blackwell directed students to ask faculty in the communications, political science, and economics departments to make attendance mandatory for certain events, suggesting that professors could then have students critique the speaker during the next class.[34] Leaflets, posters, and other advertisements needed to reach "200% coverage," such that anyone walking through campus would see event advertisements at least twice. Potential attendees should see posters on doors and in the restrooms and hear about the event on campus radio.[35]

The events themselves were as over the top as the advertising. Students used flashbulbs to "create an element of urgency and drama" during the speaker's arrival and departure. College Republican ushers oversaw seating and were "on the lookout . . . for hostile elements" of leftists entering the room. Blackwell suggested that "our people" arrive in advance and take seats throughout to prevent "the formation of solid knots of hecklers and dampen their group spirit." At least four College Republicans would be seated in a "diamond arrangement" in the crowd—one each in the front row, the back row, the far right, and the far left—to clap during pauses and to gin up excitement in their section.[36] A local minister opened with a benediction, followed by the Pledge of Allegiance and an exciting introduction of the speaker. Students planned questions for the end of the speech and provided them to the speaker in advance. During the question-and-answer session, a College Republican member selected questions from friendly audience members to take the pressure off the speaker.[37]

The Famous Foolproof Fundraising Formula

Since multiple events required considerable investment, CRNC chair Rob Polack instructed College Republican chapters to fundraise heavily. The metric was that chapters on a campus of 700 students needed a budget of seventy-five cents per student, campuses of 2,000 students needed a budget of fifty cents per student, and campuses with over 8,000 students needed a budget of thirty cents per student. For example, College Republicans at Louisiana State University, a particularly active chapter, needed to raise $3,500 (approximately $30,000 in 2023) to reflect the school's 12,000 enrolled students.[38] Executives used Brown University College Republicans' 1970 budget of $2,000 as an example in national fundraising memos.[39]

Polack advised members to budget for foreseeable expenses, such as speakers' travel and hotel costs, an official club post office box, rental fees for event spaces, and sundry "buttons, balloons and baloney." Funds were especially important for hosting social functions, such as "a hay ride, dance, bar-b-que . . . swimming parties, etc." Money also needed to be available to send representatives to Republican training sessions, including the one representative required to be present at the National Young Republican Leadership Training School each year. Every chapter also needed to furnish its own subscription costs to *National Review, Human Events,* and other conservative opinion journals.[40] Of course, if any College Republican member would have written to these magazines, they no doubt would have received a complementary subscription. Whether Polack knew of this arrangement is unclear but unlikely. Students in ISI and YAF received free magazines and books, which they resold to raise funds, and those students were often members of or worked closely alongside College Republicans.

To raise funds, College Republicans collected dues, raffled off signed copies of Goldwater's *Conscience of a Conservative* (with instructions to "have a cute co-ed draw the winning numbers"), hosted joint casino nights ("where the law permits"), and held carnivals and car washes.[41] Some clubs fundraised by borrowing and screening "really unusual" movies from the campus film club and charging a nickel for beer.[42] Chapters hosted showings of *Animal Farm* (1954) and Ronald Reagan and Robert Kennedy's 1967 CBS debate on Vietnam. Some chapters ran an Ugliest Man on Campus contest, in which dollars and coins counted as votes. Members were cautioned that "Democrats may try to needle us by voting for prominent Republicans, but we can laugh all the way to the bank."[43]

These events attracted good participation and helped raise cash, but the biggest donations were garnered following Polack's Famous Foolproof Fundraising Formula. According to the plan, each student would solicit money from two or three Republicans or conservatives they had connections to in their community. To secure the donation, members would schedule a home visit. "Arrive on time, dress neatly. Take an articulate team of two, preferably a boy and a girl," they were advised. After exchanging pleasantries, members were to shift the conversation to problems with "hostile" faculty, the "militant left wing," or the liberal university newspaper. Then they would hand over their annual budget, explaining to the homeowner that it represented the amount "necessary to adequately represent the Republican Party" on campus for a year. The last step of the plan was crucial to securing the donation: "When you are sure that they understand every item on your budget, then say the simple sentence, '*We were hoping that you would be able to help us financially to meet this budget.*' The wording of this sentence is very important. It has been developed through trial and error over several years. Among its many assets, you will note that this sentence does not end in a question mark. . . . Pause and remain silent."[44]

Assuredly, the homeowner would respond by asking for a desired contribution amount. If the homeowner were known as a person of means, such as "a prosperous farmer, a physician, an attorney, an oilman," or the like, students should ask for a hundred dollars (about $900 in 2023). Polack guaranteed that such an ask was not "audacious" but expected, and that the donor would be "flattered." Even middle-class professionals, such as a college professor, should be asked to contribute fifty dollars. Finally, members should not leave without referral contacts of the homeowner's golf buddies, Kiwanis friends, and other business associates. The students should not be shy to ask the homeowner to make introductory phone calls on their behalf, either. After receiving the donation, students were to mail a thank-you letter and assure the patron of their open invitation to club events and meetings.[45]

Mobilizing White Athletes

Though YAF purged its libertarians in 1969, the group was still interested in its own campus popularity. While it could not always count on a steady supply of active new members throughout the year, it did at least seek non-member participation in its counter events. Athletes, especially, were a key constituency of the Right's support among other students.

Some antiwar demonstrators equated the violence of contact sports with the Vietnam War. Owing to this dynamic, conservatives—particularly those at schools with large football programs, such as the University of Southern California (USC)—taunted progressives through overt patronage of the game. At USC in the fall of 1969, "where the SAE [fraternity] house makes more news than the SDS chapter," YAF alumnus Bill Saracino recalled that "the SDS at USC were openly talking about needing to get rid of the football program. That was like saying Duke [University] has to get rid of basketball today. They couldn't have picked a better issue to show what idiots they were."[46]

In dramatizing some leftist students' objections to popular contact sports, the student Right attracted crowd participation from those who cared less about politics than college athletics. For example, USC YAF was able to draw participation from fraternities, sororities, the yell squad, and dormitory friends to collaborate on a pro-administration pep rally featuring assistant coach Marv Goux and several football players. YAF riled up the audience with the school's football anthem, "Conquest," while Goux spoke about the football program's ability to bring unity to students, alumni, and community fans.[47]

For all the ways athletic violence could be used to bring white campus constituencies together, it could also be used to flaunt white supremacy at southern institutions. Southern football fans waved rebel flags at games, while the marching bands played "Dixie" during halftime performances. Mascots, such as the University of Mississippi's Colonel Reb, literally "personified the Confederacy."[48] The University of Mississippi's nickname, Ole Miss, is a reference to the moniker enslaved people gave to the wife of a plantation master. The nickname itself is traced to the college's football program, in which, as J. Hardin Hobson explains, "the men from UM took the field against their football foes . . . under a name and to chants and cheers from students that referenced the Old South and its plantation slavery system."[49]

In this way, southern football fans used the game to glorify the false Lost Cause interpretation of the Civil War, as well as to antagonize liberals and promote contemporary right-wing goals. For example, University of Alabama football fans accused sports pollsters of "playing politics" prior to a match against the University of Notre Dame. At that point in the 1966

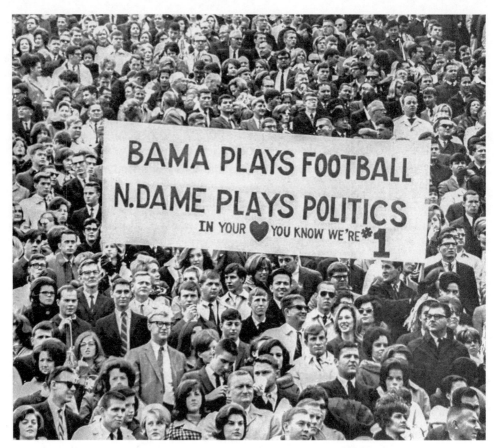

Students at the 1966 University of Alabama vs. University of Notre Dame football game. *Corolla 1967*, vol. 75, p. 229, University of Alabama Libraries Special Collections.

season, three teams—Alabama, Notre Dame, and Michigan State University—were all undefeated. In light of the numerical tie, sports analysts ranked Alabama's team in third place. The apparent reason for the lower ranking was to make a statement opposing the institution's failure to integrate.[50] A banner in the crowd proclaimed, "In your [heart] you know we're #1"—a message adapted from the 1964 presidential campaign slogan of Barry Goldwater: "In your heart, you know he's right."

The "Phony Grape Strike"

Beyond overt support for campus contact sports, conservative students found other ways to provoke their adversaries, such as counterprotesting organized labor. Conservatives in YAF, especially, disapproved of campus-based campaigns in support of the Delano grape strike by California's Filipino and Mexican farm laborers and their leaders, Dolores Huerta and Cesar Chavez. YAF had long been against labor union organizing and opposed to labor-protective legislation, such as the Wagner Act of 1935 and the Taft-Hartley Act of 1947 (though this did not stop the group from leading its own boycotts of private businesses, such as IBM and Firestone Tire, as discussed in chapter 3). Toward the end of the decade, the University of Wisconsin YAF appeared before the Wisconsin state legislature requesting that it refuse to repeal Section 14(b) of the Taft-Hartley Act, commonly referred to as the Right to Work clause. According to the students, repealing the anti-labor clause would be a "monstrous folly bordering on insanity." YAFers expressed that recent union history revealed that the leaders of these organizations ranged "from incompetents to gangsters to communists."[51]

To the outrage of capitalist college youth, clubs of pro-labor students from Stanford and the University of California lobbied their cafeterias to join the boycott by refusing to serve grapes, lettuce, onions, and other produce.[52] Saracino recalled his own opposition to the farmworker leadership: "We were very much in sympathy with the growers . . . [because] the Chavez folks were engaging in terrorism. They were going into the orchards at night and chainsawing hundreds of these massive fruit-bearing trees down at an enormous loss to the growers."[53]

As with their position against the antiwar movement, conservatives justified their opposition to the United Farm Workers (UFW) by pointing to failures of labor leadership and bad actors rather than honestly engaging with the core issues, such as Mexican and Filipino Americans' inhumane working conditions and poverty wages. Conservatives instead reflexively balked at the financial losses of business operators. Duke University YAF characterized the UFW's activities as illegitimate, calling their protest a "phony grape strike."[54] To bolster their opposition, conservatives sought out Latino workers or other labor leaders who would give credence to their reductionist anti-labor rhetoric. For example, Boston College YAF hosted a speech by Jose Mendoza, general secretary of an anti–AFL-CIO group known as the Agricultural Workers Freedom to Work Association, who denounced Chavez and the UFW.[55]

This is yet another area in which students used humor to belittle their opposition (discussed in chapter 3). YAFers facetiously served table grapes at meetings and passed out lettuce and other produce at their counter-protests. During a visit by Mark Rudd of Columbia SDS to the Rutgers

University–Newark campus, YAF organized a demonstration with posters that read: "Rudd Borrows from Low Library," "Rid Rutgers of Rudd," and "Rudd Eats Grapes."[56] At Southwestern College in Winfield, Kansas, College Republicans held a Forbidden Fruit Party on Valentine's Day in 1969 featuring California grapes. According to a student event planner, the hope was for attendees "to get smashed."[57]

At a Rutgers YAF and Veterans of Foreign Wars "grape-in," white members taunted a Black couple, there in support of the farmworkers, by offering grapes and raisin cookies. Conservatives in attendance took the stance that the farm laborers were probably well paid and well treated and that the strike actually infringed on the rights of customers to buy farm products. According to one attendee, "This wasn't an industry being struck by its employes [sic] but people looking for political gain coming from outside to organize a strike."[58] This statement echoed the common conservative suspicion that actual workforce injustices were being fabricated by foreign infiltrators—the same claim used to dismiss goals of the peace and civil rights movements. The assertion that the most powerful (employers) were being persecuted by the least powerful (farm laborers) was another complaint of those on the right, who disapproved of challenges to their preferred arrangement of "ordered" (ranked) "liberty" (anticommunism).

Significance of the Libertarian Purge

The 1969 schism between traditionalist conservatives and libertarians was not the first breakup of student groups on the right. The previous summer, traditionalists and libertarians alike, under the leadership of movement elders, had appeared to distance themselves from conspiracists and white nationalists during the 1968 presidential campaign (discussed in chapter 5). This was at the direction of *National Review* writers, whose own purges were in constant motion as they continually refined the parameters of responsible conservatism. *National Review* staff stopped publishing writers it considered too liberal, such as Peter Viereck and Clinton Rossiter, or too radical, such as Ayn Rand.[59] But the breakup of traditionalists and libertarians during the summer of 1969 was much more significant, as the libertarian wing represented a sizable portion of the Right's student movement. The schism makes clear just how strong the traditionalist commitment to resisting the Left was.

Of course, the ideological schism was not permanent, as libertarians and traditionalist conservatives have claimed over the last several decades. The schism does not even appear to have been complete even in the immediate, as traditionalists continued to use libertarian justifications to their desired ends (such as libertarian arguments against conscription, discussed in chapter 8). The purge, then, was of members who refused to behave obsequiously in response to executives' orders rather than of libertarian philosophy wholesale.

Throughout the 1970s, libertarians and anarchists appeared to chart a distinct path by creating the Libertarian Party (whose platform explicitly stated, "We condemn bigotry as irrational and repugnant"), but the party has never experienced real political success.[60] Instead, the libertarian triumph has been in mainstreaming and protecting capitalism in almost every arena of American thought and governance—to the benefit of traditionalist conservatives, whose desired ends are achieved through libertarians' neoliberal policies. The relationship continues symbiotically. While the New Right trads of the 1970s remained divorced in appearance from their former libertarian classmates, they nonetheless continued to accept generous funds from libertarian investors interested in traditionalist causes, including Charles Koch and Richard Scaife. Libertarian intellectualism—the kind promoted by economists like Friedrich Hayek and Milton Friedman—gave traditionalists the scholarly language they needed to justify the hierarchical, or "ordered," society of their visions, especially in matters of race and class.

Tell It to Hanoi

· ·

By the fall of 1969, college conservatives reached the apex of their organizational abilities as Young Americans for Freedom (YAF) transformed the student Right from a constellation of disconnected and aggrieved individuals and clubs into a distinctly traditionalist and far-reaching national organization opposed to the student Left. Having developed skills for mobilization over the previous two academic years, the upcoming 1969–70 school year would provide traditionalist students with seemingly endless opportunities to defend their position against increasingly incendiary antiwar and Black Power demonstrations.

Freedom Offensive

That semester, YAF launched its Freedom Offensive campaign to train current members, "sway the uncommitted," and "attract attention in the news media and gain public support for YAF principles and programs."[1] Specifically, the Freedom Offensive represented a coordinated national strategy to designate a handful of successful anti–New Left efforts by individual chapters and apply them nationwide. The strategy encouraged students to pursue legal action against universities under strike or occupation; promote "balanced" ideas on campuses by recruiting conservative speakers, hiring conservative faculty, challenging leftist professors and graduate assistants in the classroom, and amplifying conservative arguments in campus debates; replace progressive and moderate student government representatives with conservatives; refuse to pay fees that supported what they deemed to be "political" (leftist) causes; and continue to spread conservative messages through theatrical demonstrations and alternative campus newspapers and radio programs.[2]

With resistance to progressivism as its foremost aim, the Freedom Offensive expanded its initiatives off campus to reach an even younger youth audience: schoolchildren. YAF called for creating mandatory K–12 school courses on the differences between Americanism and communism. This idea had already taken hold in Virginia, where future Supreme Court justice Lewis F. Powell Jr., then the chair of the board of education, added a citizenship course to the K–12 curriculum in response to civil rights protests.[3] The organization assembled an action kit with step-by-step instructions on how to promote such a law, which included examples of successful state bills from Alabama, Florida, and Louisiana. The kit offered several different templates for bills for other groups (including YAF's own auxiliaries) to propose simultaneously before legislators. Receiving multiple similar bills would give legislators the impression of widespread support and increase the likelihood that at least one, perhaps considered the strongest, would pass, as opposed to a single bill being rejected outright. The kits included a petition to garner signatures of support, press releases, speeches, and a chart with legislative sessions outlined by state. A teacher-training kit was also included, along with a comprehensive bibliography and an order form for additional resources. YAF's national office pledged to pay the travel costs of prominent speakers so that they could appear before state houses to introduce the bills.[4]

A few remarkably ambitious YAF students ran for their state's higher education boards. Alan Brandstatter of the University of Southern California (USC) campaigned for one such trustee vacancy with promises to legislate "expelling, prosecuting and jailing lawbreakers" involved in campus demonstrations, replacing humanities and liberal arts courses with vocational and trade courses in California's junior colleges, and reversing the policy "of increasing taxes to meet expansion, to one of decreasing unnecessary expansion to meet tax revenue."[5]

Conservatives behind the Freedom Offensive also drew campus audiences through controversial events, such as grape-ins, mock trials, and burnings of North Vietnamese flags and effigies of peace activists. Overly theatrical debates between political clubs were excellent attention-grabbers on campus and in local media. During a typical debate—such as one that featured USC YAF and Young Republicans against representatives of the Vietnam Moratorium Committee (VMC) before an audience of one hundred—conservative students argued for "peace through strength" and "peace with honor," which entailed free elections and self-determination for the people of South Vietnam. The VMC retorted with the chicken hawk question: If conservatives were so committed to victory over communism, why weren't they enlisted?

It was a fair question, fraught with moral, classist, and racial implications. Privileged conservatives rallied for the war cause from the safety and comfort of their classrooms, thousands of miles removed from the battleground of Vietnam, where less educated, less wealthy, and less white servicemembers risked life and limb. The usual retort involved pointing to the veteran students among their club rosters and expressing some variation of the idea that "[we] expected to take our chances with the draft after graduation." A USC YAF alumnus reflected that the chicken hawk argument was a manipulative appeal to emotion: "You don't have to sit behind a machine gun to know that Communist aggression is a bad thing. . . . There are many names engraved on the Vietnam Memorial of individuals who got four years of deferments and ended up in Vietnam in the line of fire." Using this defensive reasoning, students on the right justified their temporary evasion of service. They were further incensed that peace activists described their own campus-building occupations and skirmishes with police as "war."

At the University of Wisconsin, one such debate, a forty-five-minute "verbal confrontation" between YAF and Students for a Democratic Society (SDS), drew a crowd of 150.[6] Often the excitement of such a large crowd could be ginned up by reciting popular revolutionary phrases. According to an Intercollegiate Studies Institute (ISI) alumnus who represented the Student Committee for Victory in Vietnam, debate victories were easily won through counterarguments and a familiarity with revolutionary claims: "In more than 100 debates, lectures, and teach-ins on the war, I never once left thinking I had been defeated. But the reason was that I had done my homework in preparing my 450-page honors thesis, including reading all four volumes of Ho [Chi Minh]'s selected works and everything else I could find written by the North Vietnamese. . . . My real strength was an understanding that superiority of knowledge makes a difference." This "superiority of knowledge" was, of course, something conservative movement advisers explicitly sought to provide students through ISI literature and seminars.

Supporting the War, Opposing the Draft

A final platform of the Freedom Offensive was, ironically, a draft opposition campaign. Despite sharing this goal with the New Left, YAF still demonstrated unwavering commitment to the war; it merely opposed the idea of a draft. YAF preferred an all-volunteer army, believing this was justified by the principle of freedom in the Sharon Statement. Arguing that conscription was "wasteful, economically inefficient, and a misallocation of resources," YAF members were encouraged to reach out to their politically uncommitted peers affected by the draft and segue into "the principles of volunteerism and the free market." Using a distinctly libertarian frame, traditionalist YAF leaders suggested that the New Left was not truly anti-draft but pro-communism. "These hypocrites oppose the draft only because they oppose the Vietnam War," executive Alan MacKay insisted, "and not because they oppose coercion. In fact, some of them would draft Americans to fight wars in South Africa and other places, wars which they regard as 'good' wars."[7]

For two dollars, students could purchase their own Voluntary Military Legislative Action Kit, which included a compilation of YAF literature in support of a volunteer military, a list of rhetorical responses to common "clichés of conscription," a recruitment poster in an anti-draft theme, and YAF's signature press and news releases. Members were encouraged to create their own campus posters to generate interest in anti-draft teach-ins, gather signatures to present to Congress, invite anti-draft speakers to campus, run full-page ads outlining reasons for an all-voluntary military ("Always include a YAF membership application"), and appear on radio or television news with statements prepared by the national office.[8]

Traditionalists among YAF's leadership had only weeks earlier expelled most of the libertarian chapters and hundreds of members for their anti-war (and other countercultural) attitudes, but by the fall of 1969, the group was still employing libertarian arguments against the draft when they suited the circumstance. For example, a University of Arkansas YAFer accused draft dodgers of engaging in "childish temper tantrums that will only invite repression." A self-described capitalist, the student argued that the only way to force a policy of military volunteerism was "to make men as expensive to [Uncle Sam] as they are to General Motors—and men's families." He elaborated, "Conscription is actually a tax-in-kind on the service of the draftee. I am worth $7,500 a year to a private employer, but Uncle Sam offers only $2,100—I will be taxed $5,400 per year." After referring to conscription as a violation of "slavery" per the Thirteenth Amendment, the white student's final point was an appeal to racial discrimination: "Blacks are often discriminated against by local boards comprised of whites—and perhaps the opposite."[9] But there were no majority Black draft boards. The student's libertarian romanticism highlights the factual gulf between conservative ideologues and reality as it pertained to the war and civil rights.

Still borrowing ideas from exiled libertarians, YAF called for a reinstatement of the draft bounty system. Last used during the American Civil War, the system would entice potential soldiers by paying them a bounty, which could be fundraised by community members, those opposed to the war, or parents unwilling to lose their own sons—"the market system in action."

Thus, the draft bounty would allow those with the most affluence or fund-raising connections to evade the war and remain at home, strengthening American capitalism.[10] The Right's plea to apply the "market system" conveyed a belief that people's lives should be up for bidding. It is unclear if YAF students understood the irony of their argument, as the existing student exemption already achieved this outcome. Young men who could afford college *were* effectively paying for deferment.

Others on the right continued the curious practice of provoking the peace movement's anti-drafters while arguing against conscription themselves. The Resistance, an anti-draft group of the peace movement, rallied young people to observe a National Draft Resistance Day in which male students disavowed their war obligations. Some burned their conscription cards, while others turned them over to local draft-resistance organizations, which were often headed by Catholic groups.[11] (Destroying one's draft card risked a penalty of up to five years in prison and a $10,000 fine, worth more than $80,000 in 2023.[12]) Conservatives attempted to create spectacles out of draft card turn-in events, sometimes escalating their counteractions to violence. At USC's draft card turn-in, fraternity men physically ejected peaceful organizers, who were forced to retreat off campus to a nearby church. At a University of Iowa draft card turn-in, about 125 spectators arrived to witness the impending spectacle, though no one actually submitted his draft card.[13]

Meanwhile, college conservatives at the University of Colorado, the University of Dayton, Southern Illinois University, and other schools touted their efforts to support American soldiers abroad. Their clubs held Christmas drives to collect books, gifts, videotaped messages from families, American flag pins, and anti-leftist blue buttons to ship to troops overseas or to local veterans' hospitals.[14] During the holiday season, a chapter of USC's Young Republicans mailed 500 tins of cookies and 366 woolen blankets, pairs of socks, and crutch pad covers knitted by members to wounded soldiers.[15] In this way, conservatives continued to frame their pro-war efforts as patriotic while condemning those who objected to the war and compulsory enlistment, despite being themselves opposed to the latter.

Defending Campus ROTC

The topic of the Vietnam War, which directly affected every American family with an adult male, was ideal for recruitment. This is where conservative groups realized they could attract the most authentic interest and accelerate new participation. Students on the right argued for intervention in Vietnam and against the peace movement by appealing to Cold War fears about a global communist takeover. Violence committed by a limited number of radicals was tactically attributed to the entire peace movement, which they described as anti-American. The FBI recorded 80 bombings and cases of arson directed at ROTC buildings and draft centers during the fall 1969 semester, which helped make the conservative case that antiwar activists were treasonous anarchists abetting a communist victory.[16] With no end in sight to the bombings at or near university research and recruitment centers, Nixon called for 1,000 additional FBI agents to investigate campus radicals.[17]

The student Right continued to resist the New Left using majority coalition techniques they had begun to perfect over the previous year. At Harvard, SDS led 300 students in occupying the University Hall administration building. Conservatives quickly assembled "sanitation committees" to erase occupiers' graffiti, burn effigies of SDS members, and hold signs demanding that "SDS Get Out." Students fervently passed out "Keep Harvard Open" ribbons and leaflets stating, "Take a trip, not a building" and "We favor administration takeover of Administration Building."[18] Police were summoned to end the building takeover, injuring 45 students and placing 185 under arrest. In response, thousands more students and faculty declared a campus-wide strike.[19]

In defense of the war and to spite activists, conservative students pledged their support for one of the Left's main targets, campus ROTC programs. Harvard professor of military science Colonel Robert H. Pell defended the programs as necessary to produce an educated military leadership. In a justification rooted in classism, Pell highlighted the fact that the ROTC attracted less than 5 percent of college men nationally:

> Yet out of this five percent comes 10 percent of our Congressmen,
> 15 percent of our ambassadors, 24 percent of our state governors,
> and 28 percent of business leaders earning over $100,000 per
> year. . . . Disturbing must be the knowledge that there are brilliant
> young Harvard men with God-given leadership abilities who seem
> content to waste two years of their life by allowing themselves to be
> drafted as a private. . . . An OCS program catering to high school
> graduates and college dropouts as a primary source of junior
> officers for the Army Officer Corps is unthinkable. The armed forces
> simply cannot function—nor should they be expected to function

Pro-administration students burning an effigy of SDS in counterprotest at Harvard University, Cambridge, Massachusetts, April 22, 1969. AP Photo.

in our complex society—without an officer corps comprised largely of college graduates just as most of our national institutions these days rely upon college educated men for their leadership. Who is prepared to trust their sons—let alone the nation's destiny—to the leadership of high school boys and college dropouts?[20]

In response to the antiwar declaration that a program that teaches killing has no place in a university, conservatives publicized the hypocrisy of radicals who condemned the ROTC for cultivating violence while detonating explosives and starting fires for peace.[21] Even though the buildings that leftist groups typically bombed were empty (and demonstration planners often called in evacuation warnings in advance), conservatives seized on the events without noting context, intent, or any other details that conflicted with the point they were trying to make: that leftists were nihilist criminals out to destroy the campus and the nation. These students argued that ROTC programs satisfied university missions by helping students advance their careers as officers and by boosting the defense capabilities of communities, municipalities, and states.[22] Some defended a military presence on campus as important to "avoid infringing on individual freedom" and "academic freedom."[23]

Other students, such as those in the Society for the Preservation of the American Republic (SPAR) at the University of Minnesota, were less intellectually defensive and more antagonistic. SPAR mocked antiwar demonstrators who were occupying the campus armory by theatrically marching around the building seven times and blowing trumpets in a satirical reference to the biblical Jericho wall. SPAR's signs read: "If the Walls Don't Fall, God Is on Our Side."[24]

Duke University YAF, tasked with reeducating their peers on the war (and implicitly on civil rights), promised an end to "liberal propaganda in the classrooms disguised as an education" and an end to "campus blackmail in [the] form of demands and building seizures"—a reference to the February 1969 Allen Building takeover led by the Afro-American Society.[25] YAF's official support of the ROTC was outlined in a front-page editorial in Duke's *Carolina Renaissance* in September 1969: "[ROTC] will be the nucleus of any plan to replace the draft with a volunteer army. We support ROTC because only it can provide the balanced, tolerant, and flexible military leaders our country needs today. Without ROTC, our military leadership would be the product solely of military schools, camps, and training centers. We support ROTC because it decreases militarism on campus. While radical organizations glorify and glamorize revolution and talk of the excitement of terror and sabotage, ROTC cadets learn the ugly reality of war and understand the capabilities of weapons and their ability to kill, burn, and cripple."[26]

Students at nearby North Carolina State University echoed the pro-ROTC chorus with pragmatism, declaring that "guys join ROTC not to be killers; they want the scholarship money, or they think that if they have to go [to war], being an officer is better than being a GI."[27] For this reason, YAF alumna Tricia Thackston-Ganner of the University of South Carolina spoke at the chapel of the Citadel, the Military College of South Carolina: "I talked about how military service was a positive thing, and we honored that and felt differently about the war than most." She was aware that all the students who graduated from the Citadel would be called to Vietnam as officers and felt compelled to demonstrate her deep support for them.[28]

ISI alumnus Steve Ealy of Furman University in Greenville, South Carolina, recalled that "there were campus protests, but never violent or physically directed at ROTC staff. They never had to dress in civilian clothes and change into their uniforms the way they did at some Ivy League schools." Ealy joined the ROTC despite his personal objections to the war. He explained:

> Every male student had to take the first two years at ROTC regardless of major. . . . I was a scholarship cadet, so I was committed to all four years. . . . I was watching the news in the late Sixties, and units in Vietnam were refusing to follow their platoon leaders' orders. Guys just like me, just out of college, six weeks of training, didn't know anything. I said to myself, if I was a private in a squad led by me as a lieutenant, I'd probably refuse to follow me, too. I don't know enough to keep these guys alive. There were those types of tensions. I thought about refusing my commission, but didn't because that would have killed my dad. I accepted, but by the time I graduated I was not a fan of the war. I knew enough about a policy that says, "We're good guys, they're bad guys, we want to get everyone on our side, no matter how thuggish we are." I was not happy with the policy that we pursued in Vietnam.[29]

Ealy represents a portion of conservative students who were more critical of American foreign policy as it related to the war. But for him and others, military service was ultimately a duty to country—and for Ealy in particular, both a family obligation and a payment owed for education provided—no matter how much they disliked it.

YAF, Administrators, and the Courts

A continuous drumbeat of antiwar violence throughout the fall of 1969 was helpful for conservatives to leverage in their messaging. YAF claimed that radicals were transferring guns and other weapons to campus concealed under large coats. Pointing to this as justification, YAF leaders urged students to take "physical action" to end sit-ins by "clear[ing] the buildings" and exerting their own "show of force to stop the vigilantes on the left."[30] There was no need to worry about the consequences of using aggression against other students, as YAF had set up a fund for students who might be injured or arrested while physically combating peace demonstrators.[31] YAF leaders Alan MacKay and J. Lawrence McCarthy, both attorneys, also offered free legal assistance.[32] However, there were already numerous precedents showing that administrators and police exerted force against leftist demonstrators rather than right-wing counterdemonstrators, making these guarantees for legal defense essentially symbolic. If a YAF or other counterdemonstrating student were ever actually arrested or otherwise accessed these legal defense funds, that incident would have been widely publicized by the organization. No such instances appear in the *New Guard* or other YAF records.

The largest New Left event in the fall of 1969—Vietnam Moratorium Day, organized by the National Mobilization Committee to End the War in Vietnam (the Mobe)—involved massive nationwide antiwar demonstrations on college campuses and in other public spaces on October 15. Students at over 600 colleges skipped classes in what became the nation's largest student strike to date.[33] Over 100,000 students, professors, and others participated in Vietnam Moratorium Day marches, rallies, fasts, vigils, and memorial services for the dead. Professors Howard Zinn, J. K. Galbraith, George Wald, and others spoke at the gatherings for peace.[34]

In anticipation of the event, YAF members converged across fifty-seven cities to launch a legal offensive against "militant students or spineless administrators."[35] The plan targeted thirty-two campuses believed to be the most likely to host Moratorium Day strikes, including Boston, Columbia, Dartmouth, Duke, Fordham, Georgetown, Harvard, Michigan State, Northwestern, Princeton, Rutgers, Stanford, and Tulane Universities, and nearly a dozen other state institutions.[36] Telegrams threatening lawsuits were issued directly to presidents or trustees at Adelphi, George Washington, Ohio State, Temple, and Wayne State Universities, as well as at the University of Houston, the University of Wisconsin, and Monmouth College.[37]

YAF's preemptive guide, *Legal Responses to Campus Disorder*, outlined steps that students should take as they threatened lawsuits against their administrators, trustees, and peers in advance of any strike. YAF's Don Federer urged students to push the following points: that sit-in demonstrators should be arrested for trespassing and prosecuted "to the fullest extent of the law," and that demonstrators who commit acts of violence should be "immediately expelled and never readmitted" and "unilaterally banned from using the campus and from using college facilities thereafter." Federer argued that state and private colleges "unquestionably have a legal obligation to remain open" because of the federal grants the institutions and their students receive.[38] Leaders of the organization also advised students to immediately report the appearance of out-of-state demonstrators to the Justice Department and the local FBI, which could enforce interstate anti-riot laws.[39]

This fusillade of anticipatory counteractions signaled an important advance in the course of the Right's campus activism. No longer was conservative mobilization solely reactive; rather, it had now begun to take preemptive measures, leveraging threats against institutional authorities to prevent New Left demonstrators from even attempting to strike. The intent was to force administrators to choose between the peace movement's right to demonstrate and the Right's demands for order and punishment.

In advance of the moratorium, students on the right sent telegrams to the White House requesting that Nixon publicly endorse their Loyalty Rally counterprotests.[40] The Students to Keep Wesleyan American group at Virginia Wesleyan University wrote to the president requesting "permission to fly the flag twenty four hours a day [for] four days [in] support of your stand in Vietnam and to protest the Vietnam Moratorium."[41] Loyalty Rally counterdemonstrations also included raising pro-war propaganda banners and burning Vietcong flags, as University of Minnesota SPAR did in a performance that inadvertently set fire to the pant leg of an administrator.[42] Loyalty Rallies were held at Florida Atlantic, Mount St. Mary's, and Princeton Universities; the Universities of Notre Dame, Maryland, Minnesota, and Southern California; and Brooklyn College.[43] Princeton's Undergraduates for a Stable America (whose clever acronym spelled USA) attempted to persuade students to stay in class and administrators to keep university facilities running.[44]

Other students extolled their administrations, forgoing threats in favor of praise. Most of these endorsements were enacted theatrically, through excessive shows of approval. At Cleary College in Michigan, 500 students held a pro-administration rally in which the student government presented a portrait to the vice president as a gesture of appreciation for his disciplinary policies.[45] Students at the University of Nevada showered their president and his wife with adulation on a student-declared N. Edd Miller Day. As President Miller arrived on campus, 2,000 students greeted him with applause, cheers of "We Want Edd," and a twenty-four-gun salute from the ROTC squadron. The student body president and the campus newspaper celebrated Miller's steadfast discipline by presenting him and his wife with jewelry, a plaque, and a paid weekend vacation as 1,000 balloons were released into the sky.[46]

Loyalty Rallies

On November 3, 1969, two weeks after the first moratorium, Nixon announced a plan to withdraw American troops from the ongoing war, leaving South Vietnam to defend itself against the communist North. With the time frame for American withdrawal undisclosed, the conservative student response to Vietnamization was mixed along lines of partisanship and ideology. While ultimately favoring a total victory over communism, College Republicans were in a difficult position, as they did not want to criticize the Republican president. And while YAF was technically nonpartisan, conservative ideologues could realistically chart a stronger path through allies within the GOP despite Nixon's continual letdowns than they could have if they completely parted ways with the administration.

The war was alienating veterans and potential recruits to the political right. It was also killing, maiming, and traumatizing thousands of American and Vietnamese men, women, and children. It was wrecking the domestic economy and tarnishing the nation's image abroad. To show support for Vietnamization, the College Republicans sent signatures to Nixon after the November 3 address.[47] YAF's leadership, still undecided on American withdrawal but acknowledging Nixon's decision, responded that they felt "very much alone." "Our position is one of victory," YAF insisted. "Vietnamization is fine and we're for it but not if we withdraw when our help is needed."[48]

Two weeks following Nixon's withdrawal announcement, a second, much larger Moratorium Day, involving over 600,000 participants, took place over the weekend of November 15. The moratorium included strikes, teach-ins, antiwar speeches, and singing performances in Washington, D.C. Throughout November and subsequent moratoria in December, the student Right countered with a series of "alternative weekends" and Loyalty Rallies to drown out the peace movement. During these counterstrikes, pro-war conservatives demanded that Americans "Tell it to Hanoi."

Like so many other national YAF initiatives, the "Tell It to Hanoi" campaign was originally created by one of its auxiliaries, the National Student Committee for Victory in Vietnam, and was initially billed as the "Sock It to Hanoi" campaign.[49] YAF organizers urgently asked all chapters and affiliates to rally against "surrender and defeat." The campaign consisted of teach-ins, pro-war petitions, speeches, and "Win in Vietnam" paraphernalia in a distorted echo of the antiwar actions.[50] Campus Crusade for Christ distributed anti–New Left flyers at the Washington Monument. Voices in Vital America encouraged participants to fly American flags and keep porch and vehicle lights on.[51] Washington State University YAF sold 500 patriotic-themed armbands and blue buttons to counter black antiwar bands. A teach-in at the University of Missouri included a candlelight parade and a pro-Nixon rally.[52] Duke University YAF formed the Worker-Student Alliance to Support President Nixon. Students gathered in downtown Durham, in shopping centers and in factories, distributing American flags, circulating petitions in support of the war and assuring community members "that all students do not support Mobe, that America's basic values have not failed, that our policy in Vietnam is just, and that our President is pursuing the best course for peace."[53] Students in the Florida State YAF mailed war confidence petitions to the White House on an hourly basis.[54] YAF executives mailed Nixon their own letters praising his decisions.[55] These displays of support for the president reveal that not all YAF chapters were initially in agreement about opposing Nixon's Vietnamization strategy, though they later would be.

On Veterans Day, YAFers participated in an Honor America "freedom rally" at the Washington Monument, sponsored by the American Legion and the Veterans of Foreign Wars. Comedian Bob Hope entertained a crowd of 25,000. Miniature American flags were disbursed to the crowd, a Boy Scout led the Pledge of Allegiance, and a young Black woman sang "The Star-Spangled Banner."[56] YAF, women's groups, and veterans' groups sponsored full-page newspaper ads asking patriots to "Tell It to Hanoi" and profess their commitment to fighting the Vietcong so that "40,000 young Americans have not died in vain."[57]

Two days later, on November 13, one hundred YAFers participated in a candlelight march at St. Louis University in Missouri. Participants were encouraged to wear red, white, and blue and leave their porch and car lights on. Marchers shouted, "Hell No, We Won't Quit!" and carried posters reading "The Silent Majority Becomes Outspoken."[58] The YAF chapter of Southern Illinois University collected money and Christmas gifts to mail to troops overseas.[59]

Unfazed by conservative counterefforts, an official from the Mobe, the organization that had sponsored the moratoria, dismissively stated about the student Right: "I wouldn't exactly call them competition."[60] Commenting on what they believed to be the futility of the demonstrations, one Notre Dame student and Vietnam veteran remarked, "Nixon's probably inside watching the Ohio State–Purdue football game."[61]

On December 1, between the second and third moratorium, Nixon instituted a temporary draft lottery system to make conscription more equitable, democratizing the chances for tragedy among poor and college-educated young men. The student deferment was removed, but the eligible pool of draftees was limited to nineteen-year-old men, rather than the larger pool of men between the ages of eighteen and twenty-seven. Draft board membership was also reformed to allow eighteen-year-old participation, lowered from the previous minimum age of thirty. With the chance of conscription now more equitable, antiwar demonstrations exploded.

The draft lottery was not the Nixon administration's only attempt at reforming conscription. General Lewis Hershey, head of the Selective Service Administration, had become an object of contempt among those who opposed the draft. As the three moratoria gained significant press, Nixon announced a four-star promotion for the general, prompting his retirement. The aged, irritable Hershey was strategically replaced by Curtis Tarr, a graduate of Stanford and Harvard and a former university president. One of Tarr's first decisions was to request the retirements of Selective Service officers in the hawkish conservative southern states of Mississippi, North Carolina, and Tennessee.[62] The Right viewed this series of events as a concession to the peace movement and, within the context of Vietnamization, regarded this decision as indicative of Nixon's weakness.

On December 7, in commemoration of the Pearl Harbor bombing, Boston YAF held a candlelight vigil that attracted between 1,500 and 2,500 participants and onlookers. The audience's chorus of "This Land Is Your Land" was punctuated by cries of "Bomb Hanoi!" "Bomb Red China!" and "Win the War in Vietnam!" Other participants burned a Vietcong flag. Their signs

YAF students stage a pro-war rally on the Boston Commons, demanding Americans "Tell It to Hanoi." Boston, Massachusetts, December 7, 1969. Bettmann Collection via Getty Images.

read, "Sock It to the Peaceniks!" and "Stop SDS!" One of the keynote speakers, Albert L. "Dapper" O'Neil, demanded that the United States "wipe out Hanoi" and the radical student Left. A Harvard YAF leader agreed: "The war is not hurting us as much as the critics of the war are."[63] A woman in the crowd who held up a peace sign was injured in a physical altercation with middle-aged pro-war men.[64] A *Boston Globe* reporter compared the YAF rally to a recent combative demonstration by the Black Panthers, noting "the bullying, threatening tone of the speakers, and the increasingly ugly mood of the audiences."[65]

YAF used the event as confirmation of a conservative silent majority. In an editorial in the Boston College student newspaper, YAFers pointed to the rally to make the case against "the Moratoria and the Marches": "Rallies such as these help define the rapidly coalescing discontent of those who speak quietly but firmly in a world dominated by loudmouths. Our 'peace movement' is gaining the strength of numbers, and the determination that comes with unity. The people are showing their power, and anyone with doubts about that can tell it to Hanoi!"[66]

YAF leader Randal Teague expressed that the organization would "abandon all programming to undertake a counterthrust" against the moratoria, pledging to make its alternative weekend event in December larger than the previous one.[67] Now officially opposed to the Vietnamization plan, the students declared that their support for Nixon was contingent on his commitment to escalating naval and air bombings, which they viewed as a dispensation after his pledge to withdraw ground troops. YAF printed thousands of "Tell It to Hanoi" petitions outlining its stance. On the weekend of December 13–15, YAF executives claimed to have collected 735,000 signatures and to have sponsored counter teach-ins at 600 campuses.[68]

Significance of the Freedom Offensive

The fall of 1969 proved to be another pivotal semester for conservative students in the campus wars. They were now better organized than ever, especially considering YAF's majority coalition concept and the organization's well-planned and distributed action manuals, legal kits, and education kits. YAF's national Freedom Offensive effort brought together various successful strategies tested by their own chapters, in addition to those from the College Republicans, ISI, and smaller lesser-known traditionalist groups. Even so, participation at antiwar and civil rights demonstrations was much greater than participation at conservative counterprotests. In response to this point, the student Right once again insisted that their beliefs represented a youth silent majority, attributing low group membership and event participation to the passive demeanor of most students, who, until then, had been too busy studying to bother with the unserious New Left.

According to conservatives, massive participation in peace and civil rights demonstrations was illegitimate, as these events were being bolstered by well-organized leftist outsiders. At the same time, students on the right failed to acknowledge their own significant outside mentorship and funding. Conservatives' messages depicted themselves as embodying contradictory roles: that of a youth silent majority and that of a *silenced minority* group victimized by a liberal establishment. When traditionalist groups did manage to capture large audiences, such as at Boston's "Tell It to Hanoi" rally, numbers were purposefully and consistently mentioned in their messaging, along with every small victory concerning conservative legislation, new group membership, and new club charters.

Since the serious escalation of the campus wars beginning in 1967, the Right's rhetoric steadily evolved from anticommunist fearmongering to language that was reflexively and broadly anti-leftist. After 1969, traditionalist students on the right no longer felt they needed any justification for such rhetoric since they, however inaccurately, believed their views were accepted by most. This deviation from a consistent set of ideas and claims was the product of organizers at the macro level attempting to merge disparate political, social, and cultural viewpoints into a big-tent majority coalition, whose members could only feasibly be banded together by the common goal of rejecting the New Left.

As a result, the student Right was under constant tension as a consequence of reacting to changing circumstances rather than consistently pursuing a positive vision of its own. Even the most respected arguments against the campus peace movement, such as those given by Harvard's Colonel Pell, were reduced to defending the necessity of campus ROTC programs to cultivate an elite class-based military leadership that honored traditionalist social hierarchies. Justifications for why the United States should participate in Vietnam's civil war were either assumed or considered irrelevant, as conservatives came to believe that the larger threat was not the war itself but the peace and civil rights movements on campus.

· · · · · ·

At this point in the story, it is perhaps worthwhile to review the rapid mobilization changes across the student Right in just two short years. There was much disunity and antagonism among the groups before 1967. There was also somewhat more intellectual diversity across the Right's organizations before the Columbia demonstrations in the spring of 1968, followed by an attempt to knit together majority coalitions that fall. But factions reemerged across Republican Party loyalists, Reaganites, and white nationalists during the 1968 presidential campaign. The student Right seemed to reunite around massive resistance and against calls for Black Studies programs in the spring of 1969. Then came the sizeable libertarian purge that summer. After what looked like more ideological consistency, there was a split over Vietnamization in the fall of 1969, before another round of reactive consolidation against the Nixon administration and the increasingly popular antiwar moratoria. As the spring 1970 semester approached, it became clear that the only way for the campus Right to remain a cohesive force was to incite deeper suspicions and fears concerning the New Left. They had no unifying ideas of their own.

· ·

In the aftermath of three historic moratoria spanning the fall of 1969, college campuses appeared relatively calm for the first few weeks of the new year. Several articles in the *Chronicle of Higher Education* noted a conspicuous absence of campus violence following the previous two record-setting semesters. Some changes that may have contributed to this include administrators allowing greater student participation in governance; the creation of Black studies courses at San Francisco State College, Duke University, and elsewhere; and the fracturing of Students for a Democratic Society (SDS)—the central group behind violent disruptions—into at least three distinct camps. Even the Vietnam Moratorium Committee was preparing to announce its dissolution.[1] Many radical student leaders had been arrested and were currently serving prison sentences of one to twenty-five years for violating newly enacted interstate anti-riot laws crafted by conservative legislators.[2] It seemed as if law-and-order crackdowns were working to deter new disruptions.

But the reprieve was only temporary. Nearly as soon as the spring 1970 semester began, one incident eclipsed all the previous demonstrations in size, breaking records for student arrests and remaining the largest apprehension of students by law enforcement in American history. Nearly 900 Black students were arrested at Mississippi Valley State University following a strike and demands for increased scholarship funds, building renovations, and improved faculty quality.[3] Members of the HBCU's all-white board of trustees closed the institution, banned students from campus, and denied all scholarships unless students signed a waiver revoking their right to due process.[4]

By the end of February, over twenty civil rights and antiwar demonstrations had taken place across the United States and Canada since the beginning of the year.[5] That number doubled within the first two weeks of March, as at least eighteen new demonstrations broke out on college campuses.[6] Between January and March, student protests occurred at a rate of one per day, with 23 percent categorized by the *Chronicle* as violent.[7] Conservatives, now organized entirely along the principle of defeating the Left, accelerated their mobilization into the new decade.

Reacting to Vietnamization

Despite Nixon's promise the previous fall to withdraw US troops from Vietnam, college campuses and ROTC centers were still the usual targets of radical antiwar protesters' animosity as the semester progressed. Since Nixon refused to provide a timeline for withdrawal, Young Americans for Freedom (YAF) sent eleven members to South Vietnam in March on a fact-finding mission to report on the progress of Vietnamization. David Keene confirmed that the withdrawal was underway and, out of step with many of the students in his charge, suggested that it "should have been American policy all along."[8] But along with the president's promise of Vietnamization came the implementation of the draft lottery system, which did not exempt college students. In passionate letters to Nixon, YAF assailed congressional leaders who opposed his policies, calling their stance "back-biting," "sabotage," "despicable," and "subterfuge." YAF argued that congressional debates over conscription should be public, so they could berate specific representatives whose draft views they deemed cowardly.[9]

Across the nation, students and other peace activists participated in local events on April 15 during a fourth war moratorium. Just as in the fall, conservative retribution and pro-police responses were swiftly delivered. At Pennsylvania State University, a crowd of 500 demonstrators threw glass, rocks, and bricks; twenty-four students were arrested. Before the end of the day, conservatives collected several thousand signatures on a petition to revoke the campus SDS chapter's charter and expel the demonstration organizers. The petition thanked police "for their restraint and a job well done" while apologizing for the inconvenience.[10]

The most violent protests took place after the April 18 death of Kevin Moran, a white University of California–Santa Barbara student who was misidentified and executed by police while attempting to extinguish an arsonist's fire. Over twenty-five campuses erupted in demonstrations against police brutality against the white student, with eight demonstrations involving bombings.[11] Boston YAF responded to the violence with a "Wake Up America" counterrally designed to "radicalize people to the Right, just as the Student Mobilization groups are trying to radicalize people to the Left."[12]

Executives from YAF continued sponsoring regional conferences that trained students to form majority coalitions to combat the moratoria. These training seminars urged a new militance not previously endorsed in earlier mobilization efforts. At a mid-Atlantic conference, speakers stressed the importance of meeting leftist groups with violent acts and threatening lawsuits against administrators who refused to punish radicals.[13] YAF manuals instructed members to react physically "if the situation justifies it." The contingency plan for building takeovers included baiting radicals into harming them by "putting a ring of students, preferably two deep and including a large number of girls, around the building. . . . When the leftists try to move in, the Majority Coalition line should lock arms, and make it necessary for the left to use violence against fellow students to get in the building. If they try, start yelling 'SDS brutality,' but do not resist. The left will then be in the position in which they like to put the police."[14]

In addition to strategically placed women, trainers emphasized that athletes were the most useful allies in the formation, since "being able to hold the line is more important than being able to argue philosophy when such a takeover has occurred." In the event that a building occupation was already underway, a YAF manual instructed students to "physically occupy and liberate" the vacant headquarters of the opposing club in a counter sit-in and to announce they would not leave until radicals were removed first.[15] During a strike by Black and Puerto Rican students at Queens College in New York, coalition members took over campus newspaper offices. Similarly, YAF students occupied student government and SDS chapter offices at Syracuse and Pennsylvania State Universities, as well as at the Boston office of the antiwar group Resistance.[16]

The counter sit-in strategy was also tested at Cornell, Harvard, and Stanford Universities. At Stanford, SDS launched a nine-day occupation of the Applied Electronics Laboratory (AEL), condemning the Department of Defense's military contracts with the Stanford Research Institute, which employed over a thousand university affiliates.[17] The Right could easily push back against protests like these, pointing to the potential costs of losing such an important research facility. At campuses like Stanford, federal research grants brought the university millions of dollars and employed hundreds of faculty and graduate students. During the AEL "mill-in," YAF and Young Republican members carried banners reading "SDS Is Revolting," "Reject SDS Demands," and "If You Liked Hitler, You'll Love SDS" while chanting "Pigs off campus" and guarding laboratory doors.[18] Afterward, Stanford students voted 3,924 to 1,695 against SDS demands to shut down the AEL, and 60 percent voted in favor of maintaining academic credit for the ROTC.[19] These types of campus-specific victories armed national organizations like YAF with anecdotal evidence that their chapters represented campus majorities, even if these instances were more reflective of conditions for employment and research investments than actual endorsements of the war itself.

Invasion of Cambodia

Senate investigation records indicate that a total of 4,330 bombs exploded on college campuses between January 1, 1969, and April 15, 1970.[20] The unceasing campus destruction and the number of student arrests and deaths through April 1970 well exceeded all previous incidents of violence in American higher education. But the antiwar movement's bombs, Black Power sit-ins, and retaliatory slayings by police had yet to reach a crescendo. After American intelligence discovered that enemy forces were being supplied covertly through roadways in Vietnam's neighboring nation of Cambodia, Nixon announced a ground troop invasion of neutral Cambodia on Thursday, April 30, just ten days after pledging to withdraw 150,000 troops.

Within the small conservative realm of YAF and College Republicans, students celebrated the Cambodian invasion announcement and its potential escalation of the war. Young conservatives wanted to make sure that the nearly 50,000 young American men who had lost their lives in the war to that point had not died for a stalemate. YAF affirmed Nixon's resolution by relaunching its fall "Tell It to Hanoi" campaign with an updated statement of support, reversing its previous condemnation of the Vietnamization plan: "Mr. President, We, the undersigned, stand behind you in your decisions on Cambodia and on South Vietnam. We know unless we stand and fight today, the cause of *true* peace will be dealt a fatal blow by Communist aggression."[21] Nixon thanked students from Amberton University in Texas, Mississippi State University, St. Cloud State College in Minnesota, the University of New Mexico, the University of South Florida, and Delta State College in Mississippi for their petitions of affirmation.[22]

YAF justified the incursion as a necessary step to defeat communism, insisting that Americans needed to "realize that the struggle was not really one of territorial boundaries or of nationalism. It was one of ideology."[23] If communists had infiltrated Cambodia, Americans would need to react in defense of the world. Cambodia was evidence, in YAF's view, that the domino theory of communism's spread was already being realized. Other young conservatives seemed to agree. A poll of 102,666 students from 247 campuses, conducted by the right-leaning Association of Student Governments

(ASG), reported that 40 percent of respondents supported the invasion. Among southern students, support was as high as 49 percent.[24]

Following YAF, a College Republican memo urged members to immediately initiate chapter-level programs and issue personal statements supporting the invasion to local media. College Republicans also released a statement to news services affirming the group's approval of the incursion: "[We] support the President's action to destroy the enemy sanctuaries from which they are daily raiding and killing American soldiers. It is the North Vietnamese communists who have widened this war to include South Vietnam, Laos and, now, Cambodia. I am proud of our President. He has done the right thing."[25] Beyond Nixon's small confederation of student supporters, the Cambodian invasion announcement proved disastrous in terms of campus unrest. In the week following the declaration, twenty or more new campus strikes took place each day.[26]

The Kent State Massacre

This was still not yet the crescendo. On May 1, the night following the Cambodian invasion announcement, 500 intoxicated young people shouting "Down with Nixon!" began setting fires, breaking windows, and damaging property near Kent State University in Ohio. Every police officer in the city of Kent was sent to enforce a shutdown of the area's bars and restaurants. The mayor declared a state of emergency. The university sent buses to shuttle students back to campus, where 150 members of the Ohio National Guard were on watch.[27] The following night, students set fire to the Kent State ROTC building, attacked a professor attempting to intervene, cut firefighters' hoses, and assailed defenders with rocks, breaking the collarbone of a local sheriff. The crowd of 1,000–1,500 students was dispersed with tear gas, and fourteen students were arrested. The National Guard increased its presence to 1,000 troops.[28] On May 3, National Guardsmen forced student marchers in the city to return to campus in a violent confrontation that resulted in dozens more arrests. Several students were stabbed by bayonets; two were hospitalized.[29] In the three days following the Cambodia announcement, over one hundred students were arrested in Kent State and nearby Ohio State demonstrations.[30]

James A. Rhodes, Ohio's Republican governor and prospective Senate hopeful, had sent in the National Guard to take over the university, framing this use of force as a necessary measure in protecting "merchants and people of this community." On the night of Sunday, May 3, Governor Rhodes attempted to soothe Kent residents by issuing a warning to college radicals and anyone who wished "to destroy higher education," threatening "to employ every force of law that we have under our authority."[31] Swearing full retribution, Rhodes promised to turn over an investigation by the district attorney and county prosecutor to the federal government:[32]

> We're asking the Legislature that any person throwing a rock, brick or stone at a law enforcement agency of Ohio—a sheriff, policeman, highway patrolman or national guardsman becomes a felony and, secondly, we're going to ask for legislation that any person in the administrative side or as a student—if these people are convicted whether it is a misdemeanor or a felony for participating in a riot, they're automatically dismissed—there is no hearing, no recourse and they cannot enter another State University in the State of Ohio. . . . They're the worst type of people that we harbor in America. And I want to say that they're not going to take over the campus. And the campus now is going to be part of the County and the State of Ohio. There is no sanctuary for these people to burn buildings down of private citizens—of businesses in a community and then run into a sanctuary. It's over with in Ohio.[33]

On Monday, May 4, Kent State administrators distributed 12,000 leaflets announcing that all protests were banned while the campus was under National Guard occupation. Three thousand students rallied against the National Guard presence, police brutality, and the expanding war. Of the 3,000, only 500 were "core demonstrators," while most others were sympathetic or scandalized onlookers.[34] Protesting students assailed members of the National Guard with rocks, blocks of wood with exposed nails, bottles, brickbats, and rubble. Troops armed with M1 rifles equipped with eight-round magazines directed their firearms at the students. The National Guardsmen unloaded tear gas into the crowd. A few demonstrating students captured the gas canisters and launched them back toward the soldiers.

In retaliation, over two dozen National Guardsmen unleashed a thirteen-second-long barrage that sprayed between sixty-one and sixty-seven bullets into the crowd of demonstrators, onlookers, and passersby in a parking lot. The gunshots killed four students and injured nine.[35] Guardsmen testified that their fusillade was executed in self-defense against the rock throwers, but the four white students killed were at distances ranging from 270 to 390 feet from the troops and were not all part of the demonstration. The nine white men injured were standing at distances ranging from 60 to 750 feet from the troops.[36] Despite conservatives' later insistence that the victims were radicals threatening the National Guardsmen, a witness to the shooting described most of the Kent State protesters as "clean-cut fraternity kids."[37]

On May 8, just before the end of the week, approximately one hundred FBI agents were in Kent investigating the massacre before the final National Guardsmen and highway patrol officers had left the campus.[38] YAF's David Keene informed the press that his organization had no planned counterdemonstrations, stating that they were afraid to show support for the slain "because of what might happen if they openly agree with the left." Instead, Keene encouraged all students to stay home in the aftermath of the massacre, effectively calling for silence from the 20,000 members in his charge. Reiterating the conservative claim that the victims, like most other progressives, were causing civil disobedience in bad faith, Keene explained, "Many moderate students have been taken in by cynical revolutionaries bent on using them as cannon fodder for the revolution. These are the people who will be hurt; these are the ones who will be clubbed and busted. The leaders will know what they are up to and will escape to fight another day."[39]

National Reaction to the Kent State Massacre

The Kent State carnage proved to be a flashpoint, igniting an immediate and explosive national reaction. Over 1 million students protested at roughly 1,350 colleges—nearly half of all American campuses.[40] In the first week following the shootings, 169 bombs exploded on university grounds, 900 colleges were shut down by strikes, and 35,000 National Guardsmen were deployed to stop riots at twenty-one campuses.[41] Protests took the form of student strikes, total campus shutdowns, marches, rallies, symbolic funerals, and flags flying at half-mast. Over 10,000 young people destroyed their draft cards or forfeited them to local antiwar agencies.[42]

The morning after the Kent State shootings, several members of Nixon's staff resigned, including three National Security Council staff members and the director of the Office of Students and Youth.[43] New York Young Republicans banded together with the local Young Democrats in demanding that representatives of Congress repudiate the Cambodian invasion. The National Student Association called on Congress to begin impeachment proceedings against Nixon.[44] Over 450 campuses opened chapters of Movement for a New Congress to replace sitting representatives with antiwar leaders.[45]

Two days after the massacre, 115 schools were on strike.[46] Enormous demonstrations of thousands of students marched to commemorate the slain. Three thousand students demonstrated at Southern Illinois University, and 4,000 demonstrated at Pennsylvania State University.[47] Hundreds of students at the University of Wisconsin protested; some destroyed windows and burned buildings for four nights in a row. At West Virginia University, a crowd of 3,000 students was tear-gassed by police.[48] At Boston College, fifty students captured the president's office, ransacked the ROTC building, and destroyed American flags. Students at MIT blockaded postal workers and delivery trucks from campus. Concerned about safety, administrators at Boston and Brown Universities closed dormitories and canceled classes, final exams, and commencement ceremonies.[49]

White House envoys surveyed campuses during the strikes, reporting back on the desperate need for peace between students and administrations. Even the moderates, they announced, were lost. Among college students nationally, Nixon's approval rating sank to 31 percent. His advisers cautioned that an overreaction of law and order could worsen the disastrous effects.[50] To address the backlash, Nixon informed Congress on May 6 that the United States would penetrate only twenty-two miles into Cambodia and that American forces would be removed in less than two months, by June 30, but the president's recalibration mattered little to parties on both sides of the campus wars.[51]

Despite overwhelming college opposition, an astonishing 60 percent of Americans overall approved of the National Guard's assassination of the four Kent State students. Among law enforcement, 80 percent of officers approved of federal agents' occupation on campus and in the city.[52] Campus strikes received serious condemnation from state leaders, parents, faculty, and students themselves. A faculty member at North Carolina State University described the marches on his campus as "temper tantrums," while a parent rebuked the "minority" protesters as "allowed to override authority, not attend class and break the law, when there are others who want an education."[53] Only one day after the massacre, the president of evangelical Bob Jones University announced in a chapel meeting that the Kent State victims were deserving of their deaths and injuries, stating that they "should have been shot" as penance for being brainwashed by "ungodly professors," cowardly parents, and "lawless" preachers.[54]

Keene's directive for members to be passive about the killings was ignored as conservative students continued their anti-strike initiatives and provoked peace demonstrators. At Syracuse, YAF counterprotesters held a

Pizza for Freedom rally to mock their classmates who were observing a peace fast.[55] Students at the University of Southern California (USC) replaced campus "Strike!" signs with "Open Campus" posters. USC Young Republicans instructed students on how to cross the "goon squad" picket lines. Members of the Young Republicans banded with YAF and fraternity brothers to launch another "Tell It to Hanoi" campaign, erecting information tables, passing out pro-war literature, hosting an anti-strike rally, and burning the flag of North Vietnam.[56] Others spray-painted over the street sign of the campus's former Agnew Drive after it was renamed Kent State Avenue.[57]

One day after the massacre, a handful of Tulane University YAFers and athletes engaged in fistfights with antiwar students in the presence of several hundred mourners who were gathered around the Newcomb Hall flagpole for a memorial service.[58] That morning, protesters had detonated Molotov cocktails in the ROTC barracks, setting the campus building on fire. YAF and the athletes were furious about the fire and were incredulous that administrators approved a request to lower the flag to half-mast, seemingly approving of the destruction to campus and federal property. One of the conservative students present at the Tulane antiwar demonstration was graduate history student and future Speaker of the House, Newt Gingrich.[59] Gingrich was a leader in a majority coalition group called Mobilization of Responsible Tulane Students.

The Tulane fistfight appears to be the first of several similar clashes between the student right and antiwar groups around campus flagpoles following Kent State. Days later, USC YAF, angered that the flag had been lowered to half-mast, determined to raise the flag. One YAFer fought in a tug-of-war over the pole rope against a student who attempted to keep the flag lowered. Towson State College of Maryland YAF also guarded the flagpole to prevent anyone from lowering the flag.[60] At San Diego State College, football center and twenty-six-year-old veteran Bill Pierson, who stood six feet, three inches tall and weighed 250 pounds, raised his campus flag and stood guard for hours, daring activists to attempt to lower it again.[61] It is unclear from YAF records whether each of these instances was organic, or if conservative group leaders were coordinating the flag standoffs. Either way, all of them occurred within a week of the May 4 killings, and all involved YAF, athletes, or both.

Other pro-war and anti-strike actions by majority coalitions took place nationwide. Students for Classes at the University of Bridgeport released a statement of rights and urged students to report instructors who refused to hold classes to their department chair and dean.[62] At North Carolina State University, a pro-Nixon majority coalition group named American Students for Action (ASA) organized a blood drive, circulated flyers encouraging respect for the president, and condemned peace strikes. ASA's "Peace thru Nixon" campaign reminded students that the office of the president came with a "multitude of responsibilities" that students must respect, and that elected officials needed their trust.[63] University of Tennessee YAF sent a plane over campus with a banner reading, "Give Nixon a Chance." Evangelist Billy Graham warned an audience on that same campus that given the recent events, the second coming of Christ was imminent.[64] Mount St. Mary's College held a seventy-two-hour vigil to support soldiers still on the battlefield. A group of thirty-five students from twelve colleges traveled to the White House to deliver a pro-Nixon anti-strike petition with 4,000 signatures.[65]

The best explanation for the Right's defense of the Kent State massacre was expressed by James Lacy—future national chair of YAF and eventual senior executive at the Commerce Department and general counsel for the Consumer Product Safety Commission under the Reagan administration— who was involved in the flag spectacle at USC. Lacy explained, "Those of us in the YAF group, while we felt that what happened at Kent State was a tragedy, [it] was a divisive incident politically and wasn't something that should be memorialized that way, at least on our campus."[66]

With remarkable consistency, students on the right refused to empathize with those they perceived as having different political opinions. Instead, they conceptualized compassionate responses to the tragedy as insincere gestures designed to cynically pursue a policy goal, rather than engaging with the matter of state violence against their peers. In this way, they could deflect clear transgressions of the state military (or any other authority they relied on) while demonizing those they saw as their ideological enemies. The "clean cut fraternity kids" injured and killed at Kent State were not all peace activists, but their presence (even as onlookers) at an antiwar campus event is the only detail YAFers seemed to acknowledge: if they did not want to get hurt, they should not have been at the demonstration.

Majority Coalition Lawsuits

As protests led to canceled classes or total campus shutdowns, students on the right were already prepared to sue their institutions to force them to remain open. YAF had by now disseminated lawsuit instruction manuals, made arrangements with lawyers near campuses that were likely to have strikes, and taken to using media outlets to announce their intention to sue (discussed in chapter 8). The suits accused presidents, trustees, or other administrators of a breach of contract for failing to fulfill fiduciary duties on the grounds that they had not offered classes for which tuition had already been paid.

As former YAF executive Randal Teague, who sued George Washington University, explained:

> The university, the med school, the law school, they all cancelled class because of the tear gas, and the other things. And we felt, Well, wait a minute, either our parents or ourselves had a contract with the university to provide us an education . . . [and] it turns out the real political reason was their support for students being at the demonstrations and not in class. Half a dozen of us or so brought a lawsuit against the university for breach of contract and got a temporary injunction against them and the judge ordered them to remain open.[67]

The four moratoria demonstrations between the fall of 1969 and the spring of 1970, and the hundreds of strikes in the wake of Kent State, provided numerous opportunities for YAF to obtain a legal precedent for using strike injunctions to force colleges to remain open. While trustees and students awaited these rulings, YAF formed committees to document "radicalization" and to "study the failures and policy problems of the University that permit such perversion of education objectives." Committees further aimed to "demonstrate the lack of diversity within the various departments, the actual destruction of academic freedom, and the intolerance toward and intimidation of students who do not accept the revolutionary faith."[68] Here the Right characterized protesters who were opposed to the state extrajudicially killing college students as intolerant by narrowly construing diversity as only a matter of ideological differences, rather than also comprising religious, sexual, racial, and other aspects of identity, and narrowly interpreting academic freedom as only the ability to access classroom instruction in the traditional way. It remains unclear how conservative students were systematically intimidated by administrators.

Using these justifications, students sued or threatened to sue presidents, trustees, or other administrators at the Universities of Southern California and Wisconsin; Adelphi, George Washington, Hofstra, Ohio State, and Wayne State Universities; the New York Institute of Technology; Marymount

College; and Nassau and Suffolk Community Colleges in New York.[69] Few of these lawsuits were successful, but the efforts required to legally compel administrators to keep campuses open amid violent demonstrations, arson, and bombings illustrates conservatives' commitment to using the power of the courts to force their minority will, even at the cost of campus and community safety.

Support for this type of retribution was matched by state and federal governments. Vice President Spiro Agnew personally encouraged legal recourse against administrators who had conceded to "disruptive tactics of the anti-intellectual, hardcore Leftist minorities."[70] Governor Ronald Reagan ordered all campuses within the University of California system to remain open in spite of unyielding protests and persistent bombings.[71] University administrators similarly cracked down by using enhanced law-enforcement measures. At Boston College, security provisions for the upcoming semester included an increase in the number of campus guards, with multiple guards on patrol day and night. Residence halls were not excluded from these patrols. Only one guarded gate to campus was made accessible during the night. Over holidays, police officers were supplied with a list of students authorized to be on campus. Campus guards worked with nearby city police to increase ticketing.[72] Administrators and city mayors further negotiated town-and-gown jurisdictions to increase student arrests. Nationwide, it became standard for campus police to carry firearms.

Jackson State Massacre

Concurrent with antiwar demonstrations, campus racial struggles persisted. Just eleven days after Kent State, and only three months after and eighty miles away from the site of the record-setting Valley State mass arrest, Mississippi police escalated their retribution against Black students, moving from apprehension to lethal force. After midnight on May 15, fourteen students at Jackson State University in Jackson, Mississippi, were shot by police, who fired 469 bullets and buckshot for twenty-eight seconds into a women's residence hall. This followed a racial altercation between the HBCU students and white officers the night before. Phillip Lafayette Gibbs and James Earl Green were killed, and twelve other young people, mostly Black women, were struck by bullets.

The events at Jackson State were a matter of racism and police brutality, and major national news outlets plainly reported the events as unrelated to the antiwar strikes of Kent State. As explored more fully in chapter 6, students barely reacted to the Jackson State slaying, devoting little, if any, space to it in campus newsletters and not bothering to organize any major protests in response. Progressive white students paid attention to matters of police brutality related to the war but seemed to ignore them when their chief cause was racism and the victims were Black. This same pattern played out repeatedly when white students organized mass protests following the police murders of white students like Kevin Moran, but not Black Panther organizers Fred Hampton and Mark Clark only five months prior. As after Kent State, conservatives remained silent on the matter of state violence directed against other students.

Nixon Responds to Student Unrest

According to Nixon administration records, on-campus arrests of students between 1968 and 1970 increased from 4,000 to 7,200. From 1967 to 1970, the National Guard was called to quell civil disturbances over 200 times.[73] The number of "riots" involving over 300 participants and lasting over seven hours doubled. Serious disturbances involving at least 150 participants and lasting at least three hours nearly tripled. Incidents of assault, arson, bombings, gunfire, and other violent acts nearly quadrupled. Total campus disturbances increased steadily from 105 in 1968 to 288 in 1969, and then to 307 in 1970.[74]

Facing seemingly endless protests, Nixon, who had originally been ambivalent even toward students whose support he was guaranteed, finally accepted the counsel of his advisers, including YAF's Tom Charles Huston and Pat Buchanan, and reached out to youth on the right. He did so selectively, extending invitations to minor events to an overtly conservative student demographic. The president agreed to short meetings with individual representatives from the ASG, YAF, and College Republican clubs, and made one appearance before a friendly audience of Christian evangelical students. Despite his disinclination to meet with "nutty" young conservatives, staff arranged ten-minute meetings with students to allow the president to communicate a sense of appreciation for their support.[75]

YAF, unwavering in its backing of the Cambodian invasion, sent its national chair David Keene to testify before Congress and to meet the president. Keene was introduced to a reluctant Nixon as "the most prominent youth spokesman on behalf of the President's actions" since the Cambodian invasion announcement. Well experienced in drawing attention to his group's causes, Keene had already appeared before the Republican and

Democratic National Conventions, twice on the *Today Show,* and on an NBC special about student dissent.[76]

After meeting with YAF's leader, Nixon met with College Republican chair Robert Polack, who was a senior law student at Louisiana State University and a Princeton University cum laude graduate. Nixon finally attended a Billy Graham youth rally at the University of Tennessee—his first public appearance since the massacre. Seventy-one percent of the 100,000 in attendance reportedly voted for the president.[77]

Nixon also held a series of meetings between advisers and youth representatives. The Department of Health, Education, and Welfare welcomed over 3,000 phone calls regarding campus unrest and coordinated dozens of meetings with over 1,000 young people. The White House assembled a Youth Advisory Commission to make draft selection more equitable. Members selected for the commission upheld the desirable square image.[78] While the president was finally engaging with young people, he only seemed interested in working with those who already agreed with his decisions regarding the war and who were opposed to peace strikes.

Nixon met with several college presidents and appointed faculty as special advisers to the President's Commission on Campus Unrest, under the direction of Pennsylvania governor William Scranton. Investigators included white and Black academics from Boston College and Harvard, Howard, and Stanford Universities, as well as conservative representatives from police forces in New Haven, Connecticut, and Cleveland, Ohio. Erwin D. Canham, editor of the *Christian Science Monitor,* was also an investigator.[79]

The *Report of the President's Commission on Campus Unrest,* commonly known as the Scranton Report, determined that college disturbances were a product of three factors: racial injustice, the war, and university curricula and policies. The commission urged the president to end the war in Vietnam and cultivate a sense of national unity by emphasizing commonalities shared by all Americans. For universities, the commission recommended the creation of ombudsmen to hear student grievances, a protected free speech forum on campus open to all speakers, and an expansion of financial aid for minority students.[80] YAF produced its own University Research Committee Report, challenging the Scranton Report with "markedly different" findings.[81] Nixon's response to the official report, moderate in tone, was a pledge to increase financial aid and expand enrollment access to higher education. Once again, the most hardened conservatives expressed disappointment in Nixon's perceived concessions.

Significance of Kent State for the College Right

The slayings at Kent State left conservative students at another junction in their mobilization project. Despite documented national public support for the National Guard's killing of unarmed youth, it would have been impossible for groups like YAF or the College Republicans to maintain legitimacy on campus if they continued to stand in support of the massacre, especially given the explosive national student reaction against it. Despite its own claims as a youth silent majority, YAF executives had long understood its minority status on campus and could not afford to lose the momentum it had gained in recent years. Internal YAF records indicate that across YAF's leadership, there was an acknowledgment of defeat on the war issue and a desire to "back quietly away from" pro-war rallies following the events at Kent State.[82] Jerry Norton, the only Vietnam veteran on YAF's executive board, was disillusioned with the group's unwavering pro-war stance. He asserted to Randal Teague that they had "help[ed] keep in effect a policy that others may have to die for, while being unwilling to die for it themselves."[83]

Until the official withdrawal from Vietnam in 1973, conservative students under YAF's direction focused their energies on supporting veterans and prisoners of war through groups such as Voices in Vital America, assailing draft evaders, and continuing their anti–National Student Association campaign.[84] College Republicans, under the direction of Karl Rove, Morton Blackwell, and Joseph Abate, gained independence from the Young Republican National Federation in 1970 and spent the years immediately following the Kent State massacre registering eighteen-year-old voters and promoting the Republican Party to students as the party of peace through its GO PEACE and Open Door campaigns. At odds with the majority of their peers, conservative students quietly shifted their messages from supporting the war to supporting peace through Vietnamization, as envisioned by the presidential administration that had so frequently disappointed them.

Conclusion

. . . .

After noon on January 6, 2021, approximately 2,500 right-wing conspiracists ascended the US Capitol building in Washington, D.C., in a coordinated attempt to overturn the 2020 presidential election by intimidation and force. Armed with an American flag, a cell phone, and a stun gun, Richard "Bigo" Barnett and several others ransacked Democrat and Speaker of the House Nancy Pelosi's office. A photograph shows Barnett with his feet on an office desk, holding an envelope with Pelosi's digital signature. Once outside the breached Capitol building, Barnett waved the confiscated envelope in front of an audience, insisting that he did not steal it but "put a quarter on [Pelosi's] desk even though she ain't fucking worth it. And I left her a note on her desk that says, 'Nancy, Bigo was here, you Bitch.'"[1]

Clad in a baseball cap, flannel jacket, well-worn jeans, and work boots, the sixty-year-old Barnett would have unquestionably been regarded with scoffs for his inelegant clothing, unshaven face, and profanity if he were assessed by an earlier generation of conservative activists. The Columbia University majority coalition—comprised of clean-cut students in sports coats and ties who mobilized against disheveled radicals who overtook buildings—probably would have characterized the January 6 insurrectionists the same way they did the Students for a Democratic Society (SDS) and the Student Afro-American Society (SAS): as "extortionists" and "hoodlums" who deserved "NO AMNESTY" for their violence.[2]

Yet the modern Republican Party embraces Barnett and other conspiracists charged with various federal crimes in their coup attempt to restore former president Donald Trump to office. Barnett represents the GOP's Trumpist base of nationalists whose right-wing populism has not only been accommodated but sought after by movement conservatives and provocateurs interested in uniting the party around a least common denominator: stopping a broadly conceived but ill-defined Left. In the 1960s, the up-and-coming generation mobilized around respectability, fundamentally rebuking disruptive direct action by radicals. In the years since, the Right's respectability politics have been abandoned as their obsession with combating (and mimicking) political opponents has led them to employ what

Richard "Bigo" Barnett and others in Speaker Nancy Pelosi's office on January 6, 2021. Photograph by Saul Loeb/AFP via Getty Images.

they have formerly decried as the least palatable strategies of their adversary.

The New Right

As the 1970s began, the turmoil that characterized the campus over the previous decade declined significantly. The most radical leaders of the New Left and Black Power movement were either killed, arrested, went into hiding, or graduated (many former Yippies even became Wall Street yuppies). The end of the draft brought an end to strikes and building takeovers. Some of the Right's most embattled college counteractivists, like David Keene, remained on campus in law school and carried on leading the undergraduates in their tutelage. As for the rest of the New Right (as 1960s college conservatives began calling themselves in the early 1970s) who went on to begin their careers as white-collar professionals (many taking jobs using the political connections they had made through their clubs), they did not leave their training or ideology behind.

After years of learning how laws were passed and witnessing firsthand the influence of federal and state action, the former students turned their attention to policy making in the 1970s. Over the next decades, conservatives set their sights on taking over Congress—not just the presidency—by fully capturing the Republican Party and implementing an unrelenting "politics of destruction."[3] They also founded an arsenal of think tanks, both as a complement to those that had sponsored their own training and as a supplement to the anti–New Deal infrastructure that had existed since the 1930s.

Other personalities on the Washington Beltway who were not campus activists—most notably congressional aides Paul Weyrich and Edwin Feulner, a Richard M. Weaver fellow—joined the movement and added their own contributions. Weyrich was key to bringing a new evangelical constituency, the so-called moral majority, into the fold. Together with YAF's financial interlocutors Marvin Liebman and Richard Viguerie, the New Right exponentially increased corporate giving to its nonprofits through florid direct mail marketing focused on domestic cultural issues such as abortion and gay rights (in contrast with the earlier focus on international threats such as communism).

Former YAFers, College Republicans, and ISI fellows are in their eighties now, but they remain active in Republican politics and stay connected through their clubs' national affiliates: the American Conservative Union, the Philadelphia Society, the National Conservative Political Action Committee, and the Conservative Caucus. The new organizations they have created to train the next generations in law, policy making, and communications include the Federalist Society, the American Legislative Exchange Council, the National Journalism Center, and others. These associations still function as "employment agencies" and "career funnels" to corporations with right-wing connections.[4]

A Student Silent Majority

Throughout the late 1960s, campus conservatives exhaustively claimed to represent a youth silent majority. They alleged that most of their peers agreed with them but were too busy studying or did not think it was necessary to participate in counterdemonstrations when, as they contended, the virtue of such displays was understood. The Right marketed itself as representing the cultural and political standard; it was the Left, they insisted, who were politicizing the university.

But conservatives and white progressives alike overestimated their representation on campus. Most students were moderate, if they cared about politics at all. For perspective, the total student enrollment in the fall of 1970 was 7.4 million.[5] The largest New Left club, SDS, likely had a peak membership of 30,000, though it claimed to have 100,000 active participants. Though the College Republicans was truly the largest campus club, with over 100,000 members, it claimed to have 250,000 members (and vehemently rebuked its reputation for doing nothing). YAF claimed 50,000 members, though it had 15,000–20,000 members at most.[6] ISI claimed that 30,000 students read its literature, but it is impossible to know the number of engaged readers, as most subscriptions were gifted by parents or other family members.[7] Regardless of size, the Right's *leaders* well understood that the students represented an ideological minority on campus. Organizers were thus obsessed with membership numbers and especially the number of participants or onlookers at their events and counterdemonstrations.[8] YAF's front auxiliaries, as well as its habit of claiming media credit for events that it did not create, are only two examples of its countless efforts to make college conservatism appear artificially widespread.

While conservatives were fixated on bolstering their media coverage and membership totals, they also, ironically, claimed to be oppressed and silenced. The Right's unceasing rhetoric of this sort ultimately began to wear on other students. In a letter to the editor of the Duke University YAF newspaper, a student accused the club of being "entirely too defensive" and pleaded, "If the silent majority exists, write for it and forget about the Left loudmouths." The author condemned the pessimistic attitude of the club: "The only thing YAF seems to do is pass resolutions against [reforms]. Don't you guys have any programs of your own?"[9]

YAF, College Republicans, and other groups did have programs of their own, though they regularly co-opted New Left events and slogans. Most of conservatives' programs outside the classroom were spectacles: silent vigils, mock trials, hanging effigies, and burning North Vietnamese flags. Conservative students craved mass attention, while constantly lamenting that their events were being ignored by the media and their members persecuted in the classroom.

This pursuit of attention resulted in an obsession with attractiveness (defined by physical desirability and characteristics such as agreeableness for women and machismo for men) across all clubs on the right, especially religious groups such as Campus Crusade for Christ. The Right repeatedly assailed gender nonconforming peaceniks as sissified long-haired pot smokers who refused to fight in Vietnam, as well as their own antiwar libertarians as "lazy fairies." Leveraging their straight cultural ethos, College Republicans and Campus Crusaders both purposefully fundraised on the attractive square looks of their members. College Republican manuals required that students dress their best when they made home fundraising visits. Campus Crusade's business manager expressed that donors gave for two reasons: love of Jesus or fear. From 1968 to 1970, Campus Crusade's budget rose from $8 million to $20 million (over $180 million in 2023), mostly from patrons eager to support "students who do not look like dangerous radicals."[10]

Through the majority coalition model, college conservatives exploited an opportunity to convince their peers that revolution was neither necessary nor desirable if the process was violent—before their manuals advocated their own violent techniques in 1969. Certainly some coalition students were honest in their pursuit to keep universities open and perhaps did not understand the "restoring campus order" dog whistle as a blanket call to resist peace and civil rights demands. A campaign for order was respectable packaging, which may have allowed coalition leaders to capture temporary support from students who just wanted to attend classes and football games. However, YAF, College Republicans, fraternity men, athletes, and other white conservatives openly called for the assassination of Black demonstrators and antiwar activists, and engaged in fistfights, raucous counter-rallies, property destruction, and other forms of violent misconduct themselves. When YAF announced that its Freedom Offensive program was dedicated to matching radicals' violence, it became clear that the coordinated reaction was against calls for peace and equity rather than the radical tactics used to achieve those visions.

From 1967 to 1970, campus conservatism became an attitude, an identity, and a culture that its adherents unequivocally defended. The students were united by a common objection to social change and a desire to retaliate against anyone who questioned the status quo. Under this "with us or against us" mentality, one's perception of antiwar and civil rights causes became an ideological Rorschach test. Needing only to position itself against the Left, college conservatism became remarkably intellectually flexible (if not hypocritical in the case of YAF's anti-draft stance and libertarian purge). Concurrently, a growing number of the students displayed a penchant for violence and a fascination with authoritarianism from politicians and administrators in the name of freedom.

This fickle amalgam of ideas did not place conservatism in a precarious position. Instead, it caused adherents to strengthen their main strategy: rationalize, defend, and deflect. The approach of taking a valid concern and polarizing the debate surrounding it to avoid honestly engaging with reasonable criticisms became typical after 1967. The best example is YAF's reframing of the University of Southern California's decision to lower the campus flag to half-mast in acknowledgment of the Kent State slayings, which YAF's national chair characterized as inappropriate and politically divisive. Executives at YAF, intellectuals of ISI, and conservative magazine writers smoothed over students' rhetoric in this way and helped justify their anti-left impulses by reconceptualizing certain realities that the students needed to deny. And while the national reaction to the killings at Kent State showed that conservative students' unconditional pro-war attitudes were insufficient for winning campus support no matter how they characterized the incident, their executives understood that they did not need to be popular to be effective. They only needed sources of power on their side. The former students and those who have continued to be trained by them have weaponized this fact for decades.

An Astroturf Backlash

The events covered in the previous pages complicate the understanding of conservative and right-wing backlash as grassroots (as its alumni often claim) and populist (as historians often treat it), since the main actors were students at America's colleges and universities, including some of the most elite, at a time when higher education of any kind was inaccessible to most.[11] It further challenges these ideas by documenting the impressive financial support students received from plutocratic donors. The students in this astroturf arrangement instead functioned as useful on-campus assets for a network of overlapping leaders associated with the broader conservative movement. Dozens of other academics, judges, philanthropists, military officials, governors, mayors, actors—even football coaches Marv Goux and others—supported students on the right through mentorship or funding. The assistance offered by these men was transformative to the students who admired and learned from them.

Older white women did not have the same type of charismatic influence as Buckley, Reagan, or other male heroes of the movement, and this would not change until the 1970s, when activist Phyllis Schlafly rallied significant opposition to the Equal Rights Amendment. In the era described here, women's contributions to the college Right were mostly financial. While YAF had women members on its national board and in state leadership, their presence was largely tokenism, as none of them attained authority to match that of key male figures. Tellingly, none of the dozens of former students interviewed for this study—including the women who were on YAF's national board and women who served as state chairs—credited any woman as a mentor or as otherwise having a significant influence on their political development. Of YAF's nearly 200 advisers in these years, only three women—*National Review* editor Priscilla Buckley (sister of Bill Buckley), conservative war correspondent Anna Chennault, and Birchite Alida Milliken—were listed on its advisory board. By the mid-1970s, YAF had added only one additional woman, Representative Marjorie S. Holt (R-MD), to its board.[12]

And while *National Review, Human Events, Reason,* and other journals did publish women authors, they were almost entirely of the libertarian persuasion, including Ayn Rand, Rose Wilder Lane, Isabel Paterson, and Edith Efron. None had bylines as frequently as male movement icons, and the best known of the women, Rand, was eventually banned from publishing in the most influential of the magazines, *National Review.* YAF's only known Black woman member, Myrna Bain, also published opinion pieces in the *National Review* before ultimately disavowing the Right.

Because of the close mentorship offered by key male figures, there was a direct line from conservative movement leadership to students through ISI media and seminars as well as YAF and College Republican workshops. Many of the products and activities of the student clubs were not conceived organically but were reproductions of examples offered by elders through detailed training manuals. Even ideas that were original at one campus became assigned to all if leaders were sufficiently impressed.

Alumni claims about their grassroots efforts become more suspect when considering how movement donors assumed the students' expenditures (including international travel into war zones, graduate tuition and stipends, and printing and mass mailing expenses). YAFers were trained to execute direct mail fundraisers from advisers Liebman and Viguerie, while College Republicans followed "fool-proof" solicitation scripts crafted by Robert Polack, Morton Blackwell, Karl Rove, and others. Clubs also received funds from innocuous and covert sources, such as donations from their own university trustees itemized as alumni newspaper subscriptions. Students even used the unauthorized signatures of Reagan and Nixon in their direct mail campaigns. Representatives of both politicians contacted YAF demanding they cease that practice.[13] In 1970, the College Republicans, which had just gained independence from the Young Republican National Federation, operated on a $30,000 annual budget, or about $270,000 in 2023.[14] Funding for YAF was even more impressive, with the California state organization alone benefiting from an annual operations budget of $40,000, equivalent to over $360,000 in 2023.[15]

To appreciate the influence of conservative mentors and financiers, it is helpful to compare the unsuccessful outcomes of student efforts before they received explicit guidance from movement elders, and when they did not follow directions closely. Before YAF executives produced publishing manuals and regular editorial content supplements, conservative student newspapers struggled to build readership (to say nothing of their ability to cover production and distribution expenses). Most papers were discontinued after the founding students graduated. Campus radio shows were short-lived and geographically limited to California. It does not appear that conservative campus radio stations ever received any guidance from YAF or ISI; they only received White House press releases through the Washington College News Service and its adjunct College Republicans.

Their organic and independent efforts to broadcast via print and radio failed (the only surviving papers are *American Spectator and Reason*, and neither were organic or independent, see chapter 2). It is possible their target audience was reading *National Review* and listening to the radio shows of Clarence Manion, Fulton Lewis, and others. But that would reinforce the idea that the countersphere content created by college youth was less attractive to listeners than what could be supplied directly from movement elders. Today, conservative media for students is still produced by mentors who are all thirty years of age and older, including Charlie Kirk, Candace Owens, and those associated with Turning Point USA, Campus Reform, and other right-wing youth groups.

When students began to forge their own paths to match the aggressive techniques of the New Left—a step beyond the intellectual lamentations of their bluestocking mentors until 1969—they similarly failed to win support from broad constituencies. Conservatives were best liked by their peers and received the most financial backing from patrons when they promoted goodness through their attractive physical appearances, rule following, displays of patriotism, and condemnations of violence (except when committed by US troops in Vietnam or by police against Black students). Conservative students' efficiency was maximized when they were rhetorically anti-left without being physically combative. They failed to garner respect when they were too forthright in their commitment to white supremacy (such as supporting George Wallace for president) or when they defended state violence against white liberals (such as after the Kent State massacre). The constraint of respectability politics is considerably less apparent on the right today because, as the former students came to learn, popularity is not a requisite for political power.

A Devolution of the Right?

Right-leaning students of the late 1960s were not encouraged to be violent by Buckley and his circle of gentry intellectuals *directly* (those calls from YAF in 1969 came from others on its executive board). Even during the 1968 election campaign, YAF leaders attempted to distance their students from Youth for Wallace defectors. It has also long been said that movement leaders like Buckley and Reagan tried to "write out" conspiracists associated with the John Birch Society from the conservative movement, though recently scholars of the Right, including John S. Huntington and Edward Miller, have challenged this understanding.[16] Today there are no Buckley and Reagan figures—mythic or otherwise—condemning racists, antisemites, and QAnon conspiracists in the GOP. The few Never Trumper pundits of the Right who are willing to condemn harmful charismatics do not command authority in the Republican Party.

The Republican Party's total commitment to thwarting the Left (rather than promoting its own principles) and its willingness to use punishment against its members has transformed the self-described party of ideas into a machine for minoritarian rule. The foremost figure of the modern GOP has openly embraced "very fine people, on both sides," in defense of white supremacist symbols.[17] The party had become so beholden to this singular figure that it failed to issue a new platform in 2020, simply citing its trust in then president Trump to carry out an additional four-year term without input from party representatives.[18] It cannot be overstated that because its only commitment is to reacting against the Left, the Right does not need, value, or even feign interest in a platform of ideas.

In this context, prominent historians and Never Trump pundits have mourned the "devolution" of the Republican Party, as Trumpism has become the essence of conservatism.[19] They point to the Right's obsession with culture wars—or, as they say now, "owning the libs"—rather than the ideas that animated earlier generations. Calling back to 1960s libertarian purges, contemporary traditionalists have censured or otherwise forced out so-called squishes (instead of Americans for Constitutional Action ratings, squishes are now defined by their willingness to work across the party aisle). Members such as Mitt Romney—who was the party's presidential nominee as recently as 2012—are derogatorily called RINOs (Republicans in Name Only) for expressing support for the Black Lives Matter movement or voting to appoint the first Black woman, Justice Ketanji Brown Jackson, to the Supreme Court.

One of the foremost historians of the Right has explained the party's slide into populism as a turn from the "greatest-generation, stiff-upper-lip approach" that once characterized its leaders until the early 1990s, when "patricians had given way to partisans."[20] This view is perhaps too charitable—even nostalgic—as it holds Buckley, Reagan, or some other more polished or sunny figure as a stand-in for the party and conservatism writ large. That conceptualization does not hold up to the scrutiny offered here. Decades before Pat Buchanan, Newt Gingrich, and their kindred firebrands appeared on the political mainstage in the '90s, they were picketing occupied campus buildings through majority coalitions in the '60s. They were there—*leading* their generation—all along. Republican patricians did not just give way to the partisans. They raised them.

The past landscape of conservatism was not the intellectual paradise that is implied when Never Trumpers mourn or when historians simply point out what feels lost since the reign of Buckley, Reagan, the 1990s, or some other time. For decades the Right has shown ample appetite for engaging in culture wars, amplifying white supremacists, and promoting specious tropes rather than debating substantive ideas. Populist passions spanned Buckley's greatest generation, the baby boomers he and others directed, and the generations they in turn influenced. Perhaps all that has changed, as Nicole Hemmer suggests, is that since the end of the Cold War, anticommunism no longer provides the intellectual sheath it once did.[21] For that matter, historians would do well to reconsider our understanding of anticommunism as the glue that previously bound multiple strands of conservatism when we know that, for the New Right, "anticommunism" has only ever been a euphemism. Rather, *resistance to liberalism* is what animated and bound the various factions, as it continues to. Instead of uncritically accepting the Right's coded framing, we should plainly state what was meant by their anticommunism: a wholesale rebuke of pluralism.

Nostalgists may argue that today's conservative magazines, especially *American Greatness*, blatantly encourage brutality in ways that would not have been found in 1960s editions of the genteel *National Review*. Still, the modern countersphere's endorsements of violence can be understood as a continuity rather than a break. In Buckley's own time, the *National Review* published writings of outspoken white supremacists such as Revilo Oliver, even if its editorial board blotted out direct affirmations of violence within its pages. But Oliver's thoughts on white nationalism were easily accessible in other places, such as in the John Birch Society's *American Opinion* or in his classroom at the University of Illinois, where he was tenured. Buckley gave Oliver a larger platform, and readers whose curiosities were peaked by his refined musings in *National Review* could easily find his ideas more sincerely stated in *American Opinion*. It is not a bridge too far to think that the *National Review*'s modern trafficking in violence and conspiracy theories is a logical outgrowth of an earlier time, when its editors were simply more discerning about which kinds of violence or conspiracies they viewed as publishable.

Beyond the party's transparent embrace of white nationalists, another modern complaint regarding GOP leaders is that they are too willing to engage in fraudulent posturing, especially when it comes to fundraising.[22] But the present-day Right's strategy of using fraudulent methods to promote their cause was both widespread and frequently a top-down directive of the late 1960s. Front groups producing multiple membership lists, manipulating the circumstances of a speaker's event, concealing the sources of their funds, and falsely promoting their beliefs and activities as widespread are all examples that recast apparent devolutions as continuities of an earlier era.

Instead of conceiving the modern Right as devolved in terms of its constituency, literary quality, or fundraising techniques, it is better understood as having become more transparent. Consequences for publishing conspiracies in print, online, or through entertainment news, as well as through repeating them on the campaign trail, include increases in viewership, donations, and votes.[23] Today's conservative countersphere, which functions as much as political entertainment as news, freely doles out propaganda to convince consumers of the fallacy that they represent a majority. Not only does this keep ratings, page views, and advertising revenues high, it offers a guarantee that consumers will not challenge the authoritarian structures that keep right-wing leaders in power.

The fact that Republican presidential candidates have not won a popular vote since 2004 (with the previous win being in 1988) is not lost on GOP strategists who double down on their appeals to the nationalist base rather than becoming more inclusive of the typical American. Instead, their energies are focused on making sure Americans who are likely to vote for their opposition are disenfranchised. All that is needed is a system of rules and political instruments (such as gerrymandering, the electoral college, and a stacked Supreme Court) tipped in their favor to remain in power. Procedural impediments (like the filibuster and government shutdowns), rather than popularity, guarantee their will.

Precedent, Policy, and Laws in Higher Education

Since the late 1960s, conservatives have brought about structural changes to the academy by way of precedent, policy, and laws that continue to obstruct progressive goals for higher education. Structural inequities students face pertaining to racism, sexism, ableism, classism, homophobia, and xenophobia have long histories in the university. During the era when these inequities were most visibly challenged on a national scale, too many college administrators buckled under pressure from conservative forces to protect the harmful status quo. While the research presented in this book has centered the collegiate Right's resistance to progress, it also underscores the way university decision-makers and stakeholders were themselves deeply implicated in protecting conditions that produced unequal outcomes for marginalized students. By hiding behind backlash from alumni, locals, and politicians, university decision makers effectively obscured their responsibility to correct these conditions in their willingness to respond to self-described taxpayers but not students.

From 1967 onward, the Right's attacks against progressivism in higher education were carried out through direct action (such as conducting counterdemonstrations and condemning calls for Black studies programs—and, later, ethnic and gender studies programs), supported by heavy-handed administrators, and reinforced by the ascension of retributive figures in the Republican Party who placed higher education in the purview of their authority. This three-pronged strategy brought immediate results via reprimands to students and lasting results by way of new institutional policies and state and federal legislation designed to curtail dissent on the campus.

The Right's legacy of structural changes also came about by *threatening* retribution, even if those threats were unrealized. The wave of lawsuits following the Kent State massacre in 1970 was not organic; the express purpose of those lawsuits, crafted by leaders of YAF in advance to be ready to deploy when the moment presented itself, was to set a legal precedent to force colleges to remain open once strikes began.[24] Test cases had already been developed in 1968, and there was a substantial uptick in filings in 1970 as leaders eagerly put the lawsuits into motion immediately after the massacre.[25]

Most of the student Right's lawsuits were denied, as in the following cases: *Wuelper v. University of New Hampshire* (1970), *Voegeli v. Illinois State University* (1973), *Veed v. Schwartzkopf* (1973), and *Good v. Associated Students of the University of Washington* (1975). While these test cases failed to provide legal victories, they were effective as political moves, signaling that conservatives were willing to assert themselves in matters of institutional governance through the courts. Between the time the cases were filed (mostly in 1969 and 1970) and resolved (some as late as 1975), trustees and administrators on public and private campuses felt pressure to crack down on student speech and assembly rights in anticipation of the rulings. These legal maneuvers, combined with broad support from alumni and donors, helped shape administrative decisions on matters of student conduct and the bounds of free speech and assembly on campus in the decades to come. While the Supreme Court has ruled to protect students' First Amendment guarantees, there are limitations on "time, place, and manner," as established in *Perry Education Association v. Perry Local Educators' Association* (1983). In the name of protecting campus climate, trustees and administrators now exert greater control over the "manner" of student dissent.

Today's conservative supermajority in the Supreme Court is an indication that ideological attempts to thwart reforms could have support from the highest level of the judiciary. Because the Trump administration prioritized appointing over 200 conservative judges throughout the federal system, the Right has effectively flipped the balance of appeals courts nationwide (reminiscent of 1960s organizational takeovers) and fundamentally reshaped the judiciary who will hear such cases.[26] The newest generation of students on the right are now suing institutions for implementing COVID-19 safety measures, which conservatives describe as limitations to their freedoms. To date, students have sued over 300 universities for lost tuition and in-person experiences during pandemic shutdowns (including familiar majority coalition targets: American, Columbia, and George Washington Universities).[27]

Other fundamental changes designed to curtail student dissent are the legacies of the *Report of the President's Commission on Campus Unrest* (commonly referred to as the Scranton Report), produced in the wake of the Kent State massacre. New administrative offices, such as the Office of the Ombuds and the Title IX Office, are regular institutional features that function to address policy violations internally, ensuring the institution's best interest. The administrators who head them are often practicing attorneys, and their staff typically have business degrees in fields like higher education administration.

Also working to protect institutional interests is a large bureaucracy of professionals in student accountability, student conduct, or similarly titled offices housed within student affairs departments. These conduct practitioners are trained in conflict resolution, crisis management, and counseling to help mediate policy violations.[28] They work to ensure that student and faculty behavior that violates institutional codes of conduct is addressed according to university policy to protect the institution from legal liability. A Title IX coordinator serves the same purpose regarding matters broadly related to gender discrimination and sexual violence on campus. Similarly, today's diversity, equity, and inclusion (DEI) officers regularly lead consent and diversity trainings under the guise of student inclusion and safety. While the Title IX coordinators, DEI officers, and student affairs staff who produce these workshops are generally authentic in their pursuit of these missions, their ultimate responsibilities are to communicate policy to students and keep the institution, its most senior administrators, and trustees out of the courts.

Other precedents set forth by the Scranton Report include investments in fully trained law enforcement and security units. Historically, a college security guard's duty was to regulate on-campus traffic and, acting in loco parentis, inspect and enforce parietal rules in women's residence halls.[29] In response to student demonstrations, there was a nationwide transformation of campus parking guard offices into bona fide police departments. At the same time, administrators were eager for their campus police units to expand their jurisdiction beyond the institution's physical borders and into surrounding communities, because officer arrests of Black residents were useful for justifying urban renewal programs.[30]

Today, campuses are protected by institutional police departments with qualified police officers, trained and credentialed to wield firearms and make arrests. Student conduct can be monitored, investigated, and responded to with force directly on-site when needed. University police work closely with conduct officers, Title IX coordinators, and institutional legal teams to ensure that student violations of the law (especially criminal acts of sexual assault) are handled in-house rather than brought to the courts and into the public eye.

Black Educational Justice

Over fifty years later, the legacy achievements of the student Black Power movement are still moderated by historic and contemporary conservative resistance. Though minority-centered programs and curricula have been adopted nationwide, such programs are still forced to contend with lingering charges against their legitimacy as fields of scholarly inquiry—a result of conservative countercampaigns that rebuke antiracist education.[31] As was the case in the 1970s, according to gender studies professor Roderick A. Ferguson, scholarship on race, gender, and sexuality remains "overscrutinized" in terms of its ability to meet "university standards of excellence."[32] And while the contributions of the student Black Power movement have been significant, there is still a need to extend job opportunities to more minority faculty, staff, administrators, and adjacent workers.[33] Today, only 6 percent of American faculty members are Black, and just 17 percent of college presidents are nonwhite.[34] Between 1970 and 1974, Black student enrollment soared by 56 percent.[35] Though remarkable enrollment gains have been achieved since then (nearly half of all undergraduates are students of color, and Black women are the most educated demographic in the nation as of 2019), Black students, especially Black men, continue to face unique challenges: they currently have the highest college dropout rate, the lowest six-year completion rate, and a burden of student debt disproportionate to their non-Black peers.[36]

The Right still invokes the claim of reverse oppression, though they have now extended the victimization example to include that conservatives must "pass" in the academy the same way that the LGBTQ community must conceal their real identities in the workforce and military.[37] Conservative complaints that educational policies designed to correct racial injustices instead discriminate against whites have been considered legitimate arguments in multiple Supreme Court cases, including *Regents of the University of California v. Bakke* (1978), *Parents Involved in Community Schools v. Seattle School District* (2007), and *Fisher v. University of Texas* (2016). Landmark decisions in *San Antonio Independent School District v. Rodriguez* (1973) and *Milliken v. Bradley* (1974) guaranteed inferior K–12 schooling for minority students, reducing their chances of entering and remaining in college. Nixon's appointments of four justices during the campus wars gave conservatives an unmatched legal hand in shaping those decisions, affecting federal race and education policies for decades. Reagan's appointment of anti–civil rights attorney William Rehnquist as chief justice, and Trump's appointment of three young ultraconservatives, has seemingly guaranteed legislative retractions in civil rights matters (beyond the realm of education) for the next several generations.[38] At the time of writing, the Supreme Court has yet to rule on two pending suits that could potentially repeal affirmative action protections for college admissions: *Students for Fair Admissions v. Harvard* and *Students for Fair Admissions v. University of North Carolina*.

Lingering prejudice against Black Americans, as well as a taken-for-granted association between Black activism and criminality, informs white conservative opinion on matters ranging from wealth distribution to affirmative action to paying college athletes.[39] In the months of heightened racial awareness following the murders of Breonna Taylor, George Floyd, Rayshard Brooks, and nearly 300 other Black Americans at the hands of law enforcement in the year 2020 alone, presidents of American institutions of higher learning have once again pledged antiracist commitments, which range from exploring curriculum bias to hiring more diverse faculty to addressing inequitable graduation rates of students of color.[40] Of course, none of these desired outcomes is new. The challenges that have prevented these visions from becoming reality are systemic legacies of white supremacy in the academy, which have been upheld through conservative counterefforts at every level of policy- and lawmaking.

Defunding the Academy

In the decades following the campus wars, influential conservatives have used their powerful positions to defund the academy through right-wing spending policies.[41] In response to the campus wars, libertarian economists James M. Buchanan and Nicos E. Devletoglou captured the Right's logic for defunding the university in their 1970 polemic, *Academia in Anarchy*, in which they recommended universities no longer be considered public goods. If colleges were instead treated as corporations beholden to taxpayer-shareholders, student dissent would be disincentivized. Instead, if education were viewed as a private good—a self-serving investment toward future employment—then students would pay their own way in cash or loans. The punishment for student dissent should be expulsion, and for faculty coconspirators, loss of tenure. As historian Nancy MacLean explains, the aim was and remains "to turn state universities into dissent-free suppliers of trained labor," directed by business-minded administrators rather than faculty and without any burden to taxpayers. Not only would this reduce, or ideally eliminate, public funding for universities, it would serve "the social control function" of barring low-income students from accessing them.[42]

Perhaps the best recognized precedent for neoliberalism's grip on higher education came shortly after the publication of Buchanan and Devletoglou's broadside in the form of a 1971 report to the US Chamber of Commerce, *Attack on the American Free Enterprise System*, written by Nixon-appointed Supreme Court justice Lewis F. Powell Jr. Written just a year after *Academia in Anarchy*, the Powell Memorandum recommendations read strikingly similar to ISI, Foundation for Economic Education, and The Fund for American Studies endeavors: develop academic responses to critiques of capitalism, hire professors to teach about free-market systems in graduate business schools, encourage faculty to publish exhaustively about the economic rewards of private enterprise, develop a list of capitalist intellectual speakers and demand they be given "equal time on the college speaking circuit," ensure that capitalism is well represented in economics textbooks, and devote considerable time and money to the "long-range and difficult project" of "balancing the faculties."[43] The similarities are not coincidental. The 1971 Powell Memorandum was in part a summary and analysis of right-wing campus activities already taking place.

As Ralph Wilson and Isaac Kamola explain, the Powell Memorandum provided an "open blueprint" for right-wing planners who were committed to funding a "pipeline" of conservative talent directly from the academy. Just as the memo was released in the early 1970s, the Right's nonprofit funding giant, the William Volker Fund, was closing. A new generation of financiers, especially John Birch Society cofounder Harry Bradley and fellow Birchite Charles Koch, assumed financial responsibility of right-wing academic projects (among numerous other areas of focus) for the next several decades.[44]

The Powell Memorandum also inspired YAFer Paul Weyrich to cofound the Heritage Foundation in 1973 along with beer magnate Joseph Coors, who provided the initial $250,000 investment and an additional $20,000 each month for expenditures (the initial investment would be worth approximately $2.25 million and the monthly contributions would be worth approximately $180,000 in 2023).[45] Both the Koch and Bradley Foundations continue to heavily fund the Heritage Foundation, the Cato Institute, the Reason Foundation, and numerous other conservative think tanks and educational nonprofits described at the beginning of this chapter.

The results of the Right's war on higher education has been a vast expansion of student loan debt, aid cutbacks to HBCUs and other minority-serving institutions, increased funding to for-profit colleges, and other austerity measures that disproportionately burden the nation's most marginalized students.[46] Aid is effectively redirected away from poor and minority students to the "already-advantaged" and mostly white middle class.[47] Because of the Right's strength in Congress, the federal government repeatedly fails to renew basic student protections guaranteed by the Higher Education Act of 1965, which since 1998 has been reauthorized only once (in 2008).[48]

Conservatives' austerity measures have not spared the faculty either, as administrators have chipped away at faculty participation in shared governance traditions.[49] In this modern iteration, conservative trustees and legislators have consistently worked to erode faculty protections—especially tenure—which is being challenged in several states across the country. When an institution's wealthy stakeholders have disapproved of the politics of its faculty, some universities have buckled under pressure. Best known examples include the University of North Carolina trustees' initial refusal to grant tenure to Nikole Hannah-Jones because of her antiracist *1619 Project*; Beverly Gage's resignation from Yale University's Brady-Johnson Program in Grand Strategy after objections from conservative donors; and Collin College's dismissal of multiple faculty over concerns raised by Republican legislators (including, in Lora D. Burnett's case, a Tweet critical of Mike Pence). Facing political pressure from Republican governor Ron DeSantis, officials from the University of Florida barred certain faculty members from testifying in a state voting rights case while granting permission to others whose research activity supports the Right's preferred electoral outcomes.

Conservatives in power have expanded the practice of monitoring, exposing, and banning perceived liberalism in the classroom by promoting bad-faith legislation aimed directly at faculty and curricula. Since January 2021, over 300 educational gag orders have been proposed in almost every state.[50] These bills target colleges, universities, K–12 classrooms, state agencies, and other public institutions where learning occurs, banning the teaching of certain topics the Right tactically labels "politically divisive."[51] Modern Republican-sponsored legislation of this sort requires that universities ensure "intellectual freedom & viewpoint diversity," permit students to record and share their professors' lectures, and revise "provisions related to protected expressive activity, university student governments, & codes of conduct."[52] It is clear that as long as the Right maintains political power— and as long as those furthest on the right remain the spokespeople of the Republican Party—extremists will continue to target public education for what they perceive to be its democratizing effects.

Resistance from the Right

Conservatives did not win the campus wars of the 1960s, and they failed in almost every way to meaningfully pull faculty or students to the right during their time on campus. Yet their counteractivism has by design thrown sand into the gears of the machines that drive the academy's democratic missions, then and now. Understood in historical context, it becomes clear that modern complaints about free speech or critical race theory are not genuine objections to any single type of idea or pedagogy. Instead, these grievances are part of a much larger and older campaign to subvert the academy through the elevation of conservative views and the displacement of liberal ones. The goal is fostering conservatism among younger Americans while guarding against exposure to ideas that might challenge such a worldview, regardless of their accuracy or legitimacy. Conservatives in power who view public education as the root of liberalism will undoubtably react with punishment and restrictions so long as they occupy positions of influence. And it appears that the political Right, no matter how increasingly unpopular it becomes, will continue to occupy those positions, pulling the existing levers of power and creating new ones to reject democracy and protect the minoritarian rule it has advanced over the last sixty years.

Notes

Abbreviations in the Notes

ASA   American Students for Action, c. 1969, folder 24, box 2. North Carolina State University, Student and Other Organizations, Single Folder Organizations Records, 1904–2013, North Carolina State University Special Collections, Raleigh, NC.

BG   *Boston Globe*

CHE   *Chronicle of Higher Education*

Colson Records   White House Special Files, Staff Member and Office Files: Charles W. Colson, Richard Nixon Presidential Library and Museum, National Archives and Records Administration, Yorba Linda, CA.

Corolla   University of Alabama Libraries and Special Collections, Tuscaloosa, AL.

CRNC Records   College Republican National Committee Records, Hoover Institution, Stanford University, Palo Alto, CA.

CUS   *Columbia (University) Spectator*

Dowd Papers   Patrick Dowd Papers, Hoover Institution Library and Archives, Stanford University, Palo Alto, CA.

Duke YAF   Young Americans for Freedom Papers, Duke University Archives, David M. Rubenstein Rare Book and Manuscript Library, Duke University, Durham, NC.

Duncan Papers   John J. Duncan Sr. Papers, "Young Americans for Freedom, 1965–1972," box 405, folder 5, University of Tennessee Special Collections, Knoxville, TN.

Herman Papers   Luther Russell Herman Jr. Papers, 1966–1978, North Carolina State University Special Collections, Raleigh, NC.

IU Records   Indiana University President's Office Records, 1962–1968, box 163, Student Organizations, "OUR, YAF, and others, 1965–1967" folder, Indiana University Archives, Bloomington, IN.

Knox Collection

Knox Collection of Extremist Literature, J. D. Williams Library Archives and Special Collections, University of Mississippi, Oxford, MS.

LAT   *Los Angeles Times*

May 4 Collection

Kent State University Special Collections and Archives, May 4 Collection Online Exhibit, www.kent.edu/may-4-1970.

Nixon Library

Richard Nixon Presidential Library and Museum, National Archives and Records Administration, Yorba Linda, CA.

MCCAM   *Majority Coalition Campus Action Manual,* Duncan Papers.

NCR   Nixon College Records, L-R folder 1, box 122, White House Central Files, Alphabetical Name Files Collection, Richard Nixon Presidential Library and Museum, National Archives and Records Administration, Yorba Linda, CA.

NCSU YAF   Young Americans for Freedom, North Carolina State University, Student and Other Organizations, Single Folder Organizations Records, 1904–2013, North Carolina State University Special Collections, Raleigh, NC.

NYT   *New York Times*

Powell Papers

Powell Speeches, Lewis F. Powell Jr. Papers, Washington and Lee University School of Law Scholarly Commons, Lexington City, VA.

SGEG   *Student Government Election Guide,* 1970, CRNC Records, box 8.

Tulane Archives

University Archives, Tulane University Special Collections, Tulane University, New Orleans, LA.

UW YAF Records

Young Americans for Freedom Records, 1965–1968, Series 20/3/2/2/2, University of Wisconsin-Madison Archives, Madison, Wisconsin.

Wallace Collection

George C. Wallace Collection, Alabama Department of Archives and History, Montgomery, AL.

WJBD Papers

William Jennings Bryan Dorn Papers, South Carolina Political Collections, University of South Carolina, Columbia, SC.

Introduction

1. "Dartmouth Has a Rough Reception for Wallace," *CHE,* May 17, 1967.

2. "Dartmouth Protest on Wallace Visit," *Madera (CA) Tribune,* May 4, 1967.

3. Quoted in Isserman and Kazin, *America Divided,* 208, 227.

4. Quoted in Kazin, *Populist Persuasion,* 240.

5. Robert Heitzman, "Committee Makes Decision to Suspend Demonstrators Who Participated 'Overtly,'" *Dartmouth,* May 12, 1967.

6. The Right's backlash against K–12 public education extends well before the postwar era. See Ewert, *Making Schools American*; Laats, *Other School Reformers*; Weinberg, *Red Dynamite*.

7. McVicar, "Aggressive Philanthropy," 200–201.

8. Buckley, *God and Man at Yale*, xi-xii.

9. Evans, *Revolt on the Campus*, 5.

10. MacLean, *Democracy in Chains*, 86–87.

11. Quoted in Moriyama, *Empire of Direct Mail*, 126–27.

12. For example, see Edwards, *Educating for Liberty* and *Just Right*; Rove, *Courage and Consequence*; Steinberg, *Whiplash*; Thorburn, *Generation Awakes* and *Young Americans for Freedom*; Viguerie, *New Right*; Viguerie and Franke, *America's Right Turn*.

13. See Robin, *Reactionary Mind*.

14. Histories of YAF include Andrew, *Other Side of the Sixties*; Heineman, *Campus Wars*; Klatch, *Generation Divided*; Schneider, *Cadres for Conservatism*; Thorburn, *Generation Awakes*. For the history of ISI, see Edwards, *Educating for Liberty*. Blumenthal's *Children of the Silent Majority* is the only academic monograph that incorporates College Republicans, covering the group's contributions to the Nixon campaigns of 1968 and 1972.

15. Recent academic studies provide excellent sociological analysis of modern conservative students, but historical analysis is not within their research scope. See Binder and Wood, *Becoming Right*; Binder and Kidder, *Channels of Student Activism*.

16. There also remains much to study regarding conservative evangelical institutions. See Laats, *Fundamentalist U*.

Part I

1. Major, "Bridging the Marginal and the Mainstream," 216.

Chapter 1

1. James K. Glassman, "Moral Re-armament: Its Appeal and Threat," *Harvard Crimson*, March 28, 1967.

2. Glassman, "Moral Re-armament."

3. Sack, *Moral Re-armament*.

4. Critchlow, *Conservative Ascendancy*.

5. Geiger, *American Higher Education*, 180.

6. Schoenwald, "No War, No Welfare," 21.

7. John A. Crowl, "The 'New McCarthyism'?" *CHE*, May 17, 1967.

8. Isserman and Kazin, *America Divided*, 167.

9. Altbach, "From Revolution to Apathy," 614.

10. Long, "Foundations of Student Affairs," 4–5.

11. Thelin, *Going to College in the Sixties*, 88.

12. Thelin, *Going to College in the Sixties*, 13.

13. See Cole, *Campus Color Line*; Eagles, *Price of Defiance*.

14. Rose and Mettler, "Polarization of Higher Education Policy," 42–44.

15. "How Nation's Freshmen View Themselves," *CHE*, January 13, 1967.

16. Geiger, *American Higher Education*, 188; Klatch, *Generation Divided*, 134–36.

17. Klatch, *Generation Divided*, 136.

18. Lewis F. Powell Jr., "A Strategy for Campus Peace," November 11, 1968, Powell Papers, box 117, folder 16.

19. Tuccille, *It Usually Begins with Ayn Rand*, 43.

20. Klatch, *Generation Divided*, 146–47.

21. Blumenthal, *Children of the Silent Majority*, 48.

22. Kazin, *Populist Persuasion*, 240.

23. MacLean, *Democracy in Chains*, 107.

24. Wayne Thorburn, interview with the author, July 3, 2018.

25. Edwards, *Just Right*, 173–74.

26. Thorburn, interview.

27. See Shires, *Hippies of the Religious Right*; Young, *Gray Sabbath*.

28. "Old-Time Religion Takes on New Tasks," *NYT*, August 22, 1970.

29. Quoted in Wright Rigueur, *Loneliness of the Black Republican*, 281. Other studies on Black Republicans include Farrington, *Black Republicans and the Transformation of the GOP*, and Fields, *Black Elephants in the Room*.

30. Lee Edwards, "The Founding Father of the Black Conservative Movement," Intercollegiate Studies Institute, December 3, 2019, https://isi.org/intercollegiate -review/founding-father-black-conservative-movement/.

31. "TFAS Remembers Jay Parker," Fund for American Studies, September 15, 2015, https://tfas.org/news/tfas-remembers-jay-parker/.

32. Allan Brownfeld, email message to author, August 26, 2018.

33. See Eisenmann, *Higher Education for Women*; Fass, *Outside In*; Solomon, *In the Company of Educated Women*.

34. Elizabeth Knowlton, "Letters to the Editor," *Carolina Renaissance*, December 1969, NCSU YAF Records, box 14, folder 23.

35. Patricia Thackston-Ganner, interview with the author, June 14, 2018.

36. Thackston-Ganner, interview.

37. Judith Thorburn, email message to author, July 14, 2018.

38. In 1970, the College Republican National Committee gained independence from the larger Young Republican National Federation. In this book, it is referred to by its present name, College Republicans.

39. Molly Ivins, "The Young Conservatives," *Star Tribune* (Minneapolis, MN), July 28, 1969.

40. Lipset and Raab, "The Wallace Whitelash," 34.

41. Robert L. Browning Jr. to George C. Wallace, December 1968, Wallace Collection, LPR124, box 25, folder 15.

42. Bridges, *Rise of David Duke*, 15–20.

43. Stenner, "Three Kinds of 'Conservatism,'" 142.

44. Schoenwald, "No War, No Welfare," 23.

45. J. Alan MacKay, interview with Gregory L. Schneider, September 26, 1996.

46. Bebout, "Weaponizing Victimhood," 80.

47. Malcolm G. Scully, "Faculty Members, Liberal on Politics, Found Conservative on Academic Issues," *CHE*, April 6, 1970.

48. Heale, "Sixties as History," 138. For more faculty perspectives on New Left activism, see Cronin, *Time to Stir.*

49. Schrecker, *Lost Promise*, 323.

50. Robert Ben Cason, "Cause for Controversy at Gainesville," *Tampa Bay (FL) Times*, November 12, 1967; "Supreme Court Refuses to Bar UF Loyalty Oath," *Orlando (FL) Sentinel*, November 26, 1969; "UF Professors Shun Loyalty Oath, Fired," *Bradenton (FL) Herald*, December 4, 1969.

51. Michael H. Mescon, "Academic Freedom or Academic Anarchy?" *New Guard*, December 1968.

52. "A Time Cornell Will Never Forget," *Poughkeepsie (NY) Journal*, June 9, 1969; "Brown U President Resigns," *Cumberland (MD) News*, May 10, 1969; "College Presidents Resign as Pressure Increases," *Statesman Journal* (Salem, OR), April 25, 1969; "President Resigns at CCNY; 23 Rebels Arrested at Howard," *Pittsburg (PA) Press*, May 9, 1969.

53. "SDS Oust Newsmen from Talk," *Press and Sun Bulletin* (Binghamton, NY), October 13, 1968; William A. Miller Jr., "ANSA Sets 'Time Out Day'; SDS Calls Election Strike," *CHE*, October 28, 1968.

54. Ronald A. James, "Row over SDS Is Said to Cost Colo. $1-Million," *CHE*, April 7, 1969.

55. "Goheen Raps Campus Radicals," *Central New Jersey Home News* (New Brunswick, NJ), September 23, 1968.

56. Malcolm G. Sully, "Presidents Cite Strains of Job as Many Quit," *CHE*, April 21, 1969.

57. "Would Throw SDS Out, U. of Md. Head Says," *CHE*, July 1, 1968.

58. "Boston University Students Protest," *Chicago Tribune*, March 13, 1968; "Students Call Donor 'Slum Lord'; He Withdraws Gift to Boston U," *CHE*, March 25, 1968.

59. Janda, *Prairie Power*, 73.

60. De Groot, "Ronald Reagan and Student Unrest," 121.

61. Janda, *Prairie Power*, 72.

62. Thelin, *Going to College in the Sixties*, 64.

63. "Upward and Outward," *Corolla 1967*, vol. 75, p. 138.

64. See Cummings, *Brain Magnet*; Schulman, *From Cotton Belt to Sunbelt.*

65. Williamson-Lott, *Jim Crow Campus*, 75.

66. "Upward and Outward," *Corolla 1967*, vol. 75, p. 139.

67. *MCCAM*, Duncan Papers, box 405, folder 5.

Chapter 2

1. Anthony Ripley, "Student Survey Shows 38,911 Staged 221 Protests," *NYT*, August 27, 1968.

2. The NSA's figures did not include the Columbia University strikes in April and May 1968 in their analysis, as the causes of each strike were deemed too difficult to categorize. See Cronin, *Time to Stir.*

3. De Groot, "Ronald Reagan and Student Unrest," 120, 122.

4. Nash, *Conservative Intellectual Movement*, 280.

5. Jeffrey Hart, "Secession of the Intellectuals," *National Review*, December 1, 1970.

6. Brown, *Hope and Scorn*, 163.

7. Buckley, *Rumbles Left and Right*, 134; "Buckley Calls Universities 'Submissive Ghettoes,'" *Heights* (Boston College), November 15, 1963.

8. Hart, "Secession of the Intellectuals"; De Groot, "Ronald Reagan and Student Unrest," 120.

9. See MacLean, *Democracy in Chains*; Phillips-Fein, *Invisible Hands*.

10. Edwards, *Educating for Liberty*, 114.

11. William Allen, email message to the author, July 27, 2018.

12. James Gwartney, interview with the author, August 7, 2018.

13. Edwards, *Educating for Liberty*, 97, quote on 107.

14. Edwards, *Educating for Liberty*, 80.

15. Edwards, *Educating for Liberty*, 114–15.

16. Gwartney, interview.

17. Gerald Dwyer, biographical statement shared with the author, November 8, 2018.

18. Randal Teague, interview with the author, June 13, 2018.

19. Philip E. Cleary, "From the Right," *Heights* (Boston College), April 7, 1967. For a history of the liberal foundations of the great books movement, see Lacy, *Dream of a Democratic Culture*.

20. Lee, *Creating Conservatism*, 15.

21. Gwartney, interview.

22. Quoted in Molly Ivins, "The Young Conservatives," *Star Tribune* (Minneapolis, MN), July 28, 1969.

23. Ben C. Toledano, interview with the author, September 15, 2018.

24. Ferguson, *We Demand*, 9.

25. Tullock, quoted in MacLean, *Democracy in Chains*, 106.

26. William Heberg, "What Is the Moral Crisis of Our Time?" *Intercollegiate Review*, January–March 1968.

27. "University Christian Student Center," *Corolla 1967*, vol. 75, p. 417.

28. Ratner-Rosenhagen, *Ideas That Made America*, 160.

29. Lane, "Cultivating Distrust," 157.

30. Major, "Bridging the Marginal and the Mainstream," 220.

31. Lane, "Cultivating Distrust," 157; see also Hemmer, *Messengers of the Right*.

32. Ironically, conservative journals still needed "mainstream" outlets as a foil; thus, conservatives sought to challenge other media rather than replace them. Lane explains that the presence of "liberal media" outlets allowed journals like the *National Review* to justify their own existence the way Fox News does now. See Lane, "Cultivating Distrust," 170–71.

33. Major, "Bridging the Marginal and the Mainstream," 216–17.

34. Bauer and Nadler, "Taking Conservative News Seriously," 2.

35. Major, "Bridging the Marginal and the Mainstream," 217.

36. Selden, "Neoconservative Challenge to the Undergraduate Curriculum," 96.

37. Bauer and Nadler, "Taking Conservative News Seriously," 2.

38. *Club Newsletters*, 1971, CRNC Records, box 8.

39. Morton Blackwell, interview with the author, June 15, 2018.

40. Edwards, *Educating for Liberty*, 35–36.

41. Nash, *Conservative Intellectual Movement*, 276.

42. Allen, email message.

43. *Granite*, March 17, 1969, Knox Collection, box 6, folder 22.

44. Thorburn, *Generation Awakes*, 238–39. Conservative students published dailies or weeklies at the University of California at Berkley (*Tocsin*), Los Angeles (*Student Statesman*), and Santa Barbara (*Daily Planet*); Duke (*Carolina Renaissance*), Florida Atlantic (*Florida Conservative*), Harvard, Indiana (*Alternative*), Stanford (*Arena*), and North Carolina State Universities; and the Universities of Boston (*Counterpoint*), Southern California (*Free Trojan*), Maryland (*Alternative*), Minnesota (*New Opinion*), Mississippi (*Campus Conservative*), North Carolina, San Diego State (*Evolve*), South Carolina (*Rag*), and Wisconsin (*Badger Herald*).

45. *Possibilities for Propaganda*, CRNC Records, box 8.

46. *Club Newsletters*, 1971, CRNC Records, box 8.

47. *Club Newsletters*. Later documents referred to newsletters as "a weapon of ideological struggle." See *Communications*, CRNC Records, box 8.

48. *Club Newsletters*, 1971, CRNC Records, box 8.

49. *Club Newsletters*.

50. *Student Government Election Guide*, 1970, CRNC Records, box 8. Emphasis in original.

51. *Club Newsletters*, 1971, CRNC Records, box 8.

52. *Club Newsletters*.

53. *Club Newsletters*.

54. *How to Prepare a Club Newsletter*, 1970, CRNC Records, box 8.

55. *Club Newsletters*, 1971, CRNC Records, box 8; *Communications*, CRNC Records, box 8.

56. *Club Newsletters*, 1971, CRNC Records, box 8. Emphasis in original.

57. Spillman, "Conservative Baby Boomers' Magazine," 43–44.

58. *Carolina Renaissance*, NCSU YAF Records, box 14, folder 23.

59. DiBranco, "Conservative News," 130.

60. Spillman, "Conservative Baby Boomers' Magazine," 45.

61. Schneider, *Cadres for Conservatism*, 116.

62. DiBranco, "Conservative News," 130.

63. DiBranco, "Conservative News," 134; Mostafa Heddaya, "TDR Exclusive Interview: Obamacon Jeffrey Hart," *Dartmouth Review*, October 21, 2008.

64. Charles B. Wilkinson to Rob Polack, August 25, 1969, NCR.

65. Robert C. Odle Jr., to Morton Blackwell, September 23, 1969," NCR.

66. Memo from Robert C. Odle Jr. to Mr. Krogh, June 10, 1970, NCR.

67. *State Campus News Service Guide*, 1971, CRNC Records, box 8.

68. Robert C. Odle Jr. to William A. Sievert, September 9, 1969, NCR.

69. Memo from Robert C. Odle Jr. to Mr. Krogh, June 10, 1970, NCR.

70. Memo from Robert C. Odle Jr. to Mr. Krogh, June 10, 1970, NCR; J. Bruce Whelihan to William A. Sievert, September 11, 1969, NCR.

71. Memo from Robert C. Odle Jr., to Mr. Krogh, June 10, 1970, NCR; memo from Herb Klein to the president, June 19, 1970, NCR.

72. *Possibilities for Propaganda*, 1971, CRNC Records, box 8.

73. *State Campus News Service Guide*, 1971, CRNC Records, box 8. Emphasis in original.

74. Robert C. Odle Jr. to Morton Blackwell, March 7, 1970, NCR; memo from Robert C. Odle Jr. to Morton Blackwell, February 20, 1970, NCR; memo to Chuck W. Colson re: College Republican National Committee, May 7, 1970, NCR.

75. "CRNC Program Summary," CRNC Records, box 32, Program Ideas folder.

76. "A Plan for Putting the GOP on TV News," H. R. Haldeman Collection, box 99, folder Ailes, Roger 1971, Nixon Library.

77. John Cook, "Roger Ailes' Secret Nixon-Era Blueprint for Fox News," *Gawker*, June 30, 2011.

Chapter 3

1. Lepore, *These Truths*, 624.

2. Olive Evans, "Of Schools and Riots," *NYT*, August 25, 1968.

3. General Electric and DuPont both gave regular and substantial gifts to conservative movement groups, though it does not appear that the student New Left was aware of that in their opposition to these corporations. See Brantley, *Brewing a Boycott*.

4. See Neer, *Napalm*.

5. "A Turning Point: Timeline," October 1967, University of Wisconsin, https://1967.wisc.edu/timeline/; "Dissent: Protests on the Rise across Nation," *Honolulu (HI) Advertiser*, October 23, 1967.

6. "Anti-War Students Grow More Combative," *CHE*, October 26, 1967.

7. David Keene, "Freedom, Force, and the University," *New Guard*, March 1968.

8. David Keene, "Remembering Pat Korten," *Washington Times*, April 12, 2018.

9. "Anti-War Students Grow More Combative"; "Wall of Police Turn Back War Protestors in Oakland," *Press Democrat* (Santa Rosa, CA), October 20, 1967.

10. Russell Baker, "A Day of Giving Peace a Bad Name," *Evening Sun* (Baltimore, MD), October 24, 1967.

11. Tom Lambert, "Pentagon Protest Erupts in Violence," *LAT*, October 22, 1967.

12. "Protest Tactics Draw Rebukes; Called Coercive," *CHE*, November 8, 1967.

13. "Dissent: Protests on the Rise across Nation," *Honolulu (HI) Advertiser*, October 23, 1967.

14. "Anti-War Students Grow More Combative"; "Raving, Ranting, and Rioting," *Daily News* (New York, NY), October 30, 1967.

15. "Protest Tactics Draw Rebukes," *CHE*, November 8, 1967.

16. Ian E. McNett, "Rioters Barred from Funds Appropriated for Education," *CHE*, March 25, 1968.

17. "14,000 Counted as Demonstrators on 62 Campuses," *CHE*, January 29, 1968.

18. James W. Brann, "Recruiting Lively Despite Student Protests," *CHE*, December 21, 1967.

19. John J. Camper, "Secret Research at U. of Michigan Wins Student Vote; Faculty Wary," *CHE*, April 8, 1968.

20. "Protest Tactics Draw Rebukes."

21. George L. Croft, "Harvard Students See Victory," *BG*, November 1, 1967.

22. Isserman and Kazin, *America Divided*, 211–13; Lepore, *These Truths*, 629.

23. Rowling, Sheets, and Jones, "American Atrocity Revisited," 310–11.

24. Garven Hudgins, "The Student 'Establishment,'" *San Bernardino County (CA) Sun*, March 10, 1968.

25. "Saboteurs Hit Another E. Bay PGE Tower," *San Francisco Examiner*, March 21, 1968; "Sixth Bomb Blast Rips Utility Lines in East Bay," *San Bernardino County (CA) Sun*, March 23, 1968.

26. JBW, "Student Activist Demonstrations to Fill Spring," *CHE*, April 8, 1968.

27. Steven V. Roberts, "College Walkouts Loosely Organized," *NYT*, April 27, 1968; "Students and Others on March," *Press and Sun Bulletin* (Binghamton, NY), April 27, 1968; "Student Disorders Disrupt Campuses; Buildings Seized," *CHE*, May 6, 1968.

28. "Campus Demonstrations Prelude Protest Parade," *Poughkeepsie (NY) Journal*, April 27, 1968; Michael Stern, "200,000 Cut Class in a War Protest," *NYT*, April 27, 1968.

29. Laats, "Brave Sons and Daughters True," 153.

30. "Stand on War Inappropriate, Antioch Finds," *CHE*, April 22, 1968.

31. Heineman, *Put Your Bodies upon the Wheels*, 80.

32. Meyer Liebowitz, "Peace Rally Spurs an Opposing Demonstration at Brooklyn College," *NYT*, April 27, 1968.

33. Williamson-Lott, *Jim Crow Campus*, 97.

34. Quoted in Bridges, *Rise of David Duke*, 14.

35. *How to Budget and Finance Your Club*, 1969, CRNC Records, box 8.

36. Kenneth Barry, "SDS Plans March into Low Library Tomorrow at Noon," *CUS*, April 22, 1968.

37. "YAFer Yaps Yippies, Pledges Court Action," *Hatchet* (George Washington University), September 18, 1970.

38. "Editorial: YRs Reply," *Hatchet* (George Washington University), March 25, 1971.

39. Ivins, "The Young Conservatives," July 28, 1969.

40. "What Does 'Moderate' at UW Say?" *Wisconsin State Journal* (Madison, WI), March 6, 1969.

41. "One Soft Morning," undated, UW YAF Records.

42. *Up the Hard Core! How Not to Put Volunteers to Sleep*, undated, CRNC Records, box 8.

43. "What Does 'Moderate' at UW Say?" *Wisconsin State Journal* (Madison, WI), March 6, 1969.

44. "The Sharon Statement: A Timeless Declaration of Conservative Principles," Young America's Foundation, May 4, 2016, www.yaf.org/news/the-sharon-statement/.

45. *MCCAM*, Duncan Papers, box 405, folder 5.

46. John Carbaugh to Robert M. Niemann, December 16, 1969, NCR, College, L-R folder 1, box 122.

47. Randal C. Teague, "Toward a Renewed Strategy of Anticommunism," *New Guard*, December 1967.

48. Teague, "Toward a Renewed Strategy of Anticommunism."

49. Teague, "Toward a Renewed Strategy of Anticommunism."

50. "Salute to Viva," *Reporter-Times* (Martinsville, IN), June 16, 1970; Scanlon, *Pro-War Movement*, 271–75.

51. Ronald Docksai, "YAF's Rendezvous with Destiny: 1970/71," *New Guard*, January 1971.

52. "Vietnam: Past, Present, Prospects," flyer, April 3, 1968, Duke YAF.

53. "Spring 1968 Memorandum," Robert F. Turner Papers, box 22, National Student Committee for Victory in Vietnam folder, Hoover Institution Archives.

54. "IBM Foreign Sales Prompt Active YAF Demonstration," *Heights* (Boston College), March 5, 1968.

55. Karl E. Munds to David R. Jones, March 29, 1968, WJBD Papers.

56. "6 Students Protest IBM's Red Trade," *Milwaukee, Wisconsin, Journal*, February 8, 1968; Ann Blackman, "Sibling Rivalry in the G.O.P.," *Kansas City (MO) Star*, January 10, 1971; William F. Buckley Jr., "YAF Protests Sales to Reds," *Arizona Republic* (Phoenix, AZ), March 31, 1968; "National Campaign against East-West Trade," flyer, 1968, WJBD Papers; "Students Set to Picket IBM Offices," *Corpus Christi (TX) Caller-Times*, November 15, 1967; "YAF to Picket IBM Offices," *Oneonta (NY) Star*, April 29, 1968; "Youth Group Opposes US-Communist Trade," *Star Phoenix* (Saskatoon, Saskatchewan, Canada), April 26, 1968; Earl Zarbin, "Who's on the Right? Young Americans for Freedom Say They Are," *Arizona Republic* (Phoenix, AZ), November 26, 1967.

57. "IBM Foreign Sales Prompt Active YAF Demonstration," *Heights* (Boston College), March 5, 1968; "National Campaign against East-West Trade," flyer, 1968, WJBD Papers; "YAF Pickets IBM over Red Trade," *Pittsburgh (PA) Press*, April 30, 1968.

58. "YAF Expanding Up, Down: Young Conservative of the GOP Confident," *Courier Journal* (Louisville, KY), August 28, 1965.

59. Equating culturally or politically disagreeable concepts to slavery was common on the Right, a practice popularized by F. A. Hayek in his 1943 book *The Road to Serfdom*.

60. "Moscow Circus Draws 6,500 to Civic Arena: Picket Line Thrown Up by Two Groups in Protest of Russians' Appearance Here," *Pittsburgh (PA) Post-Gazette*, October 24, 1963; "Pickets to Greet Moscow Circus: Freedom Fighters to Patrol Arena," *Pittsburgh (PA) Press*, October 23, 1963.

61. Quoted in Edwards, *Just Right*, 163; "Protesters Disrupt Mock Trial of Reds," *NYT*, February 22, 1968.

62. Testimony of David A. Keene before the Democratic Platform Committee, August 19, 1968. UW YAF Records.

63. "Blank Button Says a Lot," *Daily News* (New York, NY), May 1, 1969.

64. *SGEG*.

65. "Campus Unrest Has Passed Its Peak," *Dayton (OH) Daily News*, April 27, 1969.

66. "Campus Peace Button Is Blue," *St. Louis (MO) Post-Dispatch*, May 4, 1969; "Students Opposing Campus Disruptions to Wear Buttons," *Daily Journal* (Vineland, NJ), April 30, 1969.

67. "Youths Set FSC Rally to Finish Blue Button Drive," *Fresno (CA) Bee*, February 27, 1969.

68. Leo Rennert, "Governor Asks Campus Probe by US," *Sacramento (CA) Bee*, February 27, 1969.

69. Quoted in Klatch, *Generation Divided*, 222.

70. "'Peace on Campus' Drive Is Launched," *Central New Jersey Home News* (New Brunswick, NJ), April 30, 1969.

71. Lowell, "Time to Stir," 211.

72. YAF Order Form, Duncan Papers, box 405, folder 5.

73. Thorburn, *Generation Awakes*, 223.

74. "Inventive Students Spoof the Protests," *CHE*, March 10, 1969.

75. "New Left News: Spring 1969," Herman Papers, folder 3.

76. "Letter to Concerned Students from Wayne J. Thorburn," Duncan Papers, box 405, folder 5.

77. Thorburn, *Generation Awakes,* 225.

78. Lee Harris, "Jane Fonda Hanged in Effigy at Her USC Talk," *LAT*, April 13, 1973.

79. Bill Saracino, interview with the author, April 2, 2019.

80. Tom Dreisbach, "How Extremists Weaponize Irony to Spread Hate," *All Things Considered*, April 26, 2021.

81. Pérez, *Souls of White Jokes*, 18.

82. Pérez, *Souls of White Jokes*, 11–12.

83. Pérez, *Souls of White Jokes*, 8.

84. Sienkiewicz and Marx, *That's Not Funny*, 9–10.

85. Sienkiewicz and Marx, *That's Not Funny*, 17.

86. Buckley's own *Up from Liberalism* was an appropriation of Booker T. Washington's *Up from Slavery*.

87. "Old Time Religion Takes on New Tasks," *NYT*, August 22, 1970; Turner, *Bill Bright*, 127–28.

88. "Explo 72: Holler for Jesus," *NYT*, June 18, 1972; Edward B. Fiske, "A 'Religious Woodstock' Draws 75,000," *NYT*, June 16, 1972; "Gospel Parley to Open," *NYT*, June 12, 1972.

89. Turner, *Bill Bright*, 129.

90. Judy Klemesrud, "Rite of Spring: Beer, Beaches and Bikinis," *NYT*, March 24, 1967.

91. "In Graham's Wake—UC Religious Row," *San Francisco Examiner*, February 7, 1967; Bill Rose, "Billy Graham on UC Campus," *Oakland (CA) Tribune*, January 27, 1967; Turner, *Bill Bright*, 119–23, 126.

92. "Graham Talks to UC Students about Sex, LSD and Christ," *San Bernardino County (CA) Sun*, January 28, 1967.

93. "Billy Graham Talks to 8,000 at Rally on Berkeley Campus," *NYT*, January 28, 1967.

94. Judy Klemesrud, "Rite of Spring: Beer, Beaches and Bikinis," *NYT*, March 24, 1967.

95. Turner, *Bill Bright*, 129–31.

96. Eskridge, "One Way," 92.

97. "Old-Time Religion Takes on New Tasks."

98. David Franke, interview with the author, June 13, 2018.

99. Boisfeuillet Jones, "The Young Republican Plight," *Harvard Crimson*, July 11, 1967.

100. Juris Kaza, "Young Republicans: Power Play," *CUS*, April 22, 1968.

101. *SGEG*.

102. Advertisement to Elect Mark Leinwand College Rep to C.U.S.C., *CUS*, April 22, 1968.

103. Robert Betts, "'Silent Majority' Cools Dissidents," *Times* (Munster, IN), May 4, 1969.

104. "Junior Senator, Alabama: Sen. Jeff Sessions (R) Elected 1996; 1st term," *Congressional Quarterly's Politics in America: 107th Congress* (Washington, DC: CQ Press, 2000), https://web.archive.org/web/20141006094234/http://www.cqpress.com/ls/pia/pdfs/107/aljr-2000.pdf.

105. *SGEG*. Emphasis in original.

106. *SGEG*.

107. *SGEG*.

108. *SGEG*. Emphasis in original.

109. *SGEG*.

110. *SGEG*.

111. *SGEG*. Emphasis in original.

112. *SGEG*.

113. "Kansas State Students Reject NSA Nearly 4–1," *CHE*, December 9, 1968.

114. See Michel, *Struggle for a Better South*.

115. Williamson-Lott, *Jim Crow Campus*, 89–90.

116. "Victory at UNC," *Renaissance*, April 29, 1969, Duke YAF Papers.

117. Dennis Walsh, "N.S.A. and the Y.A.F.: Reply to a Critic," *Heights* (Boston College), March 6, 1964.

118. Robert L. Jacobson, "Student Association Offers 'Alternative' to NSA Activism," *CHE*, December 9, 1968.

119. Since at least 1961, YAF attempted to send delegates to the NSA Congress but was unable to meaningfully pull the organization to the right. See Thorburn, *Generation Awakes*, 58–61.

120. David Keene, "Freedom, Force, and the University," *New Guard*, March 1968.

Chapter 4

1. Clara Bingham, "'The Whole World Is Watching': An Oral History of the 1968 Columbia Uprising," *Vanity Fair*, March 26, 2018.

2. Robert Stulberg, "Protesters Say They Will Not Negotiate until CU Grants Disciplinary Amnesty," *CUS*, April 24, 1968.

3. Michael Stern, "1 Arrested in Park in Violent Protest," *CUS*, April 24, 1968.

4. For a discussion of Columbia's historical intrusion into Harlem, see Bradley, *Upending the Ivory Tower*, 167–96.

5. The term "urban renewal" had an explicitly racialized connotation. See Rast, *Origins of the Dual City*.

6. Robert Hessen, "Campus or Battleground? Columbia Is a Warning to All American Universities," *Barron's National Business and Financial Weekly*, May 20, 1968, UW YAF Records.

7. Kenneth Barry, "SDS Plans March into Low Library Tomorrow at Noon," *CUS*, April 22, 1968; "Columbia Truce Axed," *Press and Sun Bulletin* (Binghamton, NY), April 27, 1968; "Tired? Tired? Tired?" April 23, 1968, Columbia Libraries Online, https://exhibitions.library.columbia.edu/exhibits/show/1968/item/5534.

8. Cronin, *Time to Stir* (book), lxi.

9. See the *MCCAM*.

10. Cronin, *Time to Stir* (film), episode 3.

11. Cronin, *Time to Stir* (film), episode 3.

12. Lowell, "Time to Stir," 211.

13. "Protestors Crowd into Hamilton Hall for All-Night Vigil," *CUS*, April 24, 1968.

14. Bradley, *Upending the Ivory Tower*, 189; Kuhn, *Hardhat Riot*, 14–15; Slonecker, "Columbia Coalition," 968.

15. *Time to Stir* (film), episode 3.

16. Bingham, "'Whole World Is Watching'"; Michael Stern, "Outsiders Influence SDS Action," *CUS*, April 25, 1968.

17. Cronin, *Time to Stir* (book), lxii.

18. Bingham, "'Whole World Is Watching'"; "Columbia Truce Axed," *Press and Sun Bulletin* (Binghamton, NY), April 27, 1968; Mark Jaffe, "Protestors Roam Offices in Low," *CUS*, April 25, 1968; Robert Stulberg, "Protestors Occupy 2 New Buildings," *CUS*, April 25, 1968.

19. Spoehr, "Making Brown University's 'New Curriculum,'" 62.

20. David Burnham, "Police Guarding Gates to Campus," *NYT*, April 27, 1968.

21. "Student Disorders Disrupt Campuses; Buildings Seized," *CHE*, May 6, 1968.

22. "Silent Vigil Circular," April 27, 1968. Columbia Libraries Online, https://exhibitions.library.columbia.edu/exhibits/show/1968/item/5583.

23. Cronin, *Time to Stir* (book), lxiii.

24. Massarsky, "Primary Shades of Opposition," 220.

25. Martin Flumenbaum, "Coach Rohan Urges Restraint before Athletes in Gymnasium," *CUS*, April 26, 1968; Hurwitz, "Smartest Kid I'd Ever Met," 137.

26. Massarsky, "Primary Shades of Opposition," 221–22.

27. Flumenbaum, "Coach Rohan Urges Restraint"; Hurwitz, "Smartest Kid I'd Ever Met," 137.

28. Thoms, "Political Education and the Birth of Students," 382.

29. Rosenthal, "Life on the Ledge," 283.

30. Massarsky, "Primary Shades of Opposition," 222.

31. Paul Cronin, "The Time That Bill Barr Faced Down Protestors—Personally," *Politico*, June 7, 2020; Hurwitz, "Smartest Kid I'd Ever Met," 137.

32. "University Calls in 1,000 Police to End Demonstration as Nearly 700 Are Arrested and 100 Injured," *CUS*, April 30, 1968.

33. George Lowery, "A Campus Takeover That Symbolized an Era of Change," *Cornell Chronicle*, April 16, 2009; "University Calls in 1,000 Police."

34. Quoted in Kuhn, *Hardhat Riot*, 18.

35. Geiger, "Student Protest Movement," 182; Isserman and Kazin, *America Divided*, 218; Lowery, "Campus Takeover"; Slonecker, "Columbia Coalition," 967; "University Calls in 1,000 Police."

36. Paul Starr, "Student Group Aims to Block Amnesty," *CUS*, April 27, 1968.

37. Andrew Crane, "Body of Five Students, Five Professors, and Two Administrators Is Proposed," *CUS*, April 27, 1968; Robert Betts, "Campus Counterattack: Silent Majority Not So Silent," *Pensacola (FL) News Journal*, April 13, 1969.

38. James W. Brann, "'Changing Whole Society' Is SDS Goal at Columbia," *CHE*, May 20, 1968.

39. Bradley, *Upending the Ivory Tower*, 193.

40. "Columbia Rebels Gained Support after Use of Police, Poll Shows," *CHE*, June 10, 1968.

41. "House Votes to Deny Aid to Disruptive Students; Backlash to Sit-Ins Grows," *CHE*, May 20, 1968.

42. Isserman and Kazin, *America Divided*, 218.

43. Lowell, "Time to Stir," 210.

44. Massarsky, "Primary Shades of Opposition," 217.

45. Hessen, "Campus or Battleground?"

46. "House Votes to Deny Aid to Disruptive Students."

47. Joseph, "Dashikis and Democracy," 19; *They Demand Courageously: The 1968 Northwestern Bursar's Office Takeover*, Northwestern University Libraries Online Exhibit, https://sites.northwestern.edu/bursars1968/about/.

48. "House Votes to Deny Aid to Disruptive Students."

49. "Student Demonstrators May Lose Federal Aid."

50. Riot Act of 1968, 18 U.S.C. §§ 2101, 2102 (1999); National Mobilization Committee to End War in Vietnam v. Foran, 411 F.2d 934 (7th Cir. 1969); United States v. Dellinger, 472 F.2d 340 (7th Cir. 1972).

51. Gage, *G-man*, 653; Isserman and Kazin, *America Divided*, 219.

52. Leondra R. Kruger, "'68 Protests, Riots at Columbia Sparked Student Activism at Harvard, in Nation," *Harvard Crimson*, June 6, 1994.

53. "A Campus Rebel's Confession," *BG*, October 1, 1968.

54. Bebout, "Weaponizing Victimhood," 65.

55. Bebout, "Weaponizing Victimhood," 69.

56. *MCCAM*.

57. *MCCAM*.

58. *MCCAM*.

59. Schneider, *Cadres for Conservatism*, 114.

60. *MCCAM*.

61. *MCCAM*.

62. *MCCAM*.

63. Marc Fisher, "The Year America Unraveled," *Washington Post*, May 29, 2018.

64. Williamson-Lott, *Jim Crow Campus*, 79.

65. *MCCAM*.

66. *MCCAM*; Ernest Dunbar, "Cornell's Experience Indicates Why, All over the Country, So Much Stress Is Being Put on the Black Studies Thing," *NYT*, April 4, 1969.

67. "To All Those Concerned about the Future of the University from the Committee to Defend Individual Rights," Summer 1968. UW YAF Records.

68. *MCCAM*.

69. Alan MacKay, "Young America's Freedom Offensive," *New Guard*, March 1969.

70. "YAF to Sue Demonstrators," *Heights* (Boston College), October 14, 1969.

71. Lowell, "Time to Stir," 210.

72. Massarsky, "Primary Shades of Opposition," 219.

73. "YAF to Sue Demonstrators," *Heights* (Boston College), October 14, 1969.

74. Thorburn, *Young Americans for Freedom*, 95.

75. Ronald Docksai, "YAF's Rendezvous with Destiny: 1970/71," *New Guard*, January 1971, 143.

76. Martin Foncello, "YAF Criticizes 'Politicizing' the University," *Heights* (Boston College), October 14, 1970.

77. Janda, *Prairie Power*, 84.

78. Memo from Paul L. McKay to the Attorney General, May 10, 1969, NCR; Nixon staff member to Keith Douglas, April 11, 1969, NCR.

79. *MCCAM*.

80. Nixon staff member to Jack R. Lohrer, April 11, 1969, NCR.

81. "Informer on S.D.S. Vexes House Unit," *NYT*, August 17, 1969. After six months as an informant, Meinshausen recused himself and, with the guidance of anarchist political activist Karl Hess, urged libertarians in YAF to defect to the SDS against their greater common enemy, the US government.

82. "Stanford Defies Part of Probe Subpoena," *Los Angeles Herald-Examiner*, June 4, 1969.

83. Memorandum from Lamar Alexander for Bud Krogh, June 7, 1969, NCR.

84. Thelin, *Going to College in the Sixties*, 100.

Chapter 5

1. The majority coalition model would not be fully underway until the fall of 1968 (discussed in chapter 4). Most of the differences among these groups will be attended to by the end of the Republican National Committee convention in August 1968 and in time for the fall semester.

2. Lawrence van Gelder, "Survey Shows College Students Back McCarthy over Kennedy," *NYT*, March 17, 1968.

3. Blumenthal, *Children of the Silent Majority*, 21.

4. *1968 Project Target*, 1968, CRNC Records, box 8.

5. "Revised Schedule of the CRNC Summer Conference," August 16, 1968, CRNC Records, box 8.

6. *Project Open Door Application,* 1970, CRNC Records, box 8.

7. *Campus Voters Manual,* 1968, CRNC Records, box 8.

8. For more on how Viguerie developed his mailing lists, see Viguerie, *New Right,* 27–37.

9. *Campus Voters Manual,* 1968, CRNC Records, box 8.

10. *College Precinct Workers Manual,* 1968, CRNC Records, box 8.

11. *Campus Voters Manual,* 1968, CRNC Records, box 8.

12. *Campus Voters Manual.*

13. *Mock Convention Guide,* 1968, CRNC Records, box 8.

14. *Mock Convention Guide.*

15. Blumenthal, *Children of the Silent Majority,* 61.

16. De Groot, "Ronald Reagan and Student Unrest," 117.

17. "Not a Dime's Worth of Difference" campaign materials, 1968, Wallace Collection, box 25, folder 15.

18. John Fund, "Reagan's Famous Speech Turns 50 Today," *National Review,* October 27, 2014.

19. "Tom Charles Huston Interview Transcription," interview by Timothy Naftali, April 30, 2008, 2, Nixon Library.

20. "Tom Charles Huston Interview Transcription," 2.

21. Perlstein, *Nixonland,* 174.

22. "Tom Charles Huston Interview Transcription," 3.

23. Isserman and Kazin, *America Divided,* 226.

24. "Hecklers Disrupt Nixon Talk at Akron University," *Salem (OH) News,* October 11, 1968.

25. Blumenthal, *Children of the Silent Majority,* 30.

26. "Won't Let Government Take Your Guns—Wallace," *Akron (OH) Beacon Journal,* October 2, 1968.

27. Ian E. McNett, "All 3 Presidential Candidates Direct Appeals to Campuses," *CHE,* October 14, 1968.

28. Blumenthal, *Children of the Silent Majority,* 28.

29. Blumenthal, *Children of the Silent Majority,* 22.

30. Thorburn, *Generation Awakes,* 166.

31. Lipset and Raab, "Wallace Whitelash," 34; Paul W. Valentine, "Rightist Claims Cure for College Violence," *LAT,* May 26, 1969.

32. John Acord, "George Wallace—Candidate for Youth," Fall 1968, Wallace Collection, box 25, folder 15.

33. "YAF Pamphlet," Knox Collection, box 6, folder 22.

34. Isserman and Kazin, *America Divided,* 209.

35. Quoted in Thorburn, *Generation Awakes,* 166.

36. Quoted in Molly Ivins, "The Young Conservatives," *Star Tribune* (Minneapolis, MN), July 31, 1969.

37. Ivins, "The Young Conservatives," July 28, 1969.

38. Lipset and Raab, "Wallace Whitelash," 34.

39. Valentine, "Rightist Claims Cure for College Violence."

40. Zeskind, *Blood and Politics,* 16.

41. Valentine, "Rightist Claims Cure for College Violence."

42. Daniel M. J. Stokes to George C. Wallace, Wallace Collection, box 25, folder 15.

43. Robert L. Browning Jr. to George C. Wallace, December 1968, Wallace Collection, box 25, folder 15.

44. Ann Rodgers, "Gladewater Teen Will Lead 'Youth for Wallace,'" *Longview (TX) News-Journal*, June 16, 1968.

45. George Lardner Jr. "Campus Boost for Wallace," *Des Moines (IA) Register*, September 3, 1968; memo from Joe Fine to Ed Ewing and Cecil Jackson, April 3, 1968, Wallace Collection, box 25, folder 16; Rachel Scott, "The Youth Campaign Is On," *Detroit Free Press*, October 7, 1968; "Wallace Youth Aim at Campus," *Democrat and Chronicle* (Rochester, NY), September 3, 1968; "'Youth for Wallace' Campus Campaign Having Troubles," *Charlotte (NC) Observer*, September 4, 1968; "Wallace Youth Unit to Meet," *Dominion News* (Morgantown, WV), October 18, 1968.

46. "Youth for Wallace Newsletter," July 1968, Wallace Collection, box 25, folder 16.

47. "Stand Up for America" enrollment door flyer; telegram from John McMahan, August 24, 1968; telegram from Kentucky Youth for Wallace, August 24, 1968; and Youth for Wallace Committee enrollment form, all in Wallace Collection, box 25, folder 15.

48. Leslie E. Birchfield to Cecil C. Jackson, August 23, 1968, Wallace Collection, box 25, folder 15.

49. "Youth-for-Wallace Group Will Form," *Longview (TX) News-Journal*, June 13, 1968.

50. "A Note from the Publisher: Governor George C. Wallace, Our Choice for President of United States," *Southern Utah Free Press* (Hurricane, Utah), October 17, 1968.

51. "Solicitation to Gulf Oil Corporation from Dennis C. McMahon," August 23, 1968, Wallace Collection, box 25, folder 15; John Acord to Cecil Jackson, August 27, 1968, Wallace Collection, box 25, folder 15.

52. Memo to Cecil C. Jackson Jr. from Ed Ewing," August 12, 1968, Wallace Collection, box 25, folder 15.

53. Zeskind, *Blood and Politics*, 20–26.

54. George C. Wallace to Daniel M. J. Stokes, November 22, 1968, Wallace Collection, box 25, folder 15.

55. Berry, *Blood and Faith*, 19.

56. Revilo P. Oliver, "After Fifty Years," *Vermont Freeman* (Starksboro, VT), June 17, 1970.

57. Thorburn, *Young Americans for Freedom*, 85.

58. Blumenthal, *Children of the Silent Majority*, 26.

59. Blumenthal, *Children of the Silent Majority*, 32–34.

60. *Corolla 1969*, vol. 77, p. 46.

61. McNett, "All 3 Presidential Candidates."

62. Isserman and Kazin, *America Divided*, 221–22; Kuhn, *Hardhat Riot*, 21.

63. Paul Krassner, "Hippies, Radicals, Pranksters," *LAT*, August 31, 2017.

64. Isserman and Kazin, *America Divided*, 222.

65. "Army Riot Troops Ready," *NYT*, August 22, 1968; Steven V. Roberts, "5,000 Troops Flown to Convention Duty," *NYT*, August 26, 1968.

66. "Political Notes: Chairman Daley's Maxims," *Time*, July 18, 1969.

67. Isserman and Kazin, *America Divided*, 223; Kuhn, *Hardhat Riot*, 21.

68. "Hundreds of Protesters Block Traffic in Chicago," *NYT*, August 26, 1968.

69. "7 Yippies Arrested with Pig 'Candidate' at Chicago Center," *NYT*, August 24, 1968.

70. "Hundreds of Protesters Block Traffic in Chicago."

71. Isserman and Kazin, *America Divided*, 223.

72. "Poll Shows 71.4% Find Police Action Justified in Chicago," *NYT*, August 31, 1968.

73. Blumenthal, *Children of the Silent Majority*, 19.

74. Quoted in Ivins, "The Young Conservatives," July 30, 1969.

75. William A. Miller Jr., "ANSA Sets 'Time Out Day'; SDS Calls Election Strike," *CHE*, October 28, 1968.

76. Blumenthal, *Children of the Silent Majority*, 31.

77. *MCCAM*.

78. Thorburn, *Generation Awakes*, 223.

79. *MCCAM*.

80. *College Precinct Workers Manual*, 1968, CRNC Records, box 8.

81. David Greenberg, "The Time Nixon's Cronies Tried to Overturn a Presidential Election," *Politico*, October 10, 2020.

82. Lepore, *These Truths*, 594.

83. Lipset and Raab, "Wallace Whitelash," 27–28.

84. "Wallace Backers in City Express Disappointment," *Bridgeport (CT) Post*, November 6, 1968. For a history of the Right's claims of liberal media bias, see Hemmer, *Messengers of the Right*.

85. Drew Pearson, "Neo-Nazis Grab 'Wallace Youth' Unit," *Bradenton (FL) Herald*, April 22, 1969.

86. "Local GOP Club Supports NYA," *Montclair (CA) Tribune*, June 26, 1969.

87. Lipset and Raab, "Wallace Whitelash," 34.

88. See Michael, *Willis Carto*.

89. William B. Steel Jr. to Richard M. Nixon, President Elect, January 9, 1969, NCR, YAF folder 3, box 122.

90. Isserman and Kazin, *America Divided*, 250.

91. Gage, *G-man*, 686.

92. Jack L. Kennedy, "New Demonstrations Hit U.S. and Canadian Campuses," *CHE*, February 24, 1969; "Knowles Asks Laws to Curb Disturbances," *Kenosha (WI) News*, February 13, 1969; "TACT Wants Peace on State Campus," *Daily Chronicle* (Centralia, WA), February 8, 1969.

93. Blumenthal, *Children of the Silent Majority*, 47.

94. Matthew Storin, "Congressmen Ask College Crackdown," *BG*, April 15, 1969.

95. Memo from Dale Grubb to Bryce Harlow, February 28, 1969, NCR, folder 1, box 122.

96. Blumenthal, *Children of the Silent Majority*, 36.

97. "Campus Freedom Offensive," October 3, 1969. Duncan Papers, box 405, folder 5.

98. Robert D. Frank to Richard Nixon, February 1, 1969, NCR, folder 1, box 122.

99. M. Mackenzie, "Help College Students," *Fort Lauderdale (FL) News*, January 28, 1969.

100. Schneider, *Cadres for Conservatism*, 121.

101. Robert D. Frank to Richard Nixon, February 1, 1969, NCR, folder 1, box 122.

102. Charles E. Stuart to David T. Burhans Jr., March 24, 1969, YAF folder 3, box 122.

103. Schneider, *Cadres for Conservatism*, 121.

104. Memo from Robert C. Odle Jr. to Mr. Krogh, June 10, 1970, NCR, College, L-R folder 1, box 122.

105. "Nixon Popularity Is Found High, Especially among Young Voters," *NYT*, June 5, 1969.

106. Thorburn, *Young Americans for Freedom*, 75–76.

Chapter 6

1. Bradley, *Upending the Ivory Tower*, 100.

2. Biondi, *Black Revolution on Campus*, 1.

3. Bradley, *Upending the Ivory Tower*, 186.

4. Williamson-Lott, *Jim Crow Campus*, 73–74.

5. Lewis F. Powell Jr., "Civil Disobedience: Prelude to Revolution?" *US News and World Report*, October 30, 1967, 69.

6. Beverly Gage, *G-man*, 653.

7. Hinton, "Police Violence," 246–47.

8. Williamson-Lott, *Jim Crow Campus*, 79.

9. Rojas, *From Black Power to Black Studies*, 4.

10. A few exceptions to student Black Power resistance did appear at conservative evangelical institutions, such as Wheaton College in Illinois. See Laats, "Brave Sons and Daughters True," 146.

11. Biondi, *Black Revolution on Campus*, 53.

12. See Averbeck, *Liberalism Is Not Enough*.

13. Bristow, *Steeped in the Blood of Racism*, 139.

14. For an account of the structural racism inherent in the American legal system, see Rothstein, *Color of Law*.

15. Austin, *Up against the Wall*, 185.

16. Geiger, "Student Protest Movement," 188.

17. Ernest Dunbar, "Cornell's Experience Indicates Why, All over the Country, So Much Stress Is Being Put on the Black Studies Thing," *NYT*, April 6, 1969.

18. Bebout, "Weaponizing Victimhood," 64.

19. Cain and Dier, "Protests and Pushback," 571.

20. Harvey Hukari Jr., "Conservative as N——r," *Carolina Renaissance*, September 1969, Duke YAF.

21. Phillip Abbot Luce, "Yes, S.C., There Really Is an SDS," *New Guard*, January 1967; "12 Negroes Invade S.F. State's Daily Gater, Assault Its Editor," *Press-Tribune*

(Roseville, CA), November 7, 1967. That conservative students would be fearful of SNCC at this point in the campus wars is suspect. As historian Jelani Favors explains, SNCC was already well underway to losing its campus presence by 1968 and was essentially ineffective as a national organization. See Favors, *Shelter in a Time of Storm*, 209.

22. Quoted in Rogers, *Black Campus Movement*, 134.

23. Bridges, *Rise of David Duke*, 18.

24. "UC-Berkeley YAF's Non-Negotiable Demands," *New Guard*, Summer 1969.

25. Paul W. Valentine, "Rightist Claims Cure for College Violence," *LAT*, May 26, 1969.

26. Quoted in Molly Ivins, "The Young Conservatives," *Star Tribune* (Minneapolis, MN), July 30, 1969.

27. Averbeck, *Liberalism Is Not Enough*, 33.

28. Anthony Ripley, "Student Survey Shows 38,911 Staged 221 Protests," *NYT*, August 27, 1968.

29. Marvin Liebman, interview by Gregory L. Schneider, September 1, 1994.

30. Lewis F. Powell Jr., "The New Left on the Campus," 1966, 32, Powell Papers.

31. Austin, *Up against the Wall*, 169.

32. Quoted in Ferguson, *We Demand*, 20.

33. "Saving Orderly Society Is Ambition of SOS," *Indiana Daily Student*, February 22, 1966, IU Records.

34. Gayle Faunce, "Letter to the Editor, SOS Answer," *Indiana Daily Student*, March 2, 1966, IU Records.

35. Williamson-Lott, *Jim Crow Campus*, 85.

36. Diana Henry, "DuBois Club Recognition Withdrawn; Other News," *CHE*, March 22, 1967.

37. Isserman and Kazin, *America Divided*, 171.

38. Bradley, *Upending the Ivory Tower*, 351.

39. Dunbar, "Black Studies Thing."

40. Murray Schumach, "Columbia Rebels Fail in Protest," *NYT*, March 20, 1970.

41. Biondi, *Black Revolution on Campus*, 74.

42. T'Shaka, "Africana Studies Department History," 23–24.

43. Fred King, "Radicals Wake Up Right at UNC," *Carolina Renaissance*, September 1969; "What Does 'Moderate' at UW Say?" *Wisconsin State Journal* (Madison, WI), March 6, 1969; *MCCAM*.

44. Bradley, *Upending the Ivory Tower*, 339.

45. School Enrollment in the United States: 1970, US Department of Commerce/ Bureau of the Census, March 5, 1971, www.census.gov/content/dam/Census/library /publications/1970/demo/p20-215.pdf.

46. Bezilla, "Years of Crises."

47. Charlayne Hunter, "Black Studies Changing Schools Here," *NYT*, November 2, 1969.

48. Bradley, *Upending the Ivory Tower*, 128.

49. Dunbar, "Black Studies Thing."

50. Williamson-Lott, *Jim Crow Campus*, 116.

51. Richard Nixon, "Address at the Dedication of the Karl E. Mundt Library at General Beadle State College," Madison, South Dakota, June 3, 1969, www .presidency.ucsb.edu/documents/address-the-dedication-the-karl-e-mundt-library -general-beadle-state-college-madison-south.

52. Biondi, *Black Revolution on Campus*, 174–75.

53. Dunbar, "Black Studies Thing."

54. Hunter, "Black Studies Changing Schools."

55. Cole, *Campus Color Line*, 314.

56. "Black Studies Aid Given Guidelines," *NYT*, March 7, 1969; "US Warns Antioch on Black Studies," *NYT*, March 6, 1969.

57. Richard Eberhardt, "YAF Member Compares Dean to Commandant of Stalag 17," *Daily Reville*, December 17, 1970.

58. Bebout, "Weaponizing Victimhood," 66, 75–76.

59. Ivins, "The Young Conservatives," July 30, 1969.

60. Bridges, *Rise of David Duke*, 16.

61. Ivins, "The Young Conservatives," July 31, 1969.

62. Quoted in Ivins, "The Young Conservatives," August 1, 1969.

63. Quoted in Bradley, *Upending the Ivory Tower*, 347–48.

64. Gage, *G-man*, 684.

65. McGill, *Year of the Monkey*, 28.

66. "Racial Issue Puts Off San Jose-Texas Game," *NYT*, September 21, 1967; "San Jose Accedes to Negro Students," *CHE*, September 27, 1967.

67. "The Real Issue at San Jose," *LAT*, September 28, 1967.

68. Thelin, *Going to College in the Sixties*, 97.

69. Neelofer Lodhy, "Explore CSUN's Hidden History of Campus Activism," *Sundial* (California State University–Northridge), December 9, 2013.

70. Bradley, *Upending the Ivory Tower*, 345–60; Geiger, "Student Protest Movement in the 1968 Era in Three Acts," 186–87; Joseph, "Dashikis and Democracy," 191; George Lowery, "A Campus Takeover That Symbolized an Era of Change," *Cornell (University) Chronicle*, April 16, 2009; Rogers, *Black Campus Movement*, 127–30. For polemical perspectives of faculty and students alienated by the Cornell protests, see Bloom, *Closing of the American Mind* and Novick, Schatz, and Rahe, *Cornell in Crisis*.

71. "3 Students Slain in S.C. State Riot," *CHE*, February 26, 1968; "Carolina Youth Was Shot in Back," *NYT*, February 13, 1968; Rogers, *Black Campus Movement*, 132–33.

72. "The Other Side of Riots" invitation, March 19, 1968, Duke YAF.

73. Williamson-Lott, *Jim Crow Campus*, 91.

74. Rogers, *Black Campus Movement*, 135.

75. Patrick Chura, "Mythology of Jackson State," *CHE*, October 20, 2017.

76. Broadhurst, "We Didn't Fire a Shot," 306.

77. Gage, *G-man*, 691–92.

78. Bristow, *Steeped in the Blood of Racism*, 162–63.

79. Quoted in Bristow, *Steeped in the Blood of Racism*, 7.

80. Biondi, *Black Revolution on Campus*, 2–3.

81. "War Now First in Precipitating Student Protest," *CHE*, November 11, 1968.

82. "AU Liberalizes Visiting Rules," *Star Gazette* (Elmira, NY), October 14, 1968; James C. Smith, "Princeton Discussing Women in Dorms This Weekend," *Central New Jersey Home News* (New Brunswick, NJ), April 21, 1968; "Student Activists Do 'Important' Job," *Billings (MT) Gazette*, August 26, 1968; "Would End Dorm Rules on Women at Williams," *Times Record* (Troy, NY), October 12, 1968.

83. Bradley, *Upending the Ivory Tower*, 107.

84. Spoehr, "Making Brown University's 'New Curriculum,'" 60–61.

85. Bristow, *Steeped in the Blood of Racism*, 11.

86. Douglas Martin, "James E. Cheek, Forceful University President, Dies at 77," *NYT*, January 21, 2010.

87. Cole, *Campus Color Line*, 312.

88. Williamson-Lott, *Jim Crow Campus*, 93–94. See also Cole, *Campus Color Line*.

89. Bradley, *Upending the Ivory Tower*, 113.

90. Williamson-Lott, *Jim Crow Campus*, 116.

91. Dunbar, "Black Studies Thing."

92. See Cole, *Campus Color Line*, for how Black presidents navigated these political situations.

93. Myrna D. Bain, "Black Students and the American University," *New Guard*, May 1969.

94. Bradley, *Upending the Ivory Tower*, 337.

Chapter 7

1. Heineman, *Put Your Bodies upon the Wheels*, 80.

2. Heineman, *Put Your Bodies upon the Wheels*, 161. A former SDS member who wished to remain anonymous recalled that Dartmouth College YAF and SDS shared the same leader.

3. Timothy Bleck, "Convention of Freedom Group Here," *St. Louis (MO) Post-Dispatch*, August 27, 1969.

4. Bleck, "Convention of Freedom Group Here."

5. Bleck, "Convention of Freedom Group Here"; "YAF Parley Fight Looms: One Faction Seeks Chapter Autonomy," *Springfield (MO) Leader and Press*, August 29, 1969.

6. Bleck, "Convention of Freedom Group Here."

7. "Buckley Raps Foolish Profs," *Alton (IL) Evening Telegraph*, August 29, 1969; Malcolm G. Scully, "Conservative Students Lay Plans to 'Sock It to the Left,'" *CHE*, September 15, 1969; Doug Thompson, "To Combat Leftists, YAF Watches SIU," *Alton (IL) Evening Telegraph*, September 2, 1969; "YAF Planning Legal Action on Disorders," *Daily Capital News* (Jefferson City, MO), August 28, 1969.

8. Bleck, "Convention of Freedom Group Here"; Scully, "Conservative Students Lay Plans."

9. Klatch, *Generation Divided*, 226–27.

10. Bleck, "Convention of Freedom Group Here."

11. Schneider, *Cadres for Conservatism*, 135.

12. "YAF Facing Split as Factions Argue," *Amarillo (TX) Globe-Times*, September 23, 1969.

13. Doherty, *Radicals for Capitalism*, 357; "Rightists to Fight Student Left," *St. Louis (MO) Post-Dispatch*, August 31, 1969.

14. Doherty, *Radicals for Capitalism*, 357.

15. Scully, "Conservative Students Lay Plans."

16. Doherty, *Radicals for Capitalism*, 357; Klatch, *Generation Divided*, 232; Schneider, *Cadres for Conservatism*, 136.

17. "Rightist to Fight Student Left," *St. Louis (MO) Post-Dispatch*, August 31, 1969.

18. Klatch, *Generation Divided*, 234–35; Schoenwald, "No War," 36–40.

19. Schoenwald, "No War," 25, 38.

20. "Editorials: Political Unity," *Hatchet* (George Washington University), September 18, 1970.

21. Ron Docksai, "SDS: The Politics of Regression," *New Guard*, September 1968. Both emphases in original.

22. *Organization*, 1968, CRNC Records, box 8.

23. *Organization*.

24. "Membership and Fall Registration," August 1968, CRNC Records, box 8.

25. *Organization*, 1968, CRNC Records, box 8.

26. *Organization*.

27. *Public Programming*, undated, CRNC Records, box 8.

28. *Organization*, 1968, CRNC Records, box 8.

29. *How to Present a Public Program*, 1969, CRNC Records, box 8.

30. *Public Programming*, CRNC Records, box 8.

31. *Public Programming*.

32. *How to Present a Public Program*, CRNC Records, box 8.

33. *Public Programming*, CRNC Records, box 8.

34. *How to Present a Public Program*, CRNC Records, box 8.

35. *Public Programming*, CRNC Records, box 8.

36. *How to Present a Public Program*, CRNC Records, box 8.

37. *Public Programming*, CRNC Records, box 8.

38. *How to Budget and Finance Your Club*, 1969, CRNC Records, box 8.

39. "Sample Fund Raising Letter," 1969, CRNC Records, box 8.

40. *How to Budget and Finance Your Club*, 1969, CRNC Records, box 8.

41. *Ways and Means of Raising Money*, 1968, CRNC Records, box 8.

42. *Public Programming*, CRNC Records, box 8.

43. *How to Budget and Finance Your Club*, 1969, CRNC Records, box 8.

44. *How to Budget and Finance Your Club*. Emphasis in original.

45. *How to Budget and Finance Your Club*.

46. "USC Campus Put on Alert," *LAT*, November 21, 1969; Bill Saracino, interview with the author, April 2, 2019.

47. Saracino, interview.

48. Williamson-Lott, *Jim Crow Campus*, 91.

49. Hobson, "Football Culture at New South Universities," 43.

50. Creg Stephenson, "A Journey through Alabama's Often-Tortured Football History with Notre Dame," AL.com, January 1, 2021.

51. "Report of the University of Wisconsin YAF to the Wisconsin State Senate on Proposed Repeal of Section 14(b) of the Taft-Hartley Act," undated, UW YAF Records.

52. Phil Semas, "Students Joining Grape Boycott," *CHE*, October 28, 1968.

53. Saracino, interview.

54. "Announcements," *Renaissance*, April 29, 1969, Duke YAF Papers.

55. "YAF Balances Views on Picker's Strike," *Heights* (Boston College), November 26, 1968; "YAF Seeks Freedom," *Heights* (Boston College), November 26, 1968.

56. "YAF Told Isle Infested by Subversives," *Honolulu (HI) Star-Bulletin*, June 29, 1969.

57. "Forbidden Fruit Party Planned for Valentine's Day," *Winfield College Republican*, January 15, 1969, CRNC Records, box 8.

58. Don Drumn, "YAF Holds Grape-In, without Much Wrath," *Courier News* (Bridgewater, NJ), January 31, 1970.

59. Lane, "Cultivating Distrust of the Mainstream Media," 160.

60. Those purged in the 1969 split who have been foundational to the libertarian movement include Don Ernsberger, Dave Walter, Dave Nolan, Robert Poole, Jaret Wollstein, Roy Childs, Joe Cobb (an ISI member), and Ed Crane. See "Reminiscences and Prognostications," *Reason*, May 1978.

Chapter 8

1. Sherry Figdore, "Youth Group Pushes Battle on New Left," *Daily Register* (Red Bank, NJ), April 10, 1969; Alan MacKay, "Young America's Freedom Offensive," *New Guard*, March 1969.

2. YAF's Campus Freedom Offensive, October 3, 1969, Duncan Papers, box 405, folder 5.

3. Rahim, "Diversity to Deradicalize."

4. Figdore, "Youth Group Pushes Battle"; MacKay, "Young America's Freedom Offensive."

5. "14 Candidates Seek Junior College Board Positions on May 27," *Van Nuys (CA) News*, May 20, 1969.

6. "YAF Takes on SDS in Loud UW-M Debate," *Daily Tribune* (Wisconsin Rapids, WI), September 27, 1969.

7. Figdore, "Youth Group Pushes Battle"; MacKay, "Young America's Freedom Offensive."

8. MacKay, "Young America's Freedom Offensive."

9. Arkansas YAF press release, March 18, 1970, NCR, YAF folder 2, box 122.

10. Andrew, "Pro-war and Anti-draft," 11.

11. For a detailed study of how the Catholic Church supported antiwar efforts, see Cajka, *Follow Your Conscience.*

12. Edward Rudd, "Viet Vet Burns Card at Anti-draft Rally," *Hartford (CT) Courant*, November 1, 1968.

13. "None Turn in Draft Cards at UI Rally," *Iowa City (IA) Press Citizen*, November 15, 1968.

14. Thorburn, *Young Americans for Freedom*, 112.

15. "President of California Young GOP College Group to Speak," *LAT*, January 5, 1969.

16. Gage, *G-man*, 686.

17. Blumenthal, *Children of the Silent Majority*, 36.

18. "Campus Unrest Has Passed Its Peak," *Dayton (OH) Daily News*, April 27, 1969; Crocker Snow Jr., "All Was Quiet in Yard," *BG*, April 10, 1969.

19. George Lowery, "A Campus Takeover That Symbolized an Era of Change," *Cornell Chronicle*, April 16, 2009; Paul Sullivan, "Striking Lessons from the 1960s," *Harvard Crimson*, April 11, 2019.

20. "Col. Pell's Case for ROTC," *Harvard Crimson*, February 3, 1969.

21. Michael Berkey, "Positive Negative Steps Will Rid Campus of ROTC," *Heights* (Boston College), November 19, 1968.

22. Martin Foncello, "YAF Criticizes 'Politicizing' the University," *Heights* (Boston College), October 14, 1970.

23. Bernard Bellon, "Navy Recruiters Due Oct. 18," *Heights* (Boston College), September 27, 1971.

24. Molly Ivins, "The Young Conservatives," *Star Tribune* (Minneapolis, MN), July 28, 1969.

25. "Commitment + YAF" flyer, September 18, 1969, Duke YAF.

26. "YAF Supports Duke Faculty on ROTC Issue," *Carolina Renaissance*, September 1969. NCSU YAF.

27. "Connecting the University—the War," ASA.

28. Tricia Thackston-Ganner, interview with the author, June 14, 2018.

29. Steven Ealy, interview with the author, July 28, 2018.

30. "Students to Fight Unrest by Confronting Radicals," *BG*, August 19, 1969.

31. Peter Benchley, "Conservative Students Take on the Leftists," *Austin (TX) American*, November 2, 1969.

32. Crocker Snow Jr. "YAF Asks Arrests, Expulsion in Takeovers," *BG*, October 4, 1969.

33. Subsequent moratoria in November and December 1969 as well as the Kent State massacre in May 1970 would prompt demonstrations that surpassed this strike in participation.

34. William Davis, "2500 'Tell It to Hanoi,'" *BG*, December 8, 1969; "More Than 600 Campuses Participate in Nationwide Vietnam Moratorium," *CHE*, October 20, 1969.

35. Crocker Snow Jr., "Rightist Students May Sue Radicals," *BG*, October 4, 1969.

36. "Conservatives Pick 32 Campuses for Suits against Disruptors, Tolerant Administrators," *CHE*, October 13, 1969.

37. *MCCAM*.

38. Snow, "YAF Asks Arrests."

39. *MCCAM*.

40. Telegraph from Brooklyn College Young Americans for Freedom to the White House, October 5, 1969, NCR, YAF folder 3, box 122.

41. Telegram from Students to Keep Wesleyan American to the president, October 13, 1969, NCR, Students folder 2, box 122.

42. Ivins, "The Young Conservatives," August 1, 1969.

43. "FAU Editor Rebuffed," *Palm Beach (FL) Post*, November 12, 1969; telegraph from Brooklyn College YAF to the White House, October 5, 1969, NCR, YAF folder 3, box 122.

44. "More Than 600 Campuses Participate in Nationwide Vietnam Moratorium."

45. "500 Students Demonstrate to Show They're Happy," *CHE*, October 20, 1969.

46. RM, "Student Demonstrators Fete Nevada's President Miller," *CHE*, October 27, 1969.

47. Richard Nixon to Carol G. Abojian, January 13, 1970, NCR, College, L-R folder 1, box 122.

48. William J. Waugh, "Pro-war Students Mustering Campaign," *Intelligencer Journal* (Lancaster, PA), November 13, 1969.

49. "Young Americans for Freedom to Push 'Tell It to Hanoi' Movement for Peace," Dowd Papers, box 2.

50. Waugh, "Pro-war Students Mustering Campaign."

51. Scanlon, *Pro-war Movement*, 274.

52. Waugh, "Pro-war Students Mustering Campaign."

53. "Work in Durham While Mobe Is in Washington" flyer, November 13, 1969, Duke YAF.

54. "Moratorium Day Quiet at FSU," *Tallahassee (FL) Democrat*, November 14, 1969; "Silent Majority Honor War Dead," *Tallahassee (FL) Democrat*, November 12, 1969.

55. Ronald B. Dear to the Honorable Richard M. Nixon, January 12, 1970, NCR, YAF folder 3, box 122.

56. "Nixon Supporters Planning War Rallies," *NYT*, November 9, 1969.

57. Quoted in Andrew, "Pro-war and Anti-draft," 12.

58. "YAF Leads March against Moratorium," *St. Louis (MO) Post-Dispatch*, November 14, 1969.

59. Judith Waters, "'Exercise Freedom' Central to YAF Credo," *Edwardsville (IL) Intelligencer*, December 11, 1969.

60. Waugh, "Pro-war Students Mustering Campaign."

61. Ed Roickle, "Impressions on Washington," *Observer* (University of Notre Dame), November 20, 1969.

62. Blumenthal, *Children of the Silent Majority*, 77–78.

63. Davis, "2500 'Tell It to Hanoi'"; Gordon D. Hall, "Blazing Rhetoric or Cold Week-end," *BG*, December 12, 1969.

64. "Viet Envoy Sees GIs Out in '70," *Berkshire Eagle* (Pittsfield, MA), December 8, 1969.

65. Hall, "Blazing Rhetoric."

66. Steve MacDonald and Jeff Roche, "Right On: Tell It to Hanoi," *Heights* (Boston College), December 16, 1969.

67. Memo from Randal Teague to YAF Board of Directors, October 21, 1969, Dowd Papers, box 2.

68. "Idaho Youth's Activities Told," *Spokane (WA) Chronicle*, December 11, 1969; "YAF Campus Campaign Set to Bolster Nixon Policy," *Palladium Item* (Richmond, IN), December 12, 1969.

Chapter 9

1. Linda Charlton, "Big Rallies Are Planned, Students Protest Nixon Troop Move," *NYT*, May 2, 1970.
2. AW, "Students Get Prison Terms of 1–25 Years for Protest," *CHE*, February 9, 1970.
3. "894 Students Are Arrested at a Mississippi College," *CHE*, March 2, 1970.
4. Joseph Lelyveld, "Black Students Challenge the Order at Mississippi Valley State," *NYT*, May 25, 1970.
5. "More Than 20 Demonstrations Hit Campuses So Far This Year," *CHE*, February 24, 1970.
6. "18 Campuses Hit by Protests in Early March," *CHE*, March 16, 1970.
7. "Demonstrations Occur at Rate of One a Day in 1970," *CHE*, April 6, 1970.
8. Memo to Richard Nixon re: Meeting with David A. Keene, May 25, 1970, NCR, YAF folder 2, box 122; "YAF Team, Back from Viet, to Fight Unilateral Pullout," *Honolulu (HI) Advertiser*, April 4, 1970.
9. Randal Cornell Teague to President Nixon, February 24, 1970, NCR, YAF folder 2, box 122.
10. Bezilla, "Years of Crises."
11. "One Student Killed as Violent Protests Hit 8 Campuses," *CHE*, April 27, 1970; Winthrop Griffin, "The Isla Vista War—Campus Violence in a Class by Itself," *NYT*, August 30, 1969.
12. Stephen Kurkjian, "YAF: Wake Up America," *BG*, April 26, 1970.
13. Sherry Figdore, "Youth Group Pushes Battle on New Left," *Daily Register* (Red Bank, NJ), April 10, 1969.
14. *MCCAM.*
15. *MCCAM.*
16. M. Mackenzie, "Help College Students," *Fort Lauderdale (FL) News*, January 28, 1969; "YAF 'Liberates' NER to Expose Leftist Hypocrisy," *Heights* (Boston College), November 26, 1968.
17. Geiger, "Student Protest Movement," 187.
18. Jackie Estrada, "New Voice on Campus," *Ithaca (NY) Journal*, April 19, 1969; Judson Hand, "The Student Voice Speaks in Many Tongues, All Conflicting," *Daily News* (New York, NY), April 23, 1969.
19. "Campus Unrest Has Passed Its Peak," *Dayton (OH) Daily News*, April 27, 1969.
20. "Recap of Bombing Statistics, Period of Jan. 1, 1969, through Apr. 15, 1970," *Riots, Civil and Criminal Disorders: Hearings before the Permanent Subcommittee on Investigations of the Committee on Government Operations*, 91st Cong., 2d Sess., 5340 (1970).
21. "Tell It to Hanoi" campaign petition, May 5, 1970, NCR, YAF folder 3, box 122. Emphasis in original.

22. Richard Nixon to Harold Green, August 4, 1970, NCR, Students folder 2, box 122; Richard Nixon to John R. Hightower, August 31, 1970, NCR, YAF folder 2; Richard Nixon to Rod Norberg, August 4, 1970, NCR, Students folder 2, box 122; Richard Nixon to Deborah Doering, August 10, 1970, NCR, Students folder 2, box 122; Thomas E. Tomlinson to the president, May 23, 1970, Nixon Student Records, Students folder 2, box 122.

23. Andrew, "Pro-war and Anti-draft," 3.

24. Dennis Cogswell, "Student Sample Opposes War by 5–4 Margin," *CHE*, June 8, 1970.

25. Memo from Robert Polack to CR leadership, May 1, 1970, NCR, College, L-R folder 3, box 122.

26. Levine and Wilson, "Student Activism in the 1970s," 627.

27. "Day-by-Day Account of KSU Trouble," *Akron (OH) Beacon Journal*, May 5, 1970; "Kent State Students Demonstrate," *Newark (OH) Advocate*, May 2, 1970; Richard E. Lightner, "Student Patrols Save OSU from Third Bloody Day?" *Akron (OH) Beacon Journal*, May 1, 1970; "Students Protest Nixon's Decision," *Newark (OH) Advocate*, May 2, 1970.

28. Jerry M. Lewis and Thomas R. Hensley, "The May 4 Shootings at Kent State University: The Search for Historical Accuracy," May 4 Collection; "Kent under 'State of Emergency,'" *Akron (OH) Beacon*, May 3, 1970; "Kent State Erupts in New Riots," *Lancaster (OH) Eagle Gazette*, May 4, 1970; "Tear Gas Ends Disturbance at 3 A.M.," *Akron (OH) Beacon Journal*, May 2, 1970; "Troops Put Down Kent Disturbance," *News Journal* (Mansfield, OH), May 3, 1970.

29. Broadhurst, "'We Didn't Fire a Shot,'" 288; "Day-by-Day Account of KSU Trouble"; Geiger, "Student Protest Movement," 188–89; "Two KSU Students Are Hospitalized," *Akron (OH) Beacon-Journal*, May 4, 1970.

30. "More Than 100 Arrested in 3 Days' KSU Disorders," *Akron (OH) Beacon-Journal*, May 4, 1970.

31. Governor James A. Rhodes, Speech on Campus Disorders in Kent, May 3, 1970, Kent State University Libraries, Special Collections and Archives, https://omeka.library.kent.edu/special-collections/items/show/6234.

32. In September 1970, the Ohio legislature would pass the governor's campus riot bill, automatically suspending students and faculty for a minimum of one year as they awaited pending court cases for campus disturbances. See "Legal Chronology May 5, 1970–January 4, 1979," May 4 Collection.

33. Rhodes, Speech on Campus Disorders in Kent.

34. Lewis and Hensley, "May 4 Shootings."

35. "Day-by-Day Account of KSU Trouble"; Geiger, "Student Protest Movement," 189; John Kifner, "4 Kent State Students Killed by Troops," *NYT*, May 5, 1970; Lewis and Hensley, "May 4 Shootings."

36. Lewis and Hensley, "May 4 Shootings."

37. Quoted in Blumenthal, *Children of the Silent Majority*, 39.

38. "Legal Chronology May 5, 1970–January 4, 1979," May 4 Collection.

39. "Shun Anti-war Rally, YAF Leader Urges," *Chicago Tribune*, May 9, 1970.

40. Blumenthal, *Children of the Silent Majority*, 48.

41. Broadhurst, "'We Didn't Fire a Shot,'" 289.

42. Wells, *War Within*, 10300.

43. Kuhn, *Hardhat Riot*, 118.

44. Charlton, "Big Rallies Are Planned."

45. Blumenthal, *Children of the Silent Majority*, 87.

46. Frank J. Prial, "Students Step Up Protests on War," *NYT*, May 6, 1970.

47. Broadhurst, "'We Didn't Fire a Shot,'" 289–90; Bezilla, "Years of Crises."

48. Robert McFadden, "College Strife Spreads, over 100 Schools Closed and Up to 350 Struck," *NYT*, May 8, 1970.

49. J. W. Stillman, "Strike Hits 166 Colleges; Administrators Close B.U.," *Harvard Crimson*, May 6, 1970.

50. Blumenthal, *Children of the Silent Majority*, 34, 40.

51. "North Vietnamese Storm a U.S. Base in Cambodia," *NYT*, May 16, 1970; Stillman, "Strike Hits 166 Colleges."

52. Blumenthal, *Children of the Silent Majority*, 38.

53. Broadhurst, "'We Didn't Fire a Shot,'" 302.

54. Laats, "Brave Sons and Daughters True," 152.

55. Thorburn, *Generation Awakes*, 223.

56. "Aztec Gridder Just Protecting His Flag," *Daily News Post* (Monrovia, CA), May 15, 1970.

57. Thorburn, *Generation Awakes*, 242.

58. "1970-Campus Disturbance-Flagpole, Newcomb Hall," videorecording, May 5, 1970, Tulane University Digital Library, https://digitallibrary.tulane.edu/islandora/object/tulane%3A123642; "1970-Student Demonstration-John Hutchinson," videorecording, May 5, 1970, Tulane University Digital Library; https://digitallibrary.tulane.edu/islandora/object/tulane%3A123643.

59. "Newt Gingrich Attending a Student Demonstration," May 5, 1970, Newt Gingrich Photographs File, Tulane Archives.

60. Thorburn, *Generation Awakes*, 242.

61. "Aztec Gridder Just Protecting His Flag."

62. "Students for Classes Bulletin of Information, May 11, 1970," Colson Records, Students Pro-president folder 1, box 109.

63. "The Position of the A.S.A," ASA Records; "To all citizens, faculty, and to all students of N. C. State University," ASA Records.

64. "Billy Graham Expects Second Coming Soon," *NYT*, May 25, 1970.

65. Memorandum from Charles Colson to Rob Odle, May 15, 1970, Colson Records, Students Pro-president folder 2, box 109.

66. James Lacy, interview by Gregory L. Schneider, July 29, 1997.

67. Randal C. Teague, interview by the author, June 13, 2018.

68. Richard O. Wright, "A Preliminary Report on the University Problems Project Sponsored by the Wisconsin YAF," UW YAF Records.

69. Linda Greenhouse, "Suit Still Stirs Marymount Girls," *NYT*, May 26, 1970; Andrew H. Malcolm, "Some Colleges in Area to Reopen Today," *NYT*, May 11, 1970; McFadden, "College Strife Spreads," *NYT*, May 8, 1970; Hugh Wyatt and Gene Spagnoli, "Many Colleges Crippled," *Daily News* (New York, NY), May 11, 1970.

70. "An Exclusive Interview: Vice President Spiro T. Agnew on Campus Disorder, American Youth, etc.," *New Guard*, Summer 1970.

71. "Colleges Reopen; Protests Continue All over Nation," *Harvard Crimson*, May 12, 1970.

72. Dave Meuhing, "O'Leary Reports That Crime Is Significantly Lower This Year," *Heights* (Boston College), October 14, 1970.

73. *The Report of the President's Commission on Campus Unrest* (Washington, DC: US Government Printing Office, 1970), 12.

74. Memorandum from Fred Fielding to Chuck Colson, January 21, 1971, Colson Records, Campus Unrest folder 1, box 43.

75. This outreach was partly a strategic response to Congress holding hearings on lowering the voting age from twenty-one to eighteen. Still, Nixon needed only token student outreach, assured that college students were but a minority of young people nationwide. An eighteen-year-old silent majority could prove politically advantageous, and College Republican representatives suggested Nixon champion the issue. Memo from Herb Klein to the president, June 19, 1970, NCR, College, L-R folder 3, box 122; memorandum for Chuck W. Colson re: CRNC, May 7, 1970, Colson Records, Student Demonstrations folder, box 109.

76. Memo to Richard Nixon re: Meeting with David A. Keene, May 25, 1970, NCR, YAF folder 2, box 122.

77. Blumenthal, *Children of the Silent Majority*, 42.

78. Blumenthal, *Children of the Silent Majority*, 79, 98.

79. Leonard Garment to John A. Grasham, June 29, 1970, NCR, College, L-R folder 1, box 122.

80. *Report of the President's Commission on Campus Unrest*, 3–4, 10–13.

81. Ronald Docksai, "YAF's Rendezvous with Destiny: 1970/71," *New Guard*, January 1971.

82. Quoted in Thorburn, *Generation Awakes*, 297.

83. Memo from Jerry Norton to Randal Teague, October 1970, Dowd Papers, box 3.

84. Doug Kennell, "YAF's Opposition to Amnesty," *LAT*, April 7, 1973; Harriet van Horne, "The Youth Vote," *York (PA) Daily Record*, August 31, 1972.

Conclusion

1. "Barnett—Amended Statement of Facts," United States Attorney's Office, Capitol Breach cases: BARNETT, Richard, Case Number: 1:21-cr-38, updated January 10, 2022.

2. Robert Hessen, "Campus or Battleground? Columbia Is a Warning to All American Universities," *Barron's National Business and Financial Weekly*, May 20, 1968, UW YAF Records.

3. Hemmer, *Partisans*, 8.

4. Binder, Kidder, and Sztykowski, "Conservative Channel," 69.

5. "School Enrollment in the United States: 1970," US Department of Commerce/ Bureau of the Census, March 5, 1971, www.census.gov/content/dam/Census/library /publications/1970/demo/p20-215.pdf.

6. James Lacy, interview by Gregory L. Schneider, July 29, 1997.

7. Edwards, *Educating for Liberty*, 114.

8. Lacy, interview.

9. "Introspection," *Carolina Renaissance*, February 1970, Duke YAF.

10. "Old Time Religion Takes on New Tasks," *NYT*, August 22, 1970.

11. See Finchelstein, *From Fascism to Populism*; Kazin, *Populist Persuasion*; Müller, *What Is Populism?*; Norris, *Cultural Backlash*.

12. "YAF Pamphlet," c. 1973, Knox Collection, box 6, folder 2.

13. Lacy, interview.

14. Memorandum for Chuck W. Colson re: CRNC, May 7, 1970, Colson Records, Student Demonstrations folder, box 109.

15. Lacy, interview.

16. Erick Trickey, "Long before QAnon, Ronald Reagan and the GOP Purged John Birch Extremists from the Party," *Washington Post*, January 15, 2021; Huntington, *Far-Right Vanguard*; Cormac Kelly, "William F. Buckley and the Birchers: A Myth, a History Lesson and a Moral," *Salon*, April 3, 2021; Miller, *Conspiratorial Life*.

17. Angie Drobnic Holan, "In Context: Donald Trump's 'Very Fine People on Both Sides' Remarks (transcript)," *PolitiFact*, April 26, 2019; Doina Chiacu, "Trump Says Confederate Flag Proud Symbol of US South," *Reuters*, July 19, 2020.

18. Reid J. Epstein, "The GOP Delivers Its 2020 Platform. It's from 2016," *NYT*, August 25, 2020.

19. Kruse and Zelizer, *Myth America*, 3; Sykes, *How the Right Lost Its Mind*.

20. Hemmer, *Partisans*, 103.

21. Hemmer, *Partisans*, 2–3, 7–8.

22. See Ehrenberg, *White Nationalism and the Republican Party*; Paul Waldman, "The Right's Grift Machine Is Only Growing Stronger," *Washington Post*, February 21, 2021.

23. Terry Gross, "How the Republican Party Came to Embrace Conspiracy Theories and Denialism," August 9, 2022; Rick Klein, Alisa Wiersema, and Libby Cathey, "GOP Candidates Bring Conspiracy Theories to Trail in Trump's Defense," ABC News, August 11, 2022; Steve Reilly, Matt Stiles, Jason Paladino, and Anna Deen, "15 QAnon-Linked Candidates Have Won Key Primaries in 2022," *Grid*, July 28, 2022.

24. Richard O. Wright, "A Preliminary Report on the University Problems Project," UW YAF Records.

25. Alan MacKay, "Young America's Freedom Offensive," *New Guard*, March 1969; Randal C. Teague, "YAF: A Presence in the Room," *New Guard*, January 1971.

26. "Factbox: Donald Trump's Legacy—Six Policy Takeaways," *Reuters*, October 30, 2020; Carrie Johnson, "Wave of Young Judges Pushed by McConnell Will Be 'Ruling for Decades to Come,'" *NPR*, July 2, 2020.

27. Josh Moody, "Appeals Court Revives COVID Lawsuits," *Inside Higher Ed*, March 9, 2022.

28. Long, "Foundations of Student Affairs," 4–5.

29. Ferguson, *We Demand*, 29–30.

30. Cole, *Campus Color Line*, 70–118.

31. "A JBHE Survey: Is Black Studies Central to the Mission of a Great University?"; "Black Studies Is an Unpopular Major"; Christian, "Black Studies in the

21st Century"; "Is Black Studies Becoming an Academic Stepchild?"; Rojas, *From Black Power to Black Studies*, 6; "Rodney Dangerfield of Academic Pursuits."

32. Ferguson, *We Demand*, 10.

33. Bradley, *Upending the Ivory Tower*, 365.

34. "Race/Ethnicity of College Faculty," *National Center for Education Statistics*, https://nces.ed.gov/fastfacts/display.asp?id=61.

35. Biondi, *Black Revolution on Campus*, 4.

36. Sarah Brown, "Nearly Half of Undergraduates Are Students of Color; but Black Students Lag Behind," *CHE*, February 14, 2019.

37. Shields and Dunn, *Passing on the Right*.

38. Orfield, "Civil Rights and Federal Higher Education Policy," 32–33.

39. Feldman and Huddy, "Racial Resentment and White Opposition to Race-Conscious Programs"; Sears and Henry, "Over Thirty Years Later"; Wallsten et al., "Prejudice or Principled Conservatism?"

40. "National Trends," Mapping Police Violence, https://mappingpoliceviolence.org/nationaltrends; Tom Bartlett, "The Antiracist College: This May Be a Watershed Moment in the History of Higher Education and Race," *CHE*, February 15, 2021.

41. See Giroux, *Neoliberalism's War on Higher Education*; Sethares, *Impacts of Neoliberalism on US Community Colleges*.

42. MacLean, *Democracy in Chains*, 105, 106.

43. Lewis F. Powell Jr., "Confidential Memorandum: Attack on the American Free Enterprise System," August 23, 1971, https://scholarlycommons.law.wlu.edu/cgi/viewcontent.cgi?article=1000&context=powellmemo.

44. Wilson and Kamola, *Free Speech and Koch Money*, 17–23.

45. Brantley, *Brewing a Boycott*, 60.

46. Giroux, *Neoliberalism's War on Higher Education*; Hamilton and Nielsen, *Broke*.

47. Hillman and Orfield, *Civil Rights and Federal Higher Education*, 7.

48. Rose and Mettler, "Polarization of Higher Education Policy," 45.

49. See Gerber, *Rise and Decline of Faculty Governance*; Ginsberg, *Fall of the Faculty*.

50. "Index of Educational Gag Orders," PEN America, accessed January 2, 2023 https://docs.google.com/spreadsheets/d/1Tj5WQVBmB6SQg-zP_M8uZsQQGH09 TxmBY73v23zpyro/edit?usp=sharing.

51. Jeffrey Sachs, "Scope and Speed of Educational Gag Orders Worsening across the Country," PEN America, December 13, 2021, https://pen.org/scope-speed -educational-gag-orders-worsening-across-country/

52. Florida CS/CS/HB 233 (2021)—Postsecondary Education: www.myflorida house.gov/Sections/Bills/billsdetail.aspx?BillId=70303.

Bibliography

Primary Sources

Archival Collections

Alabama Department of Archives and History, Montgomery, AL
    George C. Wallace Collection, LPR124
Boston College Libraries, Newton, MA
    Heights student newspaper, 1967–1970
Chronicle of Higher Education, Washington, DC
    Chronicle of Higher Education archived issues, 1967–1970
Duke University David M. Rubenstein Rare Book and Manuscript Library,
    Durham, NC
    Duke Chronicle student newspaper, 1967–1970
    North Carolina Renaissance student newspaper, 1967–1970
    Young Americans for Freedom papers
George Washington University, Gelman Library Special Collections Research
    Center, Washington, DC
    Cherry Tree yearbook, 1967–1970
    Hatchet student newspaper, 1967–1970
Harvard Library Special Collections and Archives, Cambridge, MA
    Harvard Crimson student newspaper, 1967–1970
Hoover Institution Library & Archives, Stanford, CA
    College Republican National Committee Records
    Lee Edwards Papers, 1878–2004
    Marvin Liebman Papers, 1935–1992
    Patrick Dowd Papers, 1968–1971
    Young Americans for Freedom Records, 1951–2010
Indiana University Archives, Bloomington, IN
    President's Office Records, 1962–1968, Student Organizations, "OUR, YAF,
    and others, 1965–1967"
LBJ Presidential Library, Austin, TX
    White House Central Files, James Gather, "Civil Disorders on Campuses"
    White House Central Files, Mildred Stegall, "Prospects for Racial
    Violence—1968, FBI Report"
    White House Central Files, Mildred Stegall, "Student Nonviolent Coordinating
    Committee"
Louisiana State University Library Special Collections, Baton Rouge, LA
    Daily Reveille student newspaper, 1967–1970

Derek L. A. Hackett Collection

LSU Student Political Activity Collection

Young Americans for Freedom Imprints

Mississippi State University Special Collections, MSU Congressional and
      Political Research Center, Starkville, MS

   Barbara Blankenship Collection, Young Americans for Freedom

   MSU University Libraries Collection, Campus Crusade for Christ, 1966–1976

   MSU University Libraries Collection, College Republicans, 1955–1988

North Carolina State University Special Collections, Raleigh, NC

   Luther Russell Herman Jr. Papers, 1966–1978

   NCSU Student and Other Organizations, Single Folder Records,
      1904–2013, YAF, 1969

   NCSU Student and Other Organizations, Single Folder Records,
      1904–2013, American Students for Action, c. 1969

Pennsylvania State University Special Collections Archive, University Park, PA

   Office of Student Activities Records No. 1392, YAF

   Office of the Vice President for Student Affairs Records No. 1379

   PSU Department of Public Information Records No. 1257, YAF

   Student Activism Records No. 1391, YAF

Richard Nixon Presidential Library and Museum. National Archives and
      Records Administration, Yorba Linda, CA

   Campus Unrest, White House Special Files, Staff Member Office Files:
      Charles Colson

   H. R. Haldeman Collection, Ailes, Roger, 1971

   Oral History Project

   Students Pro-president, White House Special Files, Staff Member and Office
      Files: Charles W. Colson

   White House Special Files, Alphabetical Name File Collection, College L-R

   White House Special Files, Alphabetical Name File Collection, Students

   White House Special Files, Alphabetical Name File Collection, YAF

Tulane University Libraries

   Hullabaloo student newspaper, 1967–1970

   Jambalaya yearbook, 1968–1971

   Newt Gingrich Photograph File

   Special Collections Digital Library

University of Alabama Libraries Special Collections, Tuscaloosa, AL

   Corolla student yearbook, vols. 75–78 (1967–1970)

   Crimson White student newspaper collection, 1967–1972

University of Mississippi, Department of Archives & Special Collections,
      J. D. Williams Library, Oxford, MS

   Daily Mississippian student newspaper collection, 1967–1970

   Knox Collection of Extremist Literature

University of North Carolina Wilson Special Collections, Chapel Hill, NC

   UNC Ephemera Collection, Series 5, Class Strike Ephemera, 1970

University of Notre Dame Rare Books and Special Collections, Notre Dame, IN
   Observer student newspaper, 1967–1970
University of Pennsylvania Archives, Philadelphia, PA
   Vice Provost for University Life Records, Army ROTC Report, 1969
University of Tennessee Library Special Collections, Knoxville, TN
   John J. Duncan Sr. Papers
University of Wisconsin
   Insight and Outlook magazine collection
   Madison Wisconsin Conservative Club folder
   Madison YAF Records, 1965–1968
Washington and Lee University School of Law, Scholarly Commons
   Powell Speeches, Lewis F. Powell Jr. Papers

Personal Collections

Allan Brownfeld, Alexandria, VA
   Assorted writings of James A. Parker
Robert McDonald, Topanga, CA
   Manuscript of college memoir, "The Trojan Campus War"
Paul A. Rahe Jr., Hillsdale, MI
   Cornell in Crisis: A Documentary Analysis, pamphlet, 1969
Gregory L. Schneider, Topeka, KS
   YAF interview transcripts

Newspapers, Magazines, and Serial Publications

Akron Beacon Journal, OH
Alton Evening Telegraph, IL
Amarillo Globe-Times, TX
Arizona Republic, Phoenix, AZ
Atlanta Constitution, GA
Austin American, TX
Barron's National Business & Financial Weekly
Berkshire Eagle, Pittsfield, MA
Billings Gazette, MT
Boston Globe
Bradenton Herald, FL
Bridgeport Post, CT
Carolina Renaissance, North Carolina State University
Central New Jersey Home News, New Brunswick, NJ
Charlotte Observer, NC
Chicago Tribune
Chronicle of Higher Education
Columbia Spectator, Columbia University
Cornell Chronicle, Cornell University
Corpus Christi Caller-Times, TX
Courier-Journal, Louisville, KY
Courier News, Bridgewater, NJ
Cumberland News, MD
Daily Capital News, Jefferson City, MO
Daily Chronicle, Centralia, WA
Daily Journal, Vineland, NJ
Daily News, New York, NY
Daily News Post, Monrovia, CA
Daily Register, Red Bank, NJ
Daily Tribune, Wisconsin Rapids, WI
Dartmouth, Dartmouth College
Dayton Daily News, OH
Democrat and Chronicle, Rochester, NY
Des Moines Register, IA
Detroit Free Press
Dominion News, Morgantown, WV

Edwardsville Intelligencer, IL

Evening Sun, Baltimore, MD

Fort Lauderdale News, FL

Fresno Bee, CA

Guardian

Hartford Courant, CT

Harvard Crimson,
    Harvard University

Hatchet, George Washington
    University

Heights, Boston College

Honolulu Advertiser, HI

Honolulu Star-Bulletin, HI

Indiana Daily Student,
    Indiana University

Inside Higher Ed

Intelligencer Journal, Lancaster, PA

Intercollegiate Review

Iowa City Press Citizen, IA

Ithaca Journal, NY

Kansas City Star, MO

Kenosha News, WI

Lancaster Eagle Gazette, OH

Liberation, an Independent Monthly

Longview Daily News, WA

Longview News-Journal, TX

Los Angeles Herald-Examiner

Los Angeles Times

Madera Tribune, CA

Milwaukee, Wisconsin Journal

Minneapolis Tribune

Montclair Tribune, CA

Montgomery Adviser, AL

National Review

New Guard

New York Times

Newark Advocate, OH

News Journal, Mansfield, OH

Oakland Tribune, CA

Observer, University of
    Notre Dame

Oneota Star, NY

Orlando Sentinel, FL

Palladium Item, Richmond, IN

Palm Beach Post, FL

Pensacola News Journal, FL

Pittsburgh Post-Gazette, PA

Pittsburgh Press, PA

Politico

Poughkeepsie Journal, NY

Press and Sun Bulletin, Binghampton, NY

Press Democrat, Santa Rosa, CA

Press Tribune, Roseville, CA

Reporter-Times, Martinsville, IN

Reuters

Sacramento Bee, CA

Salem News, OH

Salon

San Bernadino County Sun, CA

San Francisco Chronicle

San Francisco Examiner

Southern Utah Free Press, Hurricane, UT

Spokane Chronicle, WA

Springfield Leader and Press, MO

St. Clair Chronicle, MO

St. Louis Post-Dispatch, MO

Star Gazette, Elmira, NY

Star Phoenix, Saskatoon,
    Saskatchewan, Canada

Star Tribune, Minneapolis, MN

Statesman Journal, Salem, OR

Sundial, California State
    University-Northridge

Tallahassee Democrat, FL

Tampa Bay Times, FL

Time Magazine

Times, Munster, IN

Times Record, Troy, NY

US News and World Report

Van Nuys News, CA

Vanity Fair

Vermont Freeman, Starksboro, VT

Washington Post

Washington Times

Winfield College Republican, KS

Wisconsin State Journal,
    Madison, WI

York Daily Record, PA

Other Primary Sources

Buchanan, James M., and Nicos E. Devletoglou. *Academia in Anarchy: An Economic Diagnosis*. New York: Basic Books, 1970.

Buckley, William F., Jr. *God and Man at Yale: The Superstitions of "Academic Freedom."* Chicago: Henry Regnery, 1951.

———. *Rumbles Left and Right: A Book about Troublesome People and Ideas*. New York: MacFadden Bartell, 1963.

Cain, Edward. *They'd Rather Be Right: Youth and the Conservative Movement*. New York: Macmillan, 1963.

Edwards, Lee, and Anne Edwards. *You Can Make the Difference*. New Rochelle: Arlington House, 1968.

Evans, M. Stanton. *Revolt on the Campus*. Chicago: Henry Regnery, 1961.

Hammond, John L. "Yuppies." *Public Opinion Quarterly* 50, no. 4 (Winter 1986).

Levine, Arthur, and Keith R. Wilson. "Student Activism in the 1970s: Transformation Not Decline." *Higher Education* 8, no. 6 (November 1979): 627–40.

Lipset, Seymour Martin, and Earl Raab. "The Wallace Whitelash." *Transaction: Social Science and Modern Society* 7, no. 2 (December 1969): 23–35.

Mailer, Norman. *The Armies of the Night: History as a Novel, the Novel as History*. Self-published, 1968.

McGill, William J. *The Year of the Monkey: Revolt on Campus, 1968–1969*. New York: McGraw-Hill, 1982.

Novick, Karen M., Ellen L. Schatz, and Paul A. Rahe. *Cornell in Crisis: A Documentary Analysis*. N.P.: 1969.

Scammon, Richard M., and Ben J. Wattenberg. *The Real Majority: An Extraordinary Examination of the American Electorate*. New York: Coward-McCann, 1970.

"Student Demonstrators May Lose Federal Aid." *Science News* 93, no. 21 (May 25, 1968): 493–94.

Viguerie, Richard A. *The New Right: We're Ready to Lead*. Falls Church, VA: The Viguerie Company, 1980.

Oral History Interviews and Personal Correspondence by the Author

William B. Allan, July 22, 2018

Robert Bauman, October 9, 2018

Morton Blackwell, June 15, 2018

Allan Brownfeld, August 26, 2018

Gerald P. Dwyer Jr., November 7, 2018

Steven Ealy, July 24, 2018

David Franke, June 14, 2018

James Gwartney, August 7, 2018

William Saracino, March 27, 2019, and April 2, 2019

Randal Teague, June 13, 2018

Patricia Thackston-Ganner, June 14, 2018

Judith Thorburn, July 14, 2018

Wayne Thorburn, July 3, 2018

Ben C. Toledano, August 25, 2018

Interview Transcripts Provided by Gregory L. Schneider

William F. Buckley Jr., August 16, 1994   James Lacy, July 29, 1997
Doug Caddy, March 18, 1997   Marvin Liebman, September 1, 1997
William Cotter, May 1, 1997   J. Alan MacKay, September 26, 1996
Don Devine, August 28, 1996   Howard Phillips, March 28, 1997
Robert Dolan, September 9, 1997   Ron Robinson, July 29, 1997
Frank Donatelli, August 14, 1997   William Rusher, September 17, 1994
Lee Edwards, February 22, 1995   Scott Stanley, May 15, 1997
David Franke, May 15, 1995   Wayne Thorburn, July 24, 1997
David Jones, October 10, 1994   Richard Viguerie, March 26, 1997
David Keene, September 28, 1994

Secondary Books, Articles, Theses, Dissertations, Films, and Websites

"A JBHE Survey: Is Black Studies Central to the Mission of a Great University?" *Journal of Blacks in Higher Education*, no. 31 (2001): 38–40.

Altbach, Philip G. "From Revolution to Apathy: American Student Activism in the 1970s." *Higher Education* 8, no. 6 (November 1979): 609–26.

Andrew, John A., III. *The Other Side of the Sixties: Young Americans for Freedom and the Rise of Conservative Politics.* New Brunswick, NJ: Rutgers University Press, 1997.

———. "Pro-war and Anti-draft: Young Americans for Freedom and the War in Vietnam." In *The Vietnam War on Campus: Other Voices, More Distant Drums*, edited by Marc Jason Gilbert, 1–19. Westport, CT: Praeger, 2001.

Appy, Christian G. *Working-Class War: American Combat Soldiers and Vietnam.* Chapel Hill: University of North Carolina Press, 1993.

Austin, Curtis J. *Up Against the Wall: Violence in the Making and Unmaking of the Black Panther Party.* Fayetteville: University of Arkansas Press, 2006.

Averbeck, Robin Marie. *Liberalism Is Not Enough: Race and Poverty in Postwar Political Thought.* Chapel Hill: University of North Carolina Press, 2018.

Baida, Peter. "Confessions of a Reluctant Yuppie." *American Scholar* 55, no. 1 (Winter 1985): 45.

Bauer, A. J., and Anthony Nadler. "Taking Conservative News Seriously." In *News on the Right: Studying Conservative News Cultures*, edited by Anthony Nadler and A. J. Bauer, 1–16. New York: Oxford University Press, 2020.

Bebout, Lee. "Weaponizing Victimhood: Discourses of Oppression and the Maintenance of Supremacy on the Right." In *News on the Right: Studying Conservative News Cultures*, edited by Anthony Nadler and A. J. Bauer, 64–83. New York: Oxford University Press, 2020.

Benson, Richard D. "Black Student-Worker Revolution and Reparations: The National Association of Black Students, 1969–1972." *Phylon (1960-)* 54, no. 1 (2017): 57–78.

Berry, Damon T. *Blood and Faith: Christianity in American White Nationalism.* Syracuse, NY: Syracuse University Press, 2017.

Bezilla, Michael. "Years of Crises: The 1960s." In *Penn State: An Illustrated History*. Philadelphia: University of Pennsylvania Press, 1985.

Binder, Amy J., and Jeffrey L. Kidder. *The Channels of Student Activism: How the Left and Right Are Winning (and Losing) in Campus Politics Today*. Chicago: University of Chicago Press, 2022.

Binder, Amy J., Jeffrey L. Kidder, and Zosia Sztykowski. "The Conservative Channel—Pulled Outside from the Right." In *The Channels of Student Activism: How the Left and Right Are Winning (and Losing) in Campus Politics Today*, by Amy J. Binder and Jeffrey L. Kidder, 67–89. Chicago: University of Chicago Press, 2022.

Binder, Amy J., and Kate Wood. *Becoming Right: How Campuses Shape Young Conservatives*. Princeton, NJ: Princeton University Press, 2013.

Bingham, Clara. "'The Whole World Is Watching': An Oral History of the 1968 Columbia Uprising." *Vanity Fair*, March 26, 2018.

Biondi, Martha. *The Black Revolution on Campus*. Berkeley: University of California Press, 2012.

"Black Studies Is an Unpopular Major." *Journal of Blacks in Higher Education*, no. 36 (2002): 14–15.

Bloom, Allan. *The Closing of the American Mind: How Higher Education Has Failed Democracy and Impoverished the Souls of Today's Students*. New York: Simon and Schuster, 1987.

Bloom, Joshua, and Waldo E. Martin Jr. *Black against Empire: The History and Politics of the Black Panther Party*. Oakland: University of California Press, 2016.

Blumenthal, Seth. *Children of the Silent Majority: Young Voters and the Rise of the Republican Party, 1968–1972*. Lawrence: University Press of Kansas, 2018.

Bradley, Stefan M. *Upending the Ivory Tower: Civil Rights, Black Power, and the Ivy League*. New York: New York University Press, 2018.

Brantley, Allyson P. *Brewing a Boycott: How a Grassroots Coalition Fought Coors and Remade American Consumer Activism*. Chapel Hill: University of North Carolina Press, 2021.

Bridges, Tyler. *The Rise of David Duke*. Oxford: University Press of Mississippi, 1994.

Bristow, Nancy K. *Steeped in the Blood of Racism: Black Power, Law and Order, and the 1970 Shootings at Jackson State College*. New York: Oxford University Press, 2020.

Broadhurst, Christopher J. "'We Didn't Fire a Shot, We Didn't Burn a Building': The Student Reaction at North Carolina State University to the Kent State Shootings, May 1970." *North Carolina Historical Review* 87, no. 3 (July 2010): 283–309.

Brown, Clyde, and Gayle K. Pluta Brown. "Moo U and the Cambodian Invasion: Nonviolent Anti-Vietnam War Protest at Iowa State University." In *The Vietnam War on Campus: Other Voices, More Distant Drums*, edited by Marc Jason Gilbert, 119–41. Westport, CT: Praeger, 2001.

Brown, Michael J. *Hope and Scorn: Eggheads, Experts, and Elites in American Politics*. Chicago: University of Chicago Press, 2020.

Cajka, Peter. *Follow Your Conscience: The Catholic Church and the Spirit of the Sixties*. Chicago: University of Chicago Press, 2021.

Christian, Mark. "Black Studies in the 21st Century: Longevity Has Its Place." *Journal of Black Studies* 35, no. 5 (2006): 698–719.

Cohen, Arthur M., and Carrie B. Kisker. *The Shaping of American Higher Education: Emergence and Growth of the Contemporary System*. 2nd ed. San Francisco: Jossey-Bass, 2010.

Cole, Eddie R. *The Campus Color Line: College Presidents and the Struggle for Black Freedom*. Princeton, NJ: Princeton University Press, 2020.

Critchlow, Donald. T. *The Conservative Ascendancy: How the GOP Right Made Political History*. Cambridge, MA: Harvard University Press, 2007.

———. *Republican Character: From Nixon to Reagan*. Philadelphia: University of Pennsylvania Press, 2018.

Cronin, Paul. *A Time to Stir: Columbia '68*. New York: Columbia University Press, 2018.

———. *A Time to Stir: Columbia '68*. Sticking Place Films, 2020. https://vimeo.com /454051397.

Crouchett, Lawrence. "Early Black Studies Movements." *Journal of Black Studies* 2, no. 2 (1971): 189–200.

Cummings, Alex Sayf. *Brain Magnet: Research Triangle Park and the Idea of the Idea Economy*. New York: Columbia University Press, 2020.

Dallek, Robert. *Ronald Reagan: The Politics of Symbolism*. Cambridge, MA: Harvard University Press, 1984.

De Groot, Gerard J. "Ronald Reagan and Student Unrest in California, 1966–1970." *Pacific Historical Review* 65, no. 1 (1996): 107–29. doi:10.2307/3640829.

DiBranco, Alex. "Conservative News and Movement Infrastructure." In *News on the Right: Studying Conservative News Cultures*, edited by Anthony Nadler and A. J. Bauer, 123–40. New York: Oxford University Press, 2020.

DiMaggio, Anthony. "Slanting the News: Media Bias and Its Effect." In *News on the Right: Studying Conservative News Cultures*, edited by Anthony Nadler and A. J. Bauer, 190–212. New York: Oxford University Press, 2020.

Doherty, Brian. *Radicals for Capitalism: A Freewheeling History of the Modern American Libertarian Movement*. New York: Public Affairs, 2007.

Eagles, Charles W. *The Price of Defiance: James Meredith and the Integration of Ole Miss*. Chapel Hill: University of North Carolina Press, 2014.

Edwards, Lee. *Educating for Liberty: The First Half-Century of the Intercollegiate Studies Institute*. Washington, DC: Henry Regnery, 2003.

———. *Just Right: A Life in Pursuit of Liberty*. Wilmington, DE: Intercollegiate Studies Institute, 2017.

Ehrenberg, John. *White Nationalism and the Republican Party: Toward Minority Rule in America*. New York: Routledge, 2022.

Eisenmann, Linda. *Higher Education for Women in Postwar America, 1945–1965*. Baltimore: Johns Hopkins University Press, 2006.

Eskridge, Larry. "One Way: Billy Graham, the Jesus Generation, and the Idea of an Evangelical Youth Culture." *Church History* 67, no. 1 (1998): 83–106.

Ewert, Cody Dodge. *Making Schools American: Nationalism and the Origin of Modern Educational Politics.* Baltimore: Johns Hopkins University Press, 2022.

Farber, David, and Jeff Roche, eds. *The Conservative Sixties.* New York: Peter Lang, 2003.

Farrington, Joshua D. *Black Republicans and the Transformation of the GOP.* Philadelphia: University of Pennsylvania Press, 2016.

Fass, Paula S. *Outside In: Minorities and the Transformation of American Higher Education.* New York: Oxford University Press, 1989.

Favors, Jelani M. *Shelter in a Time of Storm: How Black Colleges Fostered Generations of Leadership and Activism.* Chapel Hill: University of North Carolina Press, 2019.

Fawcett, Edmund. *Conservatism: The Fight for a Tradition.* Princeton, NJ: Princeton University Press, 2020.

Feldman, Stanley, and Leonie Huddy. "Racial Resentment and White Opposition to Race-Conscious Programs: Principles or Prejudice?" *American Journal of Political Science* 49, no. 1 (2005): 168–83.

Ferguson, Roderick A. *We Demand: The University and Student Protests.* Oakland: University of California Press, 2017.

Fields, Corey D. *Black Elephants in the Room: The Unexpected Politics of African American Republicans.* Oakland: University of California Press, 2016.

Finchelstein, Federico. *From Fascism to Populism in History.* Oakland: University of California Press, 2017.

Gage, Beverly. *G-man: J. Edgar Goover and the Making of the American Century.* New York: Viking, 2022.

Geiger, Roger L. *American Higher Education since World War II: A History.* Princeton, NJ: Princeton University Press, 2019.

———. "The Student Protest Movement in the 1968 Era in Three Acts: Inception, Confrontations, and Legacies." In *American Higher Education in the Postwar Era, 1945–1970,* edited by Roger L. Geiger, Nathan M. Sorber, and Christian K. Anderson, 170–200. New York: Routledge, 2016.

Gerber, Larry G. *The Rise and Decline of Faculty Governance: Professionalization and the Modern American University.* Baltimore: Johns Hopkins University Press, 2014.

Ginsberg, Benjamin. *The Fall of the Faculty: The Rise of the All-Administrative University and Why It Matters.* New York: Oxford University Press, 2011.

Giroux, Henry A. *Neoliberalism's War on Higher Education.* Chicago: Haymarket Books, 2014.

Greene, Robert, II. "*National Review* and the Changing Narrative of Civil Rights Memory, 1968–2016." In *News on the Right: Studying Conservative News Cultures,* edited by Anthony Nadler and A. J. Bauer, 174–89. New York: Oxford University Press, 2020.

Gurvis, Sandra. *Where Have All the Flower Children Gone?* Jackson: University Press of Mississippi, 2006.

Hamilton, Laura T., and Kelly Nielsen, eds. *Broke: The Racial Consequences of Underfunding Public Universities*. Chicago: University of Chicago Press, 2021.

Hartman, Andrew. *A War for the Soul of America: A History of the Culture Wars*. 2nd ed. Chicago: University of Chicago Press, 2019.

Hawley, George. *Making Sense of the Alt-Right*. New York: Columbia University Press, 2017.

Heale, Michael J. "The Sixties as History: A Review of the Political Historiography." *Reviews in American History* 33, no. 1 (2005): 133–52.

Heineman, Kenneth J. *Campus Wars: The Peace Movement at American State Universities in the Vietnam Era*. New York: New York University Press, 1994.

———. *Put Your Bodies upon the Wheels: Student Revolt in the 1960s*. Chicago: Ivan R. Dee, 2001.

Hemmer, Nicole. *Messengers of the Right: Conservative Media and the Transformation of American Politics*. Philadelphia: University of Pennsylvania Press, 2016.

———. *Partisans: The Conservative Revolutionaries Who Remade American Politics in the 1990s*. New York: Basic Books, 2022.

Hewitt, Christopher. *Political Violence and Terrorism in Modern America: A Chronology*. Westport, CT: Praeger Security International, 2005.

Hillman, Nicholas, and Gary Orfield, eds. *Civil Rights and Federal Higher Education*. Cambridge, MA: Harvard Education Press, 2022.

Himmelstein, Jerome. *To the Right: The Transformation of American Conservatism*. Berkeley: University of California Press, 1990.

Hinton, Elizabeth. "Police Violence." In *Myth America: Historians Take on the Biggest Legends and Lies about Our Past*, edited by Kevin M. Kruse and Julian E. Zelizer, 237–49. New York: Basic Books, 2022.

Hobson, J. Hardin. "Football Culture at New South Universities: Lost Cause and Old South Memory, Modernity, and Martial Manhood." In *The History of American College Football: Institutional Policy, Culture, and Reform*, edited by Christian K. Anderson and Amber C. Fallucca, 37–63. New York: Routledge, 2021.

Huntington, John S. *Far-Right Vanguard: The Radical Roots of Modern Conservatism*. Philadelphia: University of Pennsylvania Press, 2021.

Hurwitz, Tom. "The Smartest Kid I'd Ever Met: Memories of a Columbia Rebel." In *A Time to Stir: Columbia '68*, edited by Paul Cronin, 126–41. New York: Columbia University Press, 2018.

"Is Black Studies Becoming an Academic Stepchild?" *Journal of Blacks in Higher Education*, no. 49 (2005): 18–20.

Isserman, Maurice, and Michael Kazin. *America Divided: The Civil War of the 1960s*. 4th ed. New York: Oxford University Press, 2012.

Janda, Sarah Eppler. *Prairie Power: Student Activism, Counterculture, and Backlash in Oklahoma, 1962–1972*. Norman: University of Oklahoma Press, 2018.

Joseph, Peniel E. "Dashikis and Democracy: Black Studies, Student Activism, and the Black Power Movement." *Journal of African American History* 88, no. 2 (2003): 182–203.

Judis, John B. *William F. Buckley, Jr.: Patron Saint of the Conservatives*. New York: Simon & Schuster, 1988.

Kazin, Michael. *The Populist Persuasion: An American History*. 2nd ed. Ithaca, NY: Cornell University Press, 2017.

Keith, Michael C. "Turn On, Tune In: The Rise and Demise of Commercial Underground Radio." In *Radio Reader: Essays in the Cultural History of Radio*, edited by Michele Hilms and Loviglio, 389–404. New York: Routledge, 2002.

Klatch, Rebecca. *A Generation Divided: The New Left, the New Right, and the 1960s*. Berkeley: University of California Press, 1999.

Kruse, Kevin M., and Julian E. Zelizer. *Fault Lines: A History of the United States since 1974*. New York: W. W. Norton, 2019.

——. *Myth America: Historians Take on the Biggest Legends and Lies about Our Past*. New York: Basic Books, 2022.

Kuhn, David Paul. *The Hardhat Riot: Nixon, New York City, and the Dawn of the White Working-Class Revolution*. New York: Oxford University Press, 2020.

Laats, Adam. "Brave Sons and Daughters True: 1960s Protests at 'The Fundamentalist Harvard.'" In *American Higher Education in the Postwar Era, 1945-1970*, edited by Roger L. Geiger, Nathan M. Sorber, and Christian K. Anderson, 146–69. New York: Routledge, 2016.

——. *Fundamentalist U: Keeping the Faith in American Higher Education*. New York: Oxford University Press, 2018.

——. *The Other School Reformers: Conservative Activism in American Education*. Cambridge, MA: Harvard University Press, 2015.

Lacy, Tim. *The Dream of a Democratic Culture: Mortimer J. Adler and the Great Books Idea*. New York: Palgrave Macmillan, 2013.

Lane, Julie B. "Cultivating Distrust of the Mainstream Media." In *News on the Right: Studying Conservative News Cultures*, edited by Anthony Nadler and A. J. Bauer, 157–73. New York: Oxford University Press, 2020.

Lee, Michael J. *Creating Conservatism: Postwar Words that Made an American Movement*. East Lansing: Michigan State University Press, 2014.

Lepore, Jill. *These Truths: A History of the United States*. New York: W. W. Norton, 2018.

Lewis, George. *Massive Resistance: The White Response to the Civil Rights Movement*. London: Hodder Education, 2006.

Long, Dallas. "The Foundations of Student Affairs: A Guide to the Profession." In *Environments for Student Growth and Development: Librarians and Student Affairs in Collaboration*, edited by L. J. Hinchliffe and M. A. Wong. Chicago: Association of College & Research Libraries, 2012.

Loss, Christopher P. *Between Citizens and the State: The Politics of American Higher Education in the 20th Century*. Princeton, NJ: Princeton University Press, 2014.

Lowell, Frederick K. "A Time to Stir . . . Up Trouble." In *A Time to Stir: Columbia '68*, edited by Paul Cronin, 208–16. New York: Columbia University Press, 2018.

MacLean, Nancy. *Democracy in Chains: The Deep History of the Radical Right's Stealth Plan for America*. New York: Penguin Books, 2017.

Major, Mark. "Bridging the Marginal and the Mainstream: Methodological Considerations for Conservative News as a Subfield." In *News on the Right:*

Studying Conservative News Cultures, edited by Anthony Nadler and
A. J. Bauer, 213–31. New York: Oxford University Press, 2020.

Massarsky, Vaud E. "The Primary Shades of Opposition to the Columbia
Occupation." In *A Time to Stir: Columbia '68*, edited by Paul Cronin, 219–22.
New York: Columbia University Press, 2018.

McGirr, Lisa. *Suburban Warriors: The Origins of the New American Right*.
Princeton, NJ: Princeton University Press, 2002.

McVicar, Michael J. "Aggressive Philanthropy: Progressivism, Conservatism, and
the William Volker Charities Fund." *Missouri Historical Review* 105, no. 4
(2011): 191–212.

Menard, Louis, Paul Reitter, and Chad Wellmon, eds. *The Rise of the Research
University: A Sourcebook*. Chicago: University of Chicago Press, 2017.

Meyer, Frank S., ed. *What Is Conservatism?* Wilmington, DE: ISI Books, 2017.

Michael, George. *Willis Carto and the American Far Right*. Gainesville: University
Press of Florida, 2008.

Michel, Gregg. *Struggle for a Better South: Southern Student Organizing Committee,
1964–1969*. New York: Palgrave MacMillan, 2008.

Miller, Edward H. *A Conspiratorial Life: Robert Welch, the John Birch Society, and
the Revolution of American Conservatism*. Chicago: University of Chicago Press,
2022.

Moreton, Bethany E. "Make Payroll, Not War: Business Culture as Youth Culture."
In *Rightward Bound: Making America Conservative in the 1960s*, edited by
Bruce J. Schulman and Julian E. Zelizer, 52–70. Cambridge, MA: Harvard
University Press, 2008.

Moriyama, Takahito. *Empire of Direct Mail: How Conservative Marketing
Persuaded Voters and Transformed the Grassroots*. Lawrence: University Press
of Kansas, 2022.

Moss, Goerge Donelson. *Vietnam: An American Ordeal*. 6th ed. New York:
Routledge, 2016.

Müller, Jan Werner. *What Is Populism?* Philadelphia: University of Pennsylvania
Press, 2016.

Nadler, Anthony, and A. J. Bauer. *News on the Right: Studying Conservative News
Cultures*. New York: Oxford University Press, 2020.

Nash, George H. *The Conservative Intellectual Movement in America since 1945*.
New York: Basic Books, 1976.

Neer, Robert M. *Napalm: An American Biography*. Cambridge, MA: Harvard
University Press, 2015.

Norris, Pippa. *Cultural Backlash: Trump, Brexit, and Authoritarian Populism*.
Cambridge: Cambridge University Press, 2019.

Ogren, Christine A., and Marc A. Van Overbeke, eds. *Rethinking Campus Life:
New Perspectives on the History of College Students in the United States*. London:
Palgrave MacMillan, 2018.

Orfield, Gary. "Civil Rights and Federal Higher Education Policy." In *Civil Rights
and Federal Higher Legislation*, edited by Nicholas Hillman and Gary Orfield,
9–38. Cambridge, MA: Harvard Education Press, 2022.

Pérez, Raúl. *The Souls of White Jokes: How Racist Humor Fuels White Supremacy.* Stanford, CA: Stanford University Press, 2022.

Perlstein, Rick. *Nixonland: The Rise of a President and the Fracturing of America.* New York: Scribner, 2008.

Phillips-Fein, Kim. *Invisible Hands: The Businessmen's Crusade against the New Deal.* New York: W. W. Norton, 2009.

Rahim, Asad. "Diversity to Deradicalize." *California Law Review* 108, no. 5 (October 2020).

Rast, Joel. *The Origins of the Dual City: Housing, Race, and Redevelopment in Twentieth-Century Chicago.* Chicago: University of Chicago Press, 2019.

Ratner-Rosenhagen, Jennifer. *The Ideas That Made America: A Brief History.* New York: Oxford University Press, 2019.

Robin, Corey. *The Reactionary Mind: Conservatism from Edmund Burke to Donald Trump.* 2nd ed. New York: Oxford University Press, 2017.

"The Rodney Dangerfield of Academic Pursuits: Black Studies Wins No Respect." *Journal of Blacks in Higher Education*, no. 29 (2000): 30–31.

Rogers (Kendi), Ibram X. *The Black Campus Movement: Black Students and the Racial Reconstruction of Higher Education, 1965–1972.* New York: Palgrave MacMillan, 2012.

Rojas, Fabio. *From Black Power to Black Studies: How a Radical Social Movement Became an Academic Discipline.* Baltimore: Johns Hopkins University Press, 2007.

Rose, Deondra, and Suzanne Mettler. "The Polarization of Higher Education Policy." In *Civil Rights and Federal Higher Legislation*, edited by Nicholas Hillman and Gary Orfield, 39–52. Cambridge, MA: Harvard Education Press, 2022.

Rosenfeld, Seth. *Subversives: The FBI's War on Student Radicals, and Reagan's Rise to Power.* New York: Farrar, Status and Giroux, 2013.

Rosenthal, Michael. "Life on the Ledge." In *A Time to Stir: Columbia '68*, edited by Paul Cronin, 81–287. New York: Columbia University Press, 2018.

Rothstein, Richard. *The Color of Law: A Forgotten History of How Our Government Segregated America.* New York: W. W. Norton, 2017.

Rove, Karl. *Courage and Consequence: My Life as a Conservative in the Fight.* New York: Simon and Schuster, 2010.

Rowling, Charles M., Penelope Sheets, and Timothy M. Jones. "American Atrocity Revisited: National Identity, Cascading Frames, and the My Lai Massacre." *Political Communication* 32, no. 2 (2015): 310–30.

Sack, Daniel. *Moral Re-armament: The Reinventions of an American Religious Movement.* New York: Palgrave Macmillan, 2009.

Scanlon, Sandra. *The Pro-war Movement: Domestic Support for the Vietnam War and the Making of Modern American Conservatism.* Amherst: University of Massachusetts Press, 2013.

Schneider, Gregory L. *Cadres for Conservatism: Young Americans for Freedom and the Rise of the Contemporary Right.* New York: New York University Press, 1999.

Schoenwald, Jonathan. "No War, No Welfare, and No Damn Taxation: The Student Libertarian Movement, 1968–1972." In *The Vietnam War on Campus: Other Voices, More Distant Drums*, edited by Marc Jason Gilbert, 20–45. Westport, CT: Praeger, 2001.

———. *A Time for Choosing: The Rise of Modern American Conservatism*. Oxford: Oxford University Press, 2001.

Schrecker, Ellen. *The Lost Promise: American Universities in the 1960s*. Chicago: University of Chicago Press, 2021.

Schrum, Ethan. *The Instrumental University: Education in Service of the National Agenda after World War II*. Ithaca, NY: Cornell University Press, 2019.

Schulman, Bruce J. *From Cotton Belt to Sunbelt: Federal Policy, Economic Development, and the Transformation of the South 1938–1980*. Durham, NC: Duke University Press, 1994.

Schulman, Bruce J., and Julian E. Zelizer, eds. *Rightward Bound: Making America Conservative in the 1970s*. Cambridge, MA: Harvard University Press, 2008.

Sears, David O., and P. J. Henry. "Over Thirty Years Later: A Contemporary Look at Symbolic Racism." *Advances in Experimental Social Psychology* 37, no. 1 (2005): 95–125.

Selden, Steven. "The Neoconservative Challenge to the Undergraduate Curriculum: The Case of the Intercollegiate Studies Institute and the American Council for Trustees and Alumni." *Counterpoints* 271 (2007): 89–99.

Sethares, Greg. *The Impacts of Neoliberalism on US Community Colleges*. New York: Routledge, 2020.

Shields, Jon A., and Joshua M. Dunn Sr. *Passing on the Right: Conservative Professors in the Progressive University*. New York: Oxford University Press, 2016.

Shires, Preston. *Hippies of the Religious Right: From the Countercultures of Jerry Garcia to the Subculture of Jerry Falwell*. Waco: Baylor University Press, 2007.

Sienkiewicz, Matt, and Nick Marx. *That's Not Funny: How the Right Makes Comedy Work for Them*. Oakland: University of California Press, 2022.

Slonecker, Blake. "The Columbia Coalition: African Americans, New Leftists, and Counterculture at the Columbia University Protest of 1968." *Journal of Social History* 41, no. 4 (2008): 967–96.

Solomon, Barbara Miller. *In the Company of Educated Women*. New Haven, CT: Yale University Press, 1985.

Spillman, Daniel. "The Conservative Baby Boomers' Magazine: A History of the *American Spectator* and the Conservative Intellectual Movement, 1967–2001." PhD diss., Emory University, 2013.

Spoehr, Luther. "Making Brown University's 'New Curriculum' in 1969: The Importance of Context and Contingency." *Rhode Island History* 74, no. 2 (2016): 55–71.

Spofford, Tom. *Lynch Street: The May 1970 Slayings at Jackson State*. Kent, OH: Kent State University Press, 1988.

Steinberg, Arnold L. *Whiplash! From JFK to Donald Trump: A Political Odyssey*. Ottawa, IL: Jameson Books, 2017.

Stenner, Karen. "Three Kinds of 'Conservatism.'" *Psychological Inquiry* 20, no. 2/3 (2009): 142–59.

Stewart, Scott. "College Republicans—a Brief History," College Republican National Committee, July 24, 2002. https://web.archive.org/web/20050702072121 /http://www.crnc.org/admin/editpage/downloads/CRNChistory.pdf.

Sykes, Charlie. *How the Right Lost Its Mind.* New York: St. Martin's Press, 2017.

Thelin, John R. *Going to College in the Sixties.* Baltimore: Johns Hopkins University Press, 2018.

——. *A History of American Higher Education.* 3rd ed. Baltimore: Johns Hopkins University Press, 2019.

Thoms, John. "Political Education and the Birth of Students for a Restructured University." In *A Time to Stir: Columbia '68*, edited by Paul Cronin, 381–87. New York: Columbia University Press, 2018.

Thorburn, Wayne J. *A Generation Awakes: Young Americans for Freedom and the Creation of the Conservative Movement.* Ottowa, IL: Jameson Books, 2010.

——. *Young Americans for Freedom: Igniting a Movement.* Reston, VA: Young America's Foundation, 2017.

T'Shaka, Oba. "Africana Studies Department History: San Francisco State University." *Journal of Pan African Studies* 5 no. 7 (October 2012): 13–32.

Tuccille, Jerome. *It Usually Begins with Ayn Rand.* Revised and updated ed. Baltimore: Winkler Media, 2012.

Turner, John G. *Bill Bright and Campus Crusade for Christ: The Renewal of Evangelicalism in Postwar America.* Chapel Hill: University of North Carolina Press, 2008.

Viguerie, Richard A., and David Franke. *America's Right Turn: How Conservatives Used New and Alternative Media to Take Power.* Chicago: Bonus Books, 2004.

Wallsten, Kevin, Tatishe M. Nteta, Lauren A. McCarthy, and Melinda R. Tarsi. "Prejudice or Principled Conservatism? Racial Resentment and White Opinion toward Paying College Athletes." *Political Research Quarterly* 70, no. 1 (2017): 209–22.

Weinberg, Carl. *Red Dynamite: Creationism, Culture Wars, and Anticommunism in America.* Ithaca, NY: Cornell University Press, 2021.

Wells, Tom. *The War Within: America's Battle over Vietnam.* Berkeley: University of California Press, 2016. Kindle.

Williams, Daniel K. *God's Own Party: The Making of the Christian Right.* Oxford: Oxford University Press, 2012.

Williamson-Lott, Joy Ann. *Jim Crow Campus: Higher Education and the Struggle for a New Southern Social Order.* New York: Teacher College Press, 2018.

Wilson, Ralph, and Isaac Kamola. *Free Speech and Koch Money: Manufacturing a Campus Culture War.* London: Pluto Press, 2021.

Wright Rigueur, Leah. *The Loneliness of the Black Republican.* Princeton, NJ: Princeton University Press, 2015.

Young, Shawn David. *Gray Sabbath: Jesus People USA, the Evangelical Left, and the Evolution of Christian Rock.* New York: Columbia University Press, 2015.

Zeskind, Leonard. *Blood and Politics: The History of the White Nationalist Movement from the Margins to the Mainstream.* New York: Farrar, Straus, and Giroux, 2009.

Zimmerman, Jonathan. *The Amateur Hour: A History of College Teaching in America.* Baltimore: Johns Hopkins University Press, 2020.

Index

Note: page numbers followed by "fig" refer to figures and those followed by "n" refer to notes, with note number.

McDonald, Jack, 73
McMahon, Dennis C., 27
media countersphere, 50–51, 191.
  See also conservative countersphere
Mescon, Michael, 29–30
Meyer, Frank, 106
military recruitment, 52, 54–55
military research, 56–57
Minute Men (paramilitary group),
  27, 107
Mitchell, John, 94
the Mobe. *See* National Mobilization
  Committee to End the War in
  Vietnam (the Mobe)
mock conventions, 102–3
Modern Age (magazine), 37
Mont Pelerin Society, 6, 35
Moral Re-Armament, 13
moral traditionalism, 39
Moran, Kevin, 170, 181
moratoria, antiwar, 169, 170, 179
My Lai (1968), 57

napalm, 53
National Defense Education Act, 88
the National Guard, 17, 173, 175, 176
nationalism, 184
National Mobilization Committee to
  End the War in Vietnam (the Mobe):
  antiwar moratoria and, 165; demonstrations by, 58, 111, 112, 161; the New
  Left and, 20
National Review (magazine): concept of
  "American establishment" and, 42;
  influence of, 6, 37, 150; "liberal
  media" and, 208n32; white supremacy and, 193–94
the National Science Foundation
  (NSF), 32
National Socialist Liberation Front,
  106–7
National Socialist White People's Party,
  28, 106–7, 109, 128
National Student Association (NSA), 34,
  55, 77–78, 214n119

National Student Committee for Victory
  in Vietnam, 63, 164
National Youth Alliance (NYA), 111, 115
Nazism, 27, 106–7, 122
neo-Nazis, 110, 115, 128, 129
New Guard (magazine), 53, 106, 122, 134
the New Left. *See* student New Left
the New Right: activism of, 4, 6,
  185–86; college roots of, 5; libertarianism and, 151. *See also* student Right
newsletters, 45–47
newspapers. *See* college newspapers
New York Times (newspaper), 22–23
Nixon, Richard: approval for, 176;
  campus activism and, 95, 116;
  election of, 114; higher education
  and, 127; presidential candidacy of,
  103, 104, 105, 113; student Right and,
  110–11, 163, 167, 181–82
Nixon administration: campus activism
  and, 94; conscription reform by, 165;
  Kent State Massacre and, 175; student
  arrests and, 181; student Right and,
  104, 232n75; Vietnam War and, 16,
  115; Young Americans for Freedom
  (YAF) and, 115–17

Office of Interagency Coordination, 94
Oliver, Revilo, 109–10, 115, 194
Operation Sunshine, 72
originalism, 91
Owens, Candace, 191

Parker, Jay, 23, 138, 139
patriotism, 22
peace movement, 9, 66, 132, 156
peaceniks, 61, 187–88
Pell, Col. Robert H., 157, 159
Pelosi, Nancy, 184
Pierce, William Luther, 115
"pinko," 20
Polack, Robert, 49, 145, 146
police. *See* law enforcement
police brutality, 9, 112–13, 131, 180
political action committees, 6